D1188264

# Strange Customs

# Strange Customs: How Did They Begin?

## THE ORIGINS OF THE UNUSUAL AND OCCULT CUSTOMS, SUPERSTITIONS AND TRADITIONS

## by R. Brasch

DAVID McKAY COMPANY, INC. ● NEW YORK

**Library of Congress Cataloging in Publication Data**

Brasch, Rudolf, 1912-
   Strange customs, how did they begin?

   Includes index.
   1.  Occult sciences.   2.  Superstition.   I.  Title.
BF1411.B76       133              76-41054
ISBN 0-679-50573-3

IN MEMORY
OF
OUR DEAR PARENTS

# Contents

# Foreword

I have always been keenly interested in origins. To trace them all over the world and to explain them has been an exciting and gratifying task. And the deeper I dug, the more information I found, but also the more questions.

To have done so now in the realm of the occult has been an experience all its own. Many people are exceedingly interested in the supernatural, and for many years I have witnessed its influence on men and women in all walks of life.

Quite literally, the "occult" speaks of the "obscure," of that which is "hidden" and "concealed." To shed light on it is the ultimate purpose of this book.

As a student of Oriental languages, I have been fortunate to be able to read in their original text many of the sources of mysticism and the occult and, also, the significant Kabbalah. My understanding of Hebrew, the language in which so much of the occult first appeared, greatly helped me in the explanation of numerous practices and traditions.

Women's use of eye shadow as part of their beauty culture is not merely skin deep but rooted in man's fear of "the evil eye." Masonic "temples" perpetuate the ancient Roman augurs' divination by the flight of birds. Mourners who cover mirrors in their home unknowingly maintain a custom instituted to prevent the spirit of the deceased from haunting them.

The famous victory sign Churchill popularized during the Second World War was not of his making. The two outstretched fingers forming the V were the traditional devil's horns. For thousands of years they had been used magically to defeat the devil.

Who would ever guess that when we talk about having slept "like a log" or teach our children that pointing with the finger is rude, we really adopt and carry on occult beliefs. Even the modern cobalt treatment of malignant growths recalls "devils" once believed to inhabit German mountains.

A witch need not be a woman. But what made people assume so nevertheless? Why do the superstitious, after spilling salt, throw a pinch of it over their left shoulder? Why do Anglo-Saxon nations shun horsemeat while the French delight in it? How can we explain that green, the luscious color of verdure, came to be regarded as unlucky, while a caul is thought to bestow good fortune? What is the origin of voodoo? And is there any link between the hunchback and the "hunch" we may have?

These are a few of the many questions answered in this book.

Numerous customs practiced nowadays by the modern, enlightened generation are embedded thus in the world of the occult. This applies to throwing coins into a wishing well, jingling of money in one's pocket when seeing the new moon and pulling the wishbone of a fowl, all of which are discussed in the pages that follow.

Well known is Voltaire's aphorism that even "if God did not exist, it would be necessary to invent him." But hardly remembered is the remark of Charles Baudelaire, another Frenchman, who wrote that "the neatest trick of the devil is to convince us that he does not exist." And yet through the ages, and not least in our time, the apparent cruelty of life and the frequent brutality of men demands so much more effort to sustain belief in a benevolent God than to assume the rule of malevolent forces.

Satan and God are truly rivals—if not in the real world, they are so in man's desire and need to adopt a philosophy of life that is meaningful and makes sense, a life that is based not on wishful thinking and wrongfully placed priorities but on the realities as he sees and experiences them every day.

To be able to do so, however, demands a true understanding of what has given man the concepts of Satanism and witchcraft and all they imply, and of all that now belongs to the "sinister" side of life. How did they come into being and what do they represent and express? Surely, they concern a type of knowledge completely different from the logical laws we apply to everyday existence. Almost twenty-five hundred years ago, the Greek philosopher Heraclitus observed that "because it is sometimes so unbelievable, the truth escapes from becoming known."

All I have written is in search of truth. Therefore I have suppressed nothing. I have never attempted to ignore or cover up even the unpleasant—no matter whether it concerns the realm of the occult or its prominent, though often disguised place in religion. However I do not want anyone to imagine that by the inclusion of a specific practice or notion, I tacitly approve of it. I trust that in each case my intelligent readers will draw their own conclusion and do so on the basis of the facts I present in frankness and without bias.

We must have reason to believe and take seriously an approach to life which is out of the ordinary and do so not merely out of curiosity or, in Arthur Koestler's phrase, as "peeping Toms at the keyhole of eternity."

To debunk false ideas was yet another task I set for myself. So many of our attitudes are arrived at by wrong assumptions and, thoughtlessly taken over, are further misunderstood and misinterpreted. A further objective of this book is to go back to their very roots and original meanings and by clarifying them prove how many of their modern manifestations are unwarranted.

Satan, to begin with, was not the Evil One of modern repute. Fairies were not supernatural beings but very real men and women, desperately fighting for their survival.

The occult, certainly, is responsible for so much of what we do, say and think—or avoid. It has crept into almost every part of life and continues to this day to influence and, at times, to manipulate our existence. This book shows the occult background of the candles on the Christmas tree, the wedding ring and the *mezuzah* on the doorpost of a Jewish home.

The book also deals with the devil and the witch. It tells about astrology and explains in detail how each of the twelve houses of the Zodiac received its name. From the heights it goes to the "netherworld," to discuss hell, Hades and Gehinnom.

"Figures" of every type and shape are investigated. They include the zombie, the vampire and the black cat, and numerologically, the lucky 3, the unfortunate 13 and the reason for the royal 21-gun salute.

Two significant aims are therefore pursued in this book. First, it traces the origins of the many facets of occult phenomena and their fascinating and revealing etymology. Second, it uncovers the often unknown and unexpected influence of the supernatural on our everyday life, thought and speech, and does so in the most surprising areas.

No matter what the individual reader's personal attitude toward the occult, this book should help him understand better a dimension of life prevalent once again in our culture. Man is dissatisfied with life as it is at present. Above all, his very sense of insecurity and feeling of futility have made him reach out for something that might banish the "demon of despair." And at pressure-ridden times like these, people have always been attracted to the mystical and the occult. Only by understanding them will one be able to take up a life-style that is intelligent, positive and fulfilling.

The book can be read as a guide from the hoary background of modern mores to the perpetual and universal attempt to look into the future. Or as the individual sections are self-contained, it can be delved into at random.

As in all of my previous research of "beginnings" in the realm of customs, superstitions, sports and sex I have tried to add something new: further information and more food for thought. And all my books share one significant feature: the enormous help given me by my wife. Together we researched, watched voodoo and deciphered documents. We did so in almost every part of the world: from Iceland to Macao, in Ireland and Iran, in the depth of Africa and high up in the Andes and among Australian aborigines. Perhaps no other book but this, dealing in great part with the world of the beyond, was therefore as suitable for the choice of its dedication—to our late and beloved parents.

One last question remains, and the answer to it is not given here but left to the reader himself. If it were really possible to pierce the veil that hides from our gaze and mind all the secrets and everything that is to come, would we really want to know? Is not the very uncertainty of life one of the greatest stimuli that urges us on to strive, to work and to overcome?

R.B.

# CHAPTER ONE

# Magic

## THE SOURCE OF ALL MAGIC

Fabulous ancient Persia gave the world magic. Its name, from the old Persian word *magu*, was the original title bestowed by the Medes on their priestly class long before Zoroaster.

Like the Hebrew Levites, the priests jealously guarded their profession. Worshiping the fire, they kept it burning continuously in the temples. The earth was equally holy and to defile it with human remains they decried as sacrilegious. These priests also built the first towers of silence; here they placed the bodies of the dead for their flesh to be devoured by vultures. The faith of these magi included as well a belief in the planetary influence on the fate of man.

In the sixth century B.C., when nature worship was replaced by Zoroastrian dualism, the magu retained his position and his word was law. He wore a distinctive white robe and a tall felt cap with side flaps that covered his jaws. His numerous functions included the offering of certain animals which were regarded as creatures of the world of darkness.

But to visitors from foreign lands, the most striking aspect of the priests' ministry was its occult practices: the way they interpreted dreams and omens, appealed with incantations to invisible forces and looked into the future. Their foretelling of the future fascinated the Greeks, who believed it to be the magu's sole occupation. Adopting the name magu, the Greeks made it a part of their vocabulary and *magos* came to mean sorcerer, wizard, a person endowed with supernatural power.

The Romans borrowed the term from the Greeks, assimilating it to their own tongue as *magus*. Much better known in the plural form, *magi*, it was merely another step to call the work of the magi, magic.

Ironically, in Persia the power of the magu deteriorated. Through religious contempt shown to Zoroastrian priests by another powerful faith, their name became so debased that its modern derivation *magh* has come to mean a low-class innkeeper!

## THE THREE KINGS OF THE EAST

A popular Christmas story tells of the magi—the three kings of the East—who, following a star, came from their country to pay homage to the Christ child at Bethlehem. But going back to the original source, the Gospels, the relevant passage in Matthew (2:1) merely speaks of "magi" generally (often rendered "wise men"), with no indication of their number or that they were kings. Their traditional names, said to have been Gaspar, Melchior and Balthasar, do not appear in the New Testament either.

These fanciful details were added later and are mere fiction. Tertullian, a lawyer who became a famous Father of the Church after he converted to Christianity in A.D. 190, was the first to suggest that the magi were "almost [!] kings" (in his original Latin words, *fere reges*). By the sixth century, their royal status was taken for granted and linked with the passage in the Psalms (72:10) that referred to far-off kings who "shall bring presents" and "offer gifts."

The number of kings is generally attributed to Origen, another Father of the Church and eminent biblical scholar (who died c. A.D. 254). He believed them to be three, for, according to the Gospel, they had carried three different gifts: gold, frankincense and myrrh, and they would have done so separately.

## THE MAGIC CIRCLE

The magic circle has ruled the living and the dead almost from the moment man caught sight of the sun. The circle, in fact, was an early replica of the bright solar image. And just as the sun vanquished the darkness, its representation on earth in the form of the circle was thought to be effective against all sinister forces which shunned light.

The circle's very shape increased its antidemonic potency. Having neither beginning nor ending, it stood for eternity and infinity. It

symbolized perfection and constant renewal. It meant ultimate oneness in which there was no room for another power.

No wonder earliest cultures made frequent use of this charmed
image. They used it as a magic shield against all hostile and dangerous
agencies. This explains such peculiar symbols as the fish, the serpent
or the dragon biting its tail. The ''live'' circular figure formed by the
animal endowed its owner with an even more dynamic force with
which to counteract evil.

The beauty and perfection of the circle made it the ideal barrier
against attacks by the devil. He could not penetrate its magic line nor
find in it any dent, curve or nook he could secretly occupy to launch
his nefarious work. It was a belief that influenced some odd nine-
teenth-century architecture in the English village of Veryan, in Corn-
wall. There, five completely circular cottages had their round shape
especially chosen so that the devil would not find any corner in which
to hide.

This background of the circle explains how it assumed its significant role in the charmed work of magicians and wizards. Its purpose
was twofold. First, the magic circle would act as an invisible,
impenetrable barrier keeping out any forces that might interfere or try
to defeat the magician's occult pursuit. Second, it would serve as a
container of psychic power that would give extra, highly concentrated
strength to the magicians. Isolated and protected inside, they would
be able to cast spells and engage in other occult and mystic activities.

### The Wedding Ring and the Wreath

With all his sophistication, enlightened man does not realize how
much he unwittingly practices ancient magic.

To make sure the marital union would stay happy and love remain
strong, the man placed a magic circle on his new partner. Early
peoples used to tie a rope around the bride. Just as its lines were
unending, the magic circle thus would ensure the perpetuity of the
bond. By putting the ring on his bride's finger, the groom ''surrounded'' his good luck and thereby prevented it magically from
leaking out.

Similarly, when men pay a last tribute to the deceased, they often
put wreaths on the grave to ''honor'' the person's memory.

In reality, both customs originated from crude fear and a "protection racket."

Nothing was more frightening than being haunted by the spirit of the dead. To make sure the ghost of the deceased would stay underground and not come up to do mischief, man devised numerous precautions which he now rationalizes as hygienic and respectful, if not pious. Thus, the corpse is enclosed in a coffin with its lid firmly screwed down, the grave is filled in with heavy soil and, to top it all, a weighty, massive stone is placed above as a "memorial." But far superior to all those measures was the magic: the power of the circular wreath which, more than any other "material" practice, would tether the spirit to the body.

## POINTING THE FINGER

We teach our children that it is rude to point a finger at anyone. Why should this be so? In fact, the warning has nothing to do with etiquette or good manners. It, too, is a survivor of man's magic past. He believed that psychic power was concentrated in his finger, like in a magic cone, and by aiming at a target, he could achieve miraculous things.

It is not difficult to trace the origin of this notion to early times when man, aware of the omnipotence of sex, worshiped the phallus. It was the source of everything. He could not fail to recognize in his outstretched finger the image of the male organ, in a state of erection ready to eject its sperm. The finger thus could prove equally "productive" in the creation of both good and evil.

The use of the outstretched finger in the gesture of blessing was not a symbolic bestowal of the gift but was intended to generate good fortune for whomever it was pointed at. Conversely, men came to use the finger to inflict harm. In primitive society, the phrase "to point the finger" became synonymous with killing a person.

Eventually, the pointing finger became detached from the hand and stretched. Helped by the rod, it evolved into the magic wand, now totally independent of the hand but no less effective.

The Bible tells how Moses produced the plagues that hit Pharaoh and his people by "pointing." By stretching his hand toward the sky, he made the sun vanish and darkness envelop the land. When at

Moses' bidding Aaron pointed his rod toward the river Nile, he caused the frogs to come up and cover the land. Whether a rod or hand (this fivefold multiplication of the finger), they all reflect the identical magic of the phallus as represented by the digit. Therefore, it was not simply used as a powerful metaphor by the Egyptian magicians, who when referring to the plagues that had befallen their land, said, "This is the finger of God!" (Exod. 8:15).

Man's ancestral memory has not forgotten the original ominous connotation of the pointing finger, and he continues to decry the gesture as uncouth. But at the back of his mind remains the ancient fear.

## THE ORIGIN OF ABRACADABRA

Magicians and conjurers traditionally utter abracadabra to accomplish their tricks. The spectators know it is showmanship and that abracadabra is a word that makes no sense and has neither meaning nor power.

The assumption, however, is completely false. In abracadabra survives an age-old mystical formula. It was thought to ward off evil and to cure disease.

The first record of abracadabra dates back to Serenus Sammonicus, a second-century Roman author and the physician to Emperor Caracalla. He stated that abracadabra could serve as a potent antidote to sickness, if applied according to strict rules. There are numerous explanations as to what the strict rules were, which way the abracadabra worked and what its name signified.

Generally, abracadabra was thought to be a combination or abbreviation of several, slightly mutilated Hebrew words, and this gave rise to a multitude of confusing claims. Some authorities traced it to the Hebrew term *b'racha* or "blessing." Abracadabra, they said, really meant "pronounce the blessing." Blessing was not used in its traditional benedictory sense, however, but specifically referred to God. Speaking of him in abracadabra would drive away the evil spirits, for they were unable to tolerate hearing the divine name.

A second interpretation found in abracadabra the linking of the Hebrew "blessing"—*b'racha*—with the mystical "word" *davar*. The word of blessing was sure magically to destroy any curse.

Abracadabra was a contracted quotation from the Psalmist's call on God (Ps. 144:6) to "cast forth lightning" (in Hebrew, *b'rok barak*) to scatter the evil forces. No doubt this suggestion was based on the similarity of sound between the two.

Another view reflected Christian theology, though it drew upon the Jew's Hebrew and Aramaic tongues for the obscure word it regarded as an appeal to the Trinity. In the name of "the father (*ab*), the son (*bar*) and the holy spirit (*ru-ach ha-kodesh*)," the formula tried to expel demons. It was a method well known in the ritual of exorcism.

Another expert on the occult argued that abracadabra contained nothing godly nor did it quote from the Bible, however fragmentarily or misconstrued. On the contrary, abracadabra was the actual (Aramaic or Greek) name of a powerful demon. It could affect people in different ways. It could make them sick with ague or fever or bring them misfortune.

Once the demon had taken hold of a person, only immediate remedial action could save him by driving out the malevolent spirit. And in the world of magic, you had to fight fire with fire, like with like. By calling the name of the spirit Abracadabra, you expelled it from the victim. The spirit could not resist the "call" and, answering it, left the possessed person, who at once was restored to his former state of normalcy.

This explanation makes particular sense when one remembers that, according to magic belief, whoever knows the name of a being can control it.

Others, however, have denied any legitimate, inherent value of the term abracadabra. It existed, they believe, because of the corruption of the name Abraxas, a powerful Gnostic deity, who played a significant role in the Basilidian heretic sect of the Gnostics.

The sect was named after its founder, Basilides of Alexandria, who had claimed to have gained knowledge of the existence of the mighty god, Abraxas. This Greek name meant "hurt me not," and when uttered would magically take out the sting from any attack by demonic forces.

Going far beyond its literal meaning, Abraxas' mystical power was based primarily on the Oriental and Greek tradition of doubling letters to make figures. Individual letters of the alphabet also had a numerical value, and the seven-lettered Abraxas added up to 365. This significant figure not only stood for the number of days of the solar year, but for the number of spirits that emanated from Abraxas. Subject to him, these spirits ruled the world; they represented individual virtues, each allotted to one of the days of the year and thus the authority of Abraxas-abracadabra was both infinite and eternal.

Going back even further and more to the East, it is said that the Persians worshiped 365 different deities. And to be totally blessed, the pious had to invoke each one. This was a difficult and time-consuming task, and because of the multiplicity of names was also subject to grievous error. To omit one of the gods might play havoc with a man's life. He, therefore, contrived to combine the 365 in one word which, by the numerical value of its letters, represented the entire pantheon. This rendered the original abracadabra a fantastic, error-proof substitute, ready for use by the faithful.

Without any waste of time or fear of mistake the utterance would cast out evil spirits in man's ceaseless battle against dark forces. Having all his gods at his disposal in one word, their combined power could not be surpassed and was irresistible.

## The Application of Abracadabra

Certainly, there are few words in any tongue that have caused more speculation and diversity of interpretations. But no matter what abracadabra really meant, how it was applied concerned people most of all. And this was distinguished by a variety of methods which, in turn, depended on how it was thought the abracadabra worked.

The most widely adopted practice was based on sympathetic magic. By manipulating the abracadabra into a charm, it was believed, you could also affect the evil spirit or sickness that inflicted a person. The charm was created by a systematic reduction of abracadabra, letter by letter. As the abracadabra diminished till it reached the "vanishing point," so would the harmful influence diminish. Gradually it would disappear.

The usual form the charm took was that of an amulet. Of small size, it consisted of paper or parchment, of a thin metal sheet or even an engraved gemstone. The magic formula followed a fixed pattern. The top line contained the whole word abracadabra. On each following line, one letter was dropped till, finally, at the very bottom, one single letter was left. The occult power of the amulet was further strengthened by arranging the text in the shape of an inverted triangle.

A B R A C A D A B R A
A B R A C A D A B R
A B R A C A D A B
A B R A C A D A
A B R A C A D
A B R A C A
A B R A C
A B R A
A B R
A B
A

The triangle was chosen because it was a holy figure, the symbol of trinity and hence a powerful opponent of devilish forces.

The "abracadabra" was worn as a necklace or fixed wherever it could be most effective. Usually the charm was dispensed with after nine days. Before sunrise it was thrown backward over the left shoulder, if possible, into a stream which flowed in an easterly direction.

Each of these rituals had a significant meaning. The left side was the sinister side—that of the devil. Nine was a sacred figure, three times three. The East was linked with the rising sun which would dispel all darkness.

Some patients would actually swallow the charm so as to make it part of their system. Another group uttered the word aloud. Instead of having the formula written down in its ever diminishing size, line following line, they uttered it repeatedly and on each occasion dropped one letter, till nothing was left.

Often the original purpose of a custom is completely forgotten with the passing of time. And that happened to the abracadabra. Eventually people no longer remembered its original meaning and successive generations were mystified at its strange sound. Thus its mystic and occult efficacy was increased, particularly for those who sought it out in combating their fears and their often psychosomatically caused ailments.

## HOCUS-POCUS

People have always been gullible. It is no wonder, therefore, that those anxious to deceive traded on the ignorant person's respect for apparently superior knowledge. Anything he could not grasp necessarily contained special power. Who could check whether a foreign-sounding word or phrase was not a sham? And sham is the origin of hocus-pocus. Many have been tricked by this nonsense, not only at a conjurer's performance but when seriously seeking the origin of the term.

Some people recognized hocus-pocus as mere gabble, a spurious Latin phrase. After all, as Latin formulas were customary in the prescription of medicine that cured disease, why should not a juggler likewise work wonders with Latin words that were beyond the comprehension of the average man?

Philologists assigned its origin to the linguistic phenomenon of "reduplication." Common especially in the world of slang, it doubled up words and created such words as hoity-toity and hanky-panky. Hocus-pocus was just another phrase of that type. There was nothing mysterious behind it all.

Yet others, equally learned in the realm of language, were well aware that sometimes what was originally a man's name was adopted as a word. One recalls eighteenth-century Dr. Joseph Ignace Guillotine, an eminent Parisian physician, and the hurried meal eaten by the fourth Earl of Sandwich! Hence, these scholars claim, hocus-pocus had as its ancestor a person as well. Some identified hocus-pocus with a mythological figure and others with Mr. Ochus Bochus, whom they alleged had been a famous seventeenth-century conjurer. But neither of the claims has ever been substantiated.

Hocus-pocus has a religious basis. It was first coined, so it was said, to ridicule the Roman Catholic faith and to stress the rational superiority of Protestantism. Both share the Communion Service but differ in its meaning.

The Communion Service enacts Christ's Last Supper. Like all Jews, Jesus and his twelve disciples had joined in the traditional Passover Eve meal. An important part of it was the breaking of bread and blessing of wine, as practiced on the eve of every Sabbath and Jewish festival.

Meticulously following Jewish tradition, Jesus blessed both the bread and the wine and shared them with the rest of the company. The Gospel tells how Jesus then handed the wine to his disciples, accompanied with the words, "This is my blood." And, when sharing the bread, he pointed to it, saying "This is my body."

Catholic priests, when celebrating Mass, use the same words. When they lift up the bread, they say, "This is the body of the Lord" (*Hoc est corpus domini*). In fact, Catholics believe that at that moment the substance of the bread is actually changed into the body of Christ. This is the accepted Catholic doctrine of transsubstantiation.

Protestants deny such miraculous transformation and believe that when Jesus used the quotation, he did so symbolically. To voice their disagreement, some militant extremists parodied the sacred formula as *hocuspocus*. The underlying intention of ridicule gave hocus-pocus the originally blasphemous connotation of make-believe. And that is how *hocus-pocus dominicus* eventually became the modern conjuring formula. From mock Latin and a misquotation, hocus-pocus has been shortened to "hoax" for the Anglicized version.

## MUMBO JUMBO

Many people believed occult practices were not genuine, but were aimed at exploiting people's credulity. They were a meaningless and pretentious ritual. In fact, a mumbo jumbo.

Mumbo jumbo comes from the western Sudan in Africa, according to Mungo Park, the explorer-writer who was Sir Walter Scott's friend. He gives details about its origin in his *Travels in the Interior of Africa*, published in 1799.

Park showed that mumbo jumbo was make-believe but was invented for a very valid reason. A husband in Senegal had been greatly irritated by the constant chatter and irresponsible talk of one of his wives. This had caused such dissension at home that to reestablish peace and harmony, he was determined to silence her.

As his own word carried no weight, he deviously hired someone to impersonate Mama Dyumbo, the god of their tribe and of its territory. Mama Dyumbo was also their ancestral spirit, as indicated by the name, which in their dialect meant "the ancestor" (*Mama*) with a "pompon" (*Dyumbo*).

It is not certain whether the husband himself or a friend impersonated the god. Whoever it was did a good job, for he distinctly displayed a tuft of feathers—the pompon—on the front of his headdress. His face was disguised by a mask, and to scare the woman out of her wits, he accompanied his appearance with a terrifying, hideous noise.

The "god" then stripped the culprit naked and tied her to a tree to give her a sound beating which she would never forget.

The entire performance was gleefully watched by the members of their tribe. Giving vent to their feelings by appropriate jeers, they added their contribution and made it an even more "memorable" occasion.

Another version alleges that mumbo jumbo actually grew out of the earth and was the name of the tree (*mama jombo*) which served as a whipping post for the obstreperous woman.

No doubt, in a man-dominated society it was all done to keep the woman strictly in her place and to warn off other potential troublemakers. It would teach them to toe the line and never again threaten the men's peaceful existence. And with all the disguise, noise and chastising, the woman learned her lesson, and any other unruly wife henceforth was doubly careful to mind her words.

Through Mungo Park, Mama Dyumbo became universalized and corrupted on Western tongues into mumbo jumbo; and a figure of terror became a figure of speech.

## TREE WORSHIP

Spirits abounded. They made their home almost everywhere. It was all a matter of the lay of the land and man's geographically conditioned way of life. People felt they owed a special debt to those invisible forces on whose good will their entire existence depended. If left unpaid, the spirits would collect their dues at tremendous cost to their wayward debtor.

One of the most favored seats of the gods was the tree. In forested lands man believed his life was determined by their mysterious growth which, he was convinced, was the result of the spirit that dwelt within.

Trees gave shelter and shade. Their timber enabled man to warm himself, to build a home and to cross waters. Their fruit—as the acorn of the oak tree—would nourish his animals. The rustling of their leaves, particularly at night, was meant to convey a supernatural message. Most of all, from roots to the crown, the tree seemed to link earth and heaven.

Tree worship was one of the early forms of religion. Originally, it involved human sacrifice. People were tied to a tree and pinioned with arrows. Later the cruel custom was eliminated and the arrows were aimed straight at the tree trunk.

Both the story of Robin Hood's forays with bow and arrow in Sherwood Forest and the Swiss account of William Tell in which the hero aims an arrow at the apple placed on the young boy's head are not mere national myths. They are echoes of the once very real and widespread custom of sacrificing humans to the spirit of the wood. Thus they paid for its guidance and guardianship with the life sap of their own kind!

Ever since ancient days, arrows symbolized rain. Therefore by shooting them into the trunk of the tree, the arrows would nourish it with the life-promoting and life-preserving liquid. So deeply ingrained was the belief in the magic of trees that man did everything to ensure their growth and prevent their decay.

The oak was regarded particularly sacred, and especially so by the Druids. Its leaves were thought to contain the life-essence of the tree and its supernatural powers in concentrated form. They were an effective means by which to bestow extra vitality and renewed strength to those who needed it most.

That is why Romans crowned with a wreath of oak leaves those who had spent themselves in the execution of some extraordinary feat, and why the British used them likewise as the insignia of their army field marshals. In later centuries the leaves became the symbol of steadfastness and reliability suggested by the oak.

The ancient Hebrew prophets vehemently decried among their own people the continued Canaanite custom of deifying the tree. Tree trunks with chopped off branches were erected and worshiped. Sacred to the goddess Asherah, by whose name they were called, and no doubt symbolic of the phallus, the Asherah fulfilled an eminent role in the cult of vegetation.

The yule log, now associated with Christmas, assumed its mysterious power by joining the fertility of the earth with the life-giving warmth of the sun. Magically it was thought to help nature to overcome the darkness of winter and see the rebirth of spring.

That yew trees were grown in churchyards and cemeteries, too, had its significant meaning and message. Originally, it was not that yews were planted near churches but that churches were built near yew trees. Man observing how the yew kept on growing for many centuries, made it a symbol of his faith in immortality.

Those who nowadays continue to "touch wood" (or knock on it) for luck, do so because of the ancient tree worship. People used to summon the friendly spirit they imagined to live in the tree by knocking on its trunk. By doing this they paid it their respect but also called on its help to maintain their good luck and protect them from impending misfortune.

The influence of ancient tree worship thus continues in the modern world, even though unrecognized. A Chinese proverb has it that "if the roots are deep, there is no fear that the wind will uproot the tree." And this applies as well to its occult traditions.


## MAGIC IN NAMES

The choice of a given name is often a matter of fashion. Parents like to be with it. Annual statistics record the most favored name during the year and its selection might be influenced by the popularity of a politician or an actor or be just a crazy idea created by the media.

People forget that by falling for this temptation, they actually "date" their child for the future. All Shirleys named after Shirley Temple, for example, must be of a certain age and therefore her name is a dead giveaway at a time when the bearer least wishes to be reminded of her age.

Babies are often named after a relative. And among Christians, male offspring are frequently given the name of their father, followed by "junior," or, in the case of successive generations, by number, following the example of kings.

Jewish people (who follow the Ashkenazic tradition), however, never call a child after a living parent; this would be tantamount to wishing the father or mother dead. This tradition recalls a time when names were regarded not just as a means of identification and differentiation between one person or another, but were believed to be of great magical value.

The name, first of all, was seen as an integral part of the individual;

it determined his or her fate. Its choice, therefore, demanded utmost care and consideration.

To know the name of a person would render him into one's power. For this reason primitive races guarded their first name as a precious secret and assumed others to mislead those anxious to manipulate them. The second and fictitious name, of course, was not tied to their spirit and, therefore, could do no harm by being revealed. Among gypsies, individuals were not told their own names except once, when their mothers whispered it into their ears at birth.

In early times, God's ''name'' was kept secret. Among the Hebrews, for instance, only the high priest was entitled to use it and then only on the most sacred day, Yom Kippur. It was never written down but transmitted orally from one priestly generation to another.

The Hebrew Bible tells how Moses, on meeting God, was anxious to know the divine name. He justified his request by explaining that when approaching the Israelites on God's behalf, they were most likely to ask what the God, who sent him, was called. The answer God gave, as related in Scriptures (Exod. 3:14), has been subject to varied interpretations and originated the mysterious tetragrammaton—YHVH—the ''four-letter'' name.

Quite possibly, God evaded the issue and did not want to entrust even Moses with this vital information and just called himself ''I am who I am.'' Should Moses be asked by his people, all he would have to say was that ''I am'' had sent him.

''Change of name,'' not by deed poll but by magic, was a custom that was believed could actually change a person's fate.

It was a ritual performed especially among Jewish people, and still observed in recent times. When someone was dangerously ill and any hope of survival was very slim, as a last resort, the individual was given a new name. It was thought that by doing so the person was changed and thereby his or her destiny as well. The name was not merely a label but part of the individual's soul essence. Since the angel of death was already on his way to collect Mr. X. and, knowing only the name given to him on the death warrant, if Mr. X no longer existed, it was reasoned, death could not find him and was unable to execute (!) his mission. That is how the former Mr. X, under his new alias, had been given a new lease on life. The change of name had acted as a magic lifesaver.

Another significant custom concerning the magic of a name is linked with the belief in reincarnation. It taught that at death the body died but not its soul or spirit. It only "passed on" and would be reborn in some other creature. Possibly, this would even be a descendant which is why in some societies a newborn child was given the name of a dead ancestor. It was done not just to honor his memory, as we now rationalize the practice. It was assumed that the new human being was "ensouled" with the spirit of his dead forbear. Among Scottish Highlanders, who practiced this custom, it was called in Gaelic, "raising the spirit."

To give a name was not merely a poetic art. It could be a magic pursuit. A name was an omen. But it was also a powerful means by which to dominate people and, therefore, there was danger in being introduced. Shakespeare with all his genius was not entirely right in his depreciation of the importance of a name, in his assertion that "a rose by any other name would smell as sweet."

# CHAPTER TWO

# Numerology

## HOW NUMBERS COUNT

From the very moment numbers entered human thought, they were given a position of great importance. They were not only used for the practical purpose of counting, but were viewed as the elementals of life, becoming the foundation of the world. Just as in recent years all matter was found to consist of atoms, the numeral was seen as the basis of existence. Not an abstract concept or merely related to objects, it constituted and controlled life.

Numbers assumed an independent reality to be reckoned with. Theirs was a particular degree of distinction, even of sanctity. Therefore, they served an important role in calculating fate and determining the destiny of man and of this world. They were first noted down to express symbolic values.

The Babylonians depicted their gods by "figures"—in the numerical sense. The Mayas, on the other hand, in writing their numbers used different types of human heads to represent the numbers from 1 to 13, and zero.

The monumental pyramids, both in Egypt and Mexico, were constructed according to exact measurements. These were calculated for reasons associated with the fate of the nation, not for architectural and constructional purposes. Their true meaning has given rise to countless, and at times fantastic, speculations.

Chaldean astrologers and Persian magi were the first to discover how numbers figured in the pattern of the universe.

However, it was the sixth-century B.C. Greek philosopher Pythagoras who popularized the idea that a figure was not just an abstract number but had its own individuality. And he further taught that "all things are numerical." That is how numbers took their part in man's attempt to understand, to calculate and to control fate. Man sought to apprehend the mystical qualities of numbers and began to apply these magically so that they became an intricate part of his world of the occult.

## FIGURING IT OUT

If mysticism has employed numbers in its practices, it certainly must have been influenced greatly by the remarkable amount, and sometimes confusing ways numbers have been used throughout the history of civilization.

Why, for instance, in English, do we abbreviate "number" by the two letters "No." and not, as would be expected, by "Nr."? The peculiar contraction goes back to the Italian way of counting, in which a number was known as *numero*.

The use of numbers alone made it easy for people to study huge volumes. Only by their pagination—the numbering of the various pages—might readers know the right sequence of the thoughts presented, and follow them.

"Arab" figures are not Arab at all. They originated in India. But the fallacious designation was attached to them because in the tenth century they were introduced into Europe by the Moors, and they were Arabs.

Equally bewildering is the division of a minute into sixty "seconds." What made people choose their odd description? It was due to man's having become more time conscious. He had learned to treasure each moment and, to count it, he had added to the dial of his clocks an additional, "second" hand to indicate the passing of those shorter units of time. And they took their name after that *second* pointer.

All calculation goes back to the counting of pebbles, which, in Latin, were called *calculi*. In their democratic constitution of society, Greeks would "cast" their vote by dropping pebbles into the urn for the candidate they wished to elect.

## THE SACRED 3

"Third time" is considered lucky and the notion is closely linked with the idea of trinity, a holy concept in many races and creeds, pagan and Christian alike.

So much in life seemed to reveal a threefold basis. Life consisted of past, present and future. Man was imagined to be made up of body, soul and spirit. The ideal family was the father, the mother and the child. Three expressed the beginning, the middle and the end. And nature itself was believed to embrace the three kingdoms: animal, vegetable and mineral. Above all, it was the moon, so closely associated with the occult, which brought home to man the all-importance of the 3. The moon showed itself in three aspects: waxing, full and waning. Three, so Pythagoras taught, indeed was "the perfect number."

Thus the triangle, with its three sides, became a potent emblem, occuring as a magic sign all over the world. Because of the sanctity of it, evil forces were thought to be put off by it. Confronted by the triangle, whether in sight or sound, the devil would take his leave.

This explains why three volleys are fired over a soldier's grave. Originally, this was not done in his honor but, as in primitive pagan days, the thrice-repeated noise was imagined to frighten away the devil anxious to get hold of the soul.

The superstition against using one match for three cigarettes was linked with the sacred number 3 and not with the danger to which soldiers exposed themselves by doing so in the dark of night. The practice would offend the deity, as it would desecrate a most holy number by using it in a profane task. The 3 should be reserved only for holy occasions such as in the Greek Orthodox Church where three candles are lit on the high altar.

The deeply rooted tradition of the close unity of the 3 led to the common belief that good and bad things also happen in a series of three.

Three was a significant number among the Celts. They applied it in their magic and knew of triplets and gods they arranged in groups of three. Greek mythology, likewise, venerated the triad. There was meaning in the existence of the Three Graces, Three Furies and Three Fates.

The sanctity and inherent potency of the 3 accounts for the conviction that for a magic formula to work effectively it has to be repeated three times, and so we continue to give cheers in threes. The holiest blessing in both the Jewish and Christian faith is the threefold benediction.

## THE MEANING OF 5

The "figure" in both senses of the word has been responsible for the name and the tremendous magic efficacy attributed to the five-pointed star.

There were several significant reasons for the all-importance of five in magic. It goes back to Pythagoras who spread the idea of the vital role numbers played in the very existence and fate of the world. He taught that everything depended on them, that they were bound up with all life.

Five obtained its special value, particularly so in its control over evil spirits, through the combination of various factors.

To begin with, it was a compound of the first even and odd numbers, adding up the 2 and 3 figures that in occult tradition are endowed with deep mystical quality.

But there was so much more to the five. Man's five fingers may have pointed the way, as they produced the complete hand that could work wondrous deeds.

It was believed that man had been given five senses which alone could open up to him the world that would otherwise remain a closed book to him. It was often thought that only the use of all five together would ensure total enjoyment of anything. It was one of the reasons given for the strange custom of clinking glasses prior to drinking wine or any other alcoholic beverage. Without doing so, only four of man's senses (those of smell, sight, touch and taste) would partake of it and therefore his experience would remain merely partial. He had to hear the drink as well.

Almost every culture and mythology adopted the sacred five and saw in it a symbol of true completeness and supernatural power that could have the most beneficial or devastating results.

The instructions given to the Israelites for the building of their sacrificial altar stipulated that it had to measure five cubits both in length and in width. Young David smote the giant Goliath with five smooth pebbles he had picked up out of a brook. The Gospel speaks of the five wise virgins and the five foolish ones. And it was surely not accidental that Jesus fed the five thousand with five loaves of bread (and two fishes). Most of all, five gained supreme sacred significance in the Christian realm by the five stigmata: the five wounds on Christ's crucified body caused by the nails that pierced his hands and feet and the lance that pierced his side.

## 7—A GIFT FROM HEAVEN

The fact that 7 should be a lucky and mystical number is based on an early error. Ancient astronomers watching the skies recognized seven "planets." They incorrectly included the sun and the moon in the number.

The seven "stars" were regarded as divine, which made them sacred and luck-bringing. This concept created the seven-day week which even in Christian countries continues to honor the celestial pagan gods. Sunday pays homage to the sun and Monday to the moon, as does Saturday to the planet Saturn.

There were other factors that gave fortunate meaning to the 7, causing it to be treated with awe and respect. The early Greeks and followers of Pythagoras saw in the 7 the combination of 4 and 3—two other significant numbers which, when added up, made 7. Therefore, the 7, by its very constituents, was doubly holy and the very pinnacle of good luck.

Seven had the further distinction of being a number which was completely unrelated to any other figure in the sequence of 1 to 10. Its unequaled character bestowed on it a supernatural quality.

Seven also came to symbolize perfection and completeness. "The seven seas," for example, was never meant to be taken literally, though people often refer to them as such. Originally, the phrase was a figure of speech to denote all the seas and oceans of the world. Rudyard Kipling popularized it by choosing *The Seven Seas* as the title for a collection of poems which he stressed held only the symbolic meaning of the figure.

With celestial, astronomical and arithmetical aspects, the 7 became a mystic and sacred numeral from the earliest days. To take an oath on the 7 made it a ceremony so binding that no one would ever doubt its truth or break the promise given. That is why in biblical Hebrew the word for "swearing" is derived from the identical root as the numeral 7. Herodotus records how Arabs, for the same reason, took their oaths over seven stones which they smeared with blood. There were the Seven Wonders of the world. The Greeks had their seven sages. Rome was built on seven hills. Noah is said to have taken seven animals of each clean species into his Ark. Seven days was the period necessary to be ritually purified for a cured leper. The seventh child of a seventh child was said to be endowed with psychic powers.

Conspicuous were the seven lamps on the seven-branched candlestick of the Temple in Jerusalem.

In his vision of the future sanctuary, the prophet Ezekiel pointed to the seven steps that would lead up to it. When the dead son of the Sulamite woman was revived by Elisha, he rose up and opened his eyes after sneezing seven times.

The Jewish festivals of Passover and Tabernacles lasted seven days, and exactly seven weeks were counted between the Feast of Unleavened Bread and the Feast of Weeks which was responsible for its name. That is why Pentecost as well is so called: it falls on the fiftieth day after Easter—seven times seven days later.

The seventh day of the week, the Sabbath, is the most sacred, dedicated to God. To this very day at the Jewish solemnization of a marriage, the couple's union is sanctified by the utterance of the "seven benedictions."

Moslems believe in and popularized the existence of seven heavens, the seventh of which was the holiest of all. It was the region of pure light and the abode of God. We still thus describe the acme of happiness by saying that we are "in seventh heaven."

## A MAGICAL MULTIPLICATION TABLE

If individual figures—like the 3, 7 and 13—are distinguished by their intrinsic dynamic and magical value, it goes without saying that their multiplication or their joining of forces must result in an even more awesome potency in the minds of the superstitious.

The belief in a cat's nine lives, a royal salute, the coming of age at twenty-one and the belief in the periodic systematic destruction of civilization every fifty-two years all have their origin in this magic multiplication of sacred and mystic numbers.

## NUMBER 9

A cat has always been looked upon as a mysterious creature, somehow related to "the other world" and therefore endowed, if not with occult power, at least with the gift of telepathic communication. A cat always seemed to fall on its feet and was very tough and resilient. Hence it was thought to have not just one life but nine. Nine was the multiplication of the sacred trinitarian figure.

Man must have realized the obvious, fertile potency of the 9. The nine months of pregnancy was proof of its life-giving faculty.

Those juggling with numbers observed yet another outstanding quality and phenomenon of the 9, which added to the mystery of the figure. No matter with which other digit it was multiplied, the digits of the resulting number always added up to 9. Thus, for instance, 6 times 9 makes 54; 9 multiplied by 9 is 81, and each time the sum of the digits (5+4 and 8+1) is the selfsame 9. No wonder that those seeking the occult meaning of numbers paid special reverence to this thrice three, the perfect plural—9.

### The Cat-o'-Nine-Tails

The cat-o'-nine-tails was the whip used to punish offenders in the army and navy, and was used as recently as 1948 in Great Britain in cases of crimes of violence.

The number of its "tails" (which were actually knotted cords attached to the handle of the whip) was not accidental. The number 9 was thought to ensure that the flogging would be effective and reform the guilty party for the rest of his life. (The choice of the cat's name for this cruel instrument was due to the fact that injuries suffered by the flogging looked like scratches a cat would inflict.)

### "On Cloud 9"

A nicer application of the figure is when we talk of being "on top of cloud number 9." There is a suggestion that this figure of speech expressing rapture and ecstasy might be derived from the science of meteorology. Weather experts numbered the various cloud formations and in their numerology, "No. 9" referred to a thundercloud. To sit on top of it would certainly put a person up very high. In fact, he would be out of danger of being struck by lightning which, it was assumed, always struck downward. A person thus positioned was sure to enjoy the full benefit of the warmth and brightness of the sun.

Also very likely, "cloud number 9" was specially chosen as a figure of speech because people in the heaven of perfect bliss felt so uplifted that they would associate their state of mind with the most perfect of numbers, the holiest figure—the trinity of trinities.

## THE FIRST DOZEN

Twelve completed the original counting and the galaxy of figures. It originated with the ancient Sumerians who, it is thought, first introduced the sexagesimal system which is at its basis.

The twelve signs of the Zodiac and the subsequent division of the year into twelve months gave the number its special status. But there were even more significant reasons which account for the prominent place the 12 came to occupy in people's lives. They were fascinated by the multiple divisibility of the figure—by 2, 3 and 4—and were awed by the realization that it combined the qualities of the mystic 5 and the magic 7 which, when added up, made 12. To top it all, the sum of the digits of 12 led back to the holy trinity.

No wonder that a figure invested with such value came to dominate so much. There were the twelve tribes in the Old Testament and the twelve Apostles in the New. Hercules had to execute twelve labors and a jury is usually constituted of "twelve men good and true."

The twelfth night—January 5—had its own mystic significance far back in pre-Christian Roman times. Shakespeare's play of that name made the *Twelfth Night* especially famous.

Prior to the introduction of the decimal system, Englishmen and countries that adopted their monetary system, used to count their pennies in lots of twelve. A dozen of them made up one shilling.

Twelve, a figure so distinguished, was hard to beat. Anything following it was like an anticlimax, which is why the number 13 became so unlucky.

## THE UNLUCKY 13

The numeral 13 shares the fate of the black cat in man's ambivalent attitudes. It all depends on who and where you are, and whether the cat and the 13 mean good luck or misfortune to you.

Thirteen has not always been considered the unlucky number it is generally assumed to be now. The Aztecs saw in it a divine figure, and built 13 steps to the sacred platform on which they kept their holy fire burning for exactly four times thirteen years at a time. The Mayas, prior to the Aztecs, had worshiped "the 13 gods of the upper world" and regarded them as so holy that they saw the 13 as one collective deity.

Thirteen indeed was an important magical, if not cosmic numeral. Various myths all over the world told of a group of twelve who, by the addition of one, grew to the paramount number of thirteen. Thus, the sun, added to the twelve signs of the Zodiac, made thirteen. Indians in their temples paid homage to thirteen Buddhas.

In the Jewish faith, 13 has always had a happy and sacred connotation. Interpreting a passage in the book of Exodus (34:6-7), God was believed to reveal himself by thirteen of his attributes, all of which expressed his bountiful mercy. The divine name itself, as it appeared in the tetragrammaton—the four-lettered Yahveh (YHVH)— added up to a value of twice 13, so numerologists pointed out. (Y was the numeral for 10; H for 5 and V for 6.)

Still part of every orthodox Jewish prayerbook are the "Thirteen Principles of Faith." They were drawn up by Maimonides (or Moses ben Maimon), a twelfth-century philosopher whose constant aim was to be a "Guide of the Perplexed," the very words with which he entitled his main work. Up to this day, Jewish boys celebrate their Bar Mitzvah at the age of thirteen, when they become full and responsible members of the community.

Circumstance gave the figure 13 an especially significant role in the history of the United States. Because of the nation's original thirteen states, the American flag continues to display thirteen stripes and the American eagle to count thirteen feathers on each wing.

Thirteen was the favorite number of the German composer Richard Wagner. Not only did he take note that his name consisted of thirteen letters, but he was born in 18*13*, composed thirteen operas and completed *Tannhauser* on March 13, 1845.

It is very understandable why the notion of the unlucky 13 became so deeply rooted in man's mind. It, too, goes back to earliest times. Now part of man's ancestral memory, it has almost become an instinct.

The ability of primitive man to count was limited. He could do so up to 12 but no further. That is why no numbers beyond the 12 have an individual and independent name, but are merely composed of a combination of the description of the previous numbers. This might also explain why for no apparent reason the traditional multiplication table stops at 12 times 12.

If 12 was the end of the line, 13, which followed it, had no exact value and definite meaning at first. Hence it was an uncertain number, fraught with mystery. This enigmatic quality of the 13 made man fear the numeral and render it fateful and foreboding. This original association has never died and, unconsciously, continues to haunt and to obsess people.

No doubt a subsequent observation deepened the ominous quality attached to the 13. While 12 was a most "fortunate" number in the way it could be divided and could be seen as a multiple of 3 times 4 and 2 times 6, 13 stood on its own. Completely indivisible, it seemed not to mix with any other numbers. And because of its isolation, it came to be shunned.

These are the original causes for the attitudes about unlucky 13. All other explanations merely embellish this fear.

One example was provided by the Norse myth of the twelve gods who gathered for a banquet in Valhalla. Loki's gate-crashing of the party increased the number of gods to thirteen, which supposedly led to the death of Baldur, the most beloved of the gods.

As a child of Judaism, Christianity saw nothing evil in the number 13. Neither Jesus nor his twelve close friends shunned it. At the Last Supper, Christ and his twelve disciples made up a total of thirteen. No doubt, they had dined together many times previously, but it was this occasion that caused Christians to give the 13 its ominous meaning as a fateful number. Because Jesus and his twelve disciples had counted thirteen, it was later believed to have resulted in the crucifixion. The Last Supper and subsequent execution of Christ were seen not as a chronological sequence alone but as a chain of cause and effect. The crucifixion had actually been the consequence of the presence of thirteen at Christ's last celebration of the Jewish Passover eve. It was all a matter not of *post hoc* but *propter hoc*.

At least this idea became fixed in many Christian minds centuries after the event. It seemed only to confirm the widespread pagan tradition of the disastrous effect of 13.

Later, when Satanic cults tried to ridicule Christian tradition, they introduced the Black Mass as a mockery of the Last Supper and the Holy Communion service which evolved from it. When the followers of black magic met in their secret covens, it was said that on each occasion they made sure to number thirteen: twelve ordinary witches plus their leader or "warlock." The Christian Church was convinced that the Satanic cult had deliberately chosen this quorum, and, like so many features of its Black Mass, was deriding the Church's sacred tradition. One theory holds that it was the association of the number 13 with witchcraft and devilry that caused Christians to decry the numeral as evil. As an omen of misfortune and an integral part of Satanism, no good could come of it. By proclaiming 13 the most unlucky of numbers, the Christians felt they could keep people away from the Satanic gatherings, a practice so abominable in their eyes.

It was like a chain reaction which by diverse means seemed determined to establish 13 as the unlucky number. The malevolence of the number was further reinforced by the thirteenth card in the fortune-telling deck: it represented Death and was depicted as a skeleton carrying a scythe.

Belief in the unlucky 13 is the real reason why the thirteen loaves bakers once supplied in bulk were never called by their real number but described as "a baker's dozen." Some people did not dare even to utter the unfortunate number. More so, the thirteenth loaf was regarded as a special bribe for the devil so he would not spoil the sale or the bread.

Perhaps to make the irrational fear of 13 respectable, the very sophisticated liked to refer to it as "triskaidekaphobia," a word derived from the Greek *triskaideka* (13) and *phobia* (fear).

## 21 GUNS

A royal salute of 21 guns is not as "odd" a number as might at first appear. The figure was endowed with tremendous magical power brought about by the multiplication of two vital numbers: three times seven makes twenty-one. It was chosen with utmost care to welcome the king and those representing him, not out of honor but for protection against possible attacks by devilish forces.

The devil himself had his weak spots. He was very allergic to noise which would make him depart hurriedly. And what could be better and louder than the violent bang made by the firing of a gun! But to repeat this twenty-one times made absolutely sure the departure of the archfiend and thereby the safety of the king. Bombarding the devil with three times seven blasts was beyond his endurance.

The identical magic background of 21—as the multiple of the lucky 3 and sacred 7—caused man to believe that at the age of 21 life was renewed. It was a year of destiny. Reaching it, life started all over again, a fact legally recognized by giving citizens full responsibility and declaring a person to have come "of age." This magic spell has now been broken by our much faster life-style, and in many countries the prosaic 18 (years) has taken the place of the magic 21.


## A MAGIC RENEWAL OF LIFE

The ancient Mayan civilization was very "figure" conscious, and it introduced the first symbol for zero ever used. Counting for nothing, it could mean everything.

Mayas believed that certain numbers determined the very fate of man and the universe. These were 4, 7 and 13, which continued to play a significant part in the lives, the joys and fears, of the Toltecs and Aztecs who followed the Mayas. They applied and embodied these figures in their temples and pyramids, as can still be verified in their monuments and constructions.

Thirteen steps on each of its four sides led up to a famous altar platform near Mexico City. Four times the sacred thirteen added up to fifty-two steps, a number significantly identical with that of the weeks in the year.

The 52 became their most sacred figure. It was of cosmic significance. Life, they believed, consisted of cycles, each of which counted exactly that number of years.

Consequently, a fire was kept burning continuously for fifty-two years on the altar platform. Its flames, it was thought, ensured the survival of all living things, of nature and the universe. In fact, these flames were imagined to nourish the sun.

But at the end of the fifty-second year, the fire was extinguished. An era had come to an end. And all through the country, in its observance, people put out the fires in their homes and broke all their vessels. Then everyone anxiously waited for a certain star to reach its zenith. Coinciding with that occurrence, the sacred fire was rekindled in a solemn ritual. Runners standing by, lit torches from its flames which they carried to every part of the country, hastening along to bring the happy message of the rebirth of life.

The home fires, too, were now relit and new vessels made to replace those destroyed. Life had started all over again and the sun would shine on it—with its gifts of light, warmth and fertility—till this cycle, too, would be complete at the end of another four times thirteen years.

## THE DANGER OF BEING COUNTED

That people getting on in years are loathe to reveal their age is easily understood. Everyone likes to stay young.

But no satisfactory explanation is apparent for the odd biblical account of the disastrous effect of the census taken by King David to establish the exact number of his men of war. He did so against the advice of Joab, his chief in command (2 Sam. 24 and 1 Chron. 21).

The Bible reports that the moment the "counting of heads" had been completed, a plague broke out which within three days killed 70,000 men. It further mentions that David had embarked on the entire venture because Satan had enticed him "to count the people."

This "motivation" is the key that helps to understand the original reason for people's resistance throughout the ages against "taking stock" of any kind. They were most reticent to reveal their "vital" statistics, no matter whether this concerned their age, their fortune or the population of their country.

Even in our modern "enlightened" era a custom prevails among some Jewish people who, when asking a person's age, preface their inquiry by saying, "up to a hundred and twenty." This odd remark is really meant as a kind of countermagic that would annul any possible harm caused by revealing the number of years one had lived so far.

By giving away the number of your years, your fortune or your population—just like once upon a time by revealing your "real" name—you delivered yourself or the people into the power of the devil. Knowing the "right number," one gained power over the person to whom the figure not only referred but whom it actually represented.

Figures were not just a matter of mental calculation or cold statistics. They were identified with the individual to whom they belonged. Whoever got hold of them "possessed" and could manipulate the fate of this person for better or, mostly, for worse.

## THE ODDS HAVE IT

To enumerate the significance of numbers and the influence they have exerted on man is part of history and civilization. They certainly have been responsible for many of man's anticipations and apprehensions.

There are varied reasons why a specific figure should be linked with good or ill fortune. It may have its basis in a single historical incident or a mere coincidence. Or it could have been started by an alert mind with a keen sense of observation, or be the result of a deeply rooted but unexplained occult tradition or inevitably stumbled upon by repetitious experience.

Man ever concerned with his fate carefully watched the effect of each figure. He took note of the association of a number with a certain event and then never forgot their link. This gave that figure a permanent place in the realm of magic.

A man's life was regarded (by the Psalmist) to last "three score years and ten." If he was specially vigorous, it could extend to eighty years.

Passengers arriving by the latest jet planes may be put into quarantine. If so, they would observe the early tradition of the magic figure 40. This is the literal meaning of the Italian *quaranta*. It was thought to work wonders. If a person afflicted by a disease was kept in isolation for exactly forty days—not a day less or more—he would be cured.

The Bible has many references to the number 40. Noah and his family spent forty days in the Ark as did Moses on Mount Sinai to receive the divine revelation. The Israelites wandered through the desert for forty years, and Jonah gave the people of Nineveh forty days to repent. For forty days Jesus was tempted in the wilderness.

With the notable exception of 40, even numbers were always regarded as unlucky. Since they could be divided and thereby diminished in their value, they were considered as foreboding dissolution and death. But there was "divinity in odd numbers," in the words of Shakespeare. And because of it, 3, 7, 9 and 21 were inimical to evil forces which, scared by them, would do everything to shun them.

Examples of the belief in the lucky odd number could be culled from all over the world. A tradition tells that the legendary Roman king Numa Pompilius had added an extra day to those months of the calendar which unfortunately counted an even number of days. Chinese pagodas always have an odd number of stories which may vary anywhere between three and thirteen.

## WHEN YOUR NUMBER IS UP

At times of war soldiers and civilians exposed to mortal danger often adopt a fatalistic attitude. Somehow, they feel, destiny must have decreed in advance who should die. Therefore, it was no use to fret and to fear. It was said that no man could escape his fate if "his number was up."

On the other hand, the very same people would acknowledge a narrow escape by noting with relief that the bullet that had just missed them had done so not accidentally or by sheer luck but because, as they would put it, "my number wasn't on it"!

These were not mere colloquial phrases. They were the surviving belief that fate selected the individuals who were to die and magically executed its decision.

Children's games of "counting one out" such as "eenie, meenie, miney, mo," have the same numerological and magic origin. Like many other nursery rhymes, they have a lethal background in magic.

They go back to the days of the Druids, who decided by a count whose number was up to drop out and be sacrificed to the gods.

The origin of the word "decimation" has the same basis. Derived from the Latin for 10 (*decem*), it recalls the Roman punishment of army mutineers or surviving enemy soldiers after a victorious battle. One out of each batch of ten men was picked by lot to be executed.

## A REVELATION OF THE RITUAL

It is expected that there is magic in any ritual. This is the reason why those solemnizing it—whether in witchcraft or religion—meticulously follow the "order" prescribed and handed down with care from one generation to another. To deviate even in a minute degree from the right sequence, or to omit one detail, would spoil the efficacy of the act performed.

This also explains the strong objections raised by some people to any updating or changing of the traditional order of a rite. They do so not because of any sentimentalism on their part, an innate love of traditional tunes, words or ceremonies. The fundamental reason is their unconscious fear that any change might destroy the magic potency of the solemn practice.

Any rite and ritual literally reveals this anxious concern. Both terms are derived from the Indo-European root *ri* which actually speaks of a "number" and of "counting." A ritual, therefore, was the correct pattern in which each part "counted" and was allotted its proper place. And unless the right sequence was maintained, the magic just would not work. It was the most crucial condition for its success.

The rosary used in Roman Catholicism owes its very existence to this. Its purpose was to help worshipers keep an exact account of the number of prayers they had said, for without completing the prescribed amount, their entire devotion might prove futile. Very appropriately then, a rosary was known earlier in Europe as *calculi* and *numeralia*.

The reason Jewish people call both their Passover Eve celebration and their daily prayer book by the Hebrew terms for "order" (*seder* and *siddur* respectively) has the same origin. Only if the "order of worship" was properly followed, and the Passover ritual observed in the right "sequence," would both attain their desired end in approaching and influencing the supernatural.

Of course, nowadays all these origins are in the process of being forgotten and the names and practices have been to a great extent "rationalized."

## WORDS COUNT

The magic of numbers extended to words as well. This is the basis of what came to be known as numerology. Numerology claims that every word has its numerical value which determines its good or bad fortune, or other circumstances linked with it.

It all started in the East where assessing how much a word "counted" was easy. Babylonian, Hebrew and Greek writing had no separate numbers. Letters doubled for them in the sequence of the alphabet.

Typical was Hebrew, the ancient sacred tongue. The first letter—the *aleph*—stood also for 1, the second—the *bet*—for 2, and so on. And thus each of the twenty-two consonants (biblical Hebrew had no written vowels; they were a much later addition) constituted an entire range of figures. The last, the twenty-second letter—the *tav*—originally the shape of a cross or key, "counted" 400.

It followed that any name or word represented a number as well. All that had to be done was to add up the individual values of each of its letters. The sum arrived at was taken to indicate the character or fate of the person or object so named.

But going beyond such speculation and simple calculation, another and more complex procedure evolved. This not only determined the numerical value of a word, but also sought out another word or concept whose letters added up to the equivalent figure. The meaning of this numerically equivalent term was then related to the original with which it was interchangeable. Representing the identical "amount" was thought to establish an occult link between both: the latter revealing the fate, future or character of whatever or whomever the former described.

The earliest reference to such use of the numerical value of a word and its magic significance goes back to an inscription of King Sargon II of Assyria, the eighth-century B.C. potentate. It recorded that the wall he had built for Khorsabad measured exactly 16,283 cubits. He had determined its length by assessing the numerical value of his name. His powerful name thus would protect the city.

Interpretations of the Bible made equal use of this "science of numbers." When, for instance, it tells how Jacob in a dream saw a ladder that led from the earth to heaven, it was noted that the numerical value of *sulam*—Hebrew for "ladder"—corresponded to that of "Sinai," both individually "adding up" to 130. Hence it was deduced that the revelation on "Sinai" was the "ladder" that joined God in heaven with man on earth.

Mysticism, and the Kabbalah in particular, applied numerology in their speculations, and with its aid tried to discover the hidden meanings in words and names.

It was merely another step for modern numerology to develop. Working out complicated systems based on the ancient methods, it used them to detect the destiny of people and nations. It assigned to them the lucky numbers they should favor and warned them of the figures they ought to shun.

Though numbers now have become totally independent and lost their original link with letters, and therefore can no longer be "identified," numerology has not died out.

# CHAPTER THREE

# Occult Superstitions and Customs

## HOUSEWARMING

A "housewarming" nowadays is a social get-together arranged to introduce friends to a new home. Originally it was arranged not for the entertainment of the guests invited, but out of deep concern with the spirit world.

In every epoch and culture there has been a focal point in the home around which people gathered. Today it is the television set. In front of it the family gathers in silent communion, not with each other but with the T.V. screen.

In earlier times the source of attention was the hearth, which symbolically and literally formed the very center of the home.

The flames of the fire burning in the grate have always mystified man. The shapes they take and their constant flicker seem to reveal a live force, a supernatural being dwelling within.

The ancient Greeks and Romans believed the fire itself was part of the divine sun. Thus, for them the hearth became the humble, earthbound temple occupied by their domestic gods. These house gods were worshiped throughout the year as the keepers and guardians of the household and its food supply. In their honor the fire was kept burning in the hearth. Soon the fire itself was regarded as sacred and as representing life, and it was never allowed to go out.

Even as the original notion of the divine nature of the hearth became less clear, its influence on man's life continued. The ancient Greek and Roman house gods were replaced by fairies, brownies and other spirits who were thought to have taken possession of the hearth and on whose goodwill the family's life and luck depended. The entire family was cared for by these spirits of the hearth. To please them in every possible way and to keep them warm would make everybody happier. To neglect their welfare would displease them and one would have to pay the inevitable consequences. Hence, prior to going to bed, people especially tidied up the grate. To keep the fire burning and thereby the goblins well satisfied, they put on a new log or fresh peat.

In certain regions, tending the hearth was the duty of the woman of the house and was conducted with deep reverence, accompanied by special invocations asking for protection.

It followed that when people moved into a new home, they were truly concerned it might lack a protecting spirit and the spirits that had looked after them would stay behind in the old house. It is not just by way of metaphor that we continue to speak of a home having or lacking a special atmosphere.

Therefore when people moved from one place to another, they took live embers from the old grate, to start at once a fire in the new hearth. By this "housewarming" they ensured continuation of their good fortune. They had brought with them the very spirits that belonged to and had looked after their family for so many years previously. And that is how housewarming parties have their roots in the occult. And it is in this "spirit" that they survive.

### WHY PEACOCK FEATHERS ARE BAD LUCK

Man has always kept his eyes open and carefully observed everything around him. He has always asked questions, wondering about a myriad of whys and wherefores. He was convinced that everything in life had a purpose and that there was nothing without a cause. So when man saw peacocks strutting about with their gorgeous tail feathers spread out, he was convinced that the feathers' countless eyes must have been placed there for some significant reason.

Greek myth gave its own interpretation for the eyes on the peacock's tail, linking them with jealousy among the very "human" gods.

Hera was distressed over the constant unfaithfulness of her husband, Zeus, and she knew of the affair he was having with his latest mistress, Io.

To conceal Io, Zeus changed her into a heifer. He hoped the

innocently grazing "animal" would not rouse Hera's suspicions. But he had not reckoned with a wife's jealousy, for she could not be deceived even by the cleverest scheming and subterfuge.

Hera, knowing the true identify of the heifer, enlisted the help of Argus, the hundred-eyed giant, to keep watch on the "animal-mistress" and thereby prevent any tryst between her and amorous Zeus. Argus was the best choice for the purpose. He was renowned for keeping open at least two of his eyes at all times.

Hera, unfortunately, could not outwit Zeus, who remained master of the situation. He commanded his son Hermes to put Argus to sleep by the sound of his magic flute and by songs so soporific that not even the faithful Argus could resist dozing off. The moment his hundred eyes had closed, Hermes slew him by severing his head.

In her grief and rage, Hera transferred the eyes of her loyal servant to the tail of her favorite bird, the peacock. It is one of the strangest living memorials. Renewed with each generation, the colorful, brilliant display of the male peacock perpetuates the death of a vigilant hero for the goddess of monogamy.

The peacock thus became sacred to both Greeks and Romans, who revered and cared for it as the treasured guardian of their temples, wifely virtues and conjugal rights. The numerous eyes on its tail were regarded as the gods' never-resting watchfulness. Thus the bird became part of sanctuaries. Only priests were allowed to handle the sacred bird. For an ordinary mortal to do so was a sacrilegious crime punished by death, and to possess even one of its feathers was to defy sacred tradition.

However, it was the fear of the devil and of the evil eye that were primarily responsible for the assigning of magic powers to the bird. The numerous wide-open eyes on the tail intrigued the ancients. When haunted by fears they assumed the eyes belonged to the devil or were a perilous increase of the evil eye. To live constantly under their stare would expose the entire household to the malevolent influence of the power of darkness.

The belief was reinforced centuries later by a Moslem legend which held that the peacock had opened the gate to Paradise to admit Iblis, the devil, thus enabling him to cause man's fall. The bird's early association with the Evil One has never been forgotten. No one could ever trust the peacock again. Worse still, the devil might take advantage of its spectacular plumage, tempting people to take it home and thereby place themselves within the power of an ever-vigilant traitor.

As time went on, the peacock became a symbol of immortality and resurrection. People noticed that its feathers did not fade or lose their luster. This might have given rise to the fallacious notion that the bird's flesh never decayed either. Because of the flesh's assumed incorruptibility, it became customary to use the bird's plumage at funerals, and was meant to indicate that the deceased person was not really dead. His spirit survived and his eventual rebirth was assured. The presence of the feathers would actually help the deceased in his life hereafter.

The custom had its side effect, however. Because of their use at funerals, the peacock's feathers became closely linked with death. And people, forgetting their original protective association and symbolism, started to dread the presence of peacock feathers in their home. The feathers were no longer an assurance of immortality but an omen of doom—a telling example of how ignorance of the origin can confuse and lead to sad misunderstandings.

## The Pope's Fans

Christians adopted the ancient belief that recognized the peacock as a symbol of immortality, and used it in their ceremonial and sacred art.

When the early Christians were forced to practice their religion in hiding, they decorated the walls of the catacombs with a peacock motif to express their new faith and belief in Christ's resurrection. Centuries later, artists used peacock feathers in their ornamentation of churches to embellish or depict angels' wings. When the Crusaders returned from the East, they brought feathers of the bird with them as treasured and venerated possessions.

Today, when the pope is borne in solemn procession in his "portable chair" (*sedia gestatoria*), attendants accompanying him on each side carry two huge fans, known by their original Latin term, *flabella*. They are made either of peacock feathers or ostrich plumage on which are sewn the eye spots, and are attached to two long staffs. Probably the fans once served a practical purpose: to cool the air and keep flies and other insects away from the pontiff. But the many-eyed peacock feathers became symbolic of the ever-watchful eyes of the Catholic Church and the pope. Use of the fans on Easter Sunday is all the more significant; they symbolized the additional message of Christ's resurrection.

# COINS

## Throwing Coins into a Well

Throwing coins into a well for good luck is a custom observed all over the world. Coins tossed into the Trevi Fountain in Rome by visitors are thought to ensure their return to the Eternal City. In Shiraz, Iran, Persians use this means to pay honor to Saadi, their world-renowned national poet. A pool for that purpose is part of his magnificent mausoleum.

However lightly we may now treat such "offerings," their origins can be traced to the distant past when people were convinced that a spirit dwelt at the bottom of each fountain. Wells were their sacred abode, and unless one paid them a tribute willingly, they would raise it by sending misfortune.

In remote days, to quench the divine thirst of the spirit, men gave what was most precious to them: their own flesh and blood. Human offerings were the price paid for good luck. Young Mayan girls drowned in the Well of Sacrifice in Chichén Itzá, Mexico, did not have to be forced to give their lives for their people's good fortune. They regarded the sacrifice a privilege. They believed that the indwelling spirit or rain god would acknowledge their self-sacrifice and would marry them, and they would live happily ever after in his palace at the bottom of the well.

Eventually, "civilization" replaced the deadly sacrifice with money tokens. The throwing of coins into a fountain continues to *pay* homage to and buy the protection of the spirit "possessing" it.

## The Coin Under the Mast

To place a coin beneath the mainmast of a ship is a time-honored custom and superstition among shipbuilders. It goes back to ancient Greek myth and the most ominous journey on a boat any person could ever make.

Those who had departed this life and were destined for Elysium had to cross the River Styx situated in the lower world in order to reach the "islands of the blessed."

Charon owned the monopoly rights to convey the shades, and his was the only ferry making the trip. He charged a set fee—one obolus—and anyone who did not have the toll money was refused passage.

To avoid such eventuality, the Greeks introduced the custom of burying the dead with a coin placed either into the mouth or hand of the deceased. Thus he had the money ready to pay his passage to the underworld and was assured safe arrival.

Similar considerations for safety in crossing the seas led to the custom of paying protection money in advance to the spirits ruling the ocean. Symbolically, in the form of a coin, it was placed under the mast of a ship prior to launching.

## Cutting Friendship

Many a lucky charm, it was firmly believed, would "work" only if it was obtained as a gift. To purchase or acquire it by any other means rendered it ineffective. But the giving of presents has not always been as innocuous and friendly a custom as is now imagined. At times, a free gift was not welcomed but would cause suspicion and fear. Like the Trojan horse, it might bear not joy and fortune but doom and disaster.

Still frequently observed is the custom never to give a knife or a pair of scissors as a gift. The usual explanation is that the sharp instrument would cut the friendship between the giver and the recipient. To avoid this, the actual presentation is converted into a mock purchase. In exchange for the gift the donor is handed a small coin. Thus it is no longer a present but a sale.

The root of this transaction is tied to practices commonly associated with black magic. In its practice, sharp instruments or simple objects such as pins and needles infused with nefarious powers, were handed to the innocent victim and duly fulfilled their destructive mission. The spell only worked if the victim accepted the object unconditionally, that is, without being asked, he paid for it, however little. By this simple action he was able to discharge any potential danger hidden in the knife, scissors or camouflaged weapon.

## THE SINISTER OR LEFT SIDE OF LIFE

Ours is a right-oriented world. It has been so from almost the very beginning of mankind. "Rightness" began as a physiological fact. Primitive man already must have felt the heart beating on his left side. And as dead people's hearts had stopped beating, he reasoned that the heart must be the very source of life. Consequently, to pierce it would kill a person, and experience showed that this was so. It followed that in a world so full of hostility and aggressiveness, anyone keen on preserving his life had to protect first of all this most vulnerable part of his body. He did so by holding a shield (or before that perhaps a flat stone) in front of the heart. And as this was on his left side, he naturally used his left hand. This kept the right hand free to do the actual fighting. By constant practice in handling the sword (or whichever form of weapon he employed), the right inevitably became the stronger hand.

Since most men's strength was on the right side it was only natural that evil forces would look for men's weak spots. Thus, they positioned themselves on the left, recognizing they were safer there and would be more successful in launching an attack from that side.

That is how, eventually, *sinister*—the Latin word for "left"— assumed its unfortunate connotation to describe all that is ominous, evil and foreboding.

This was one of the reasons why ancient augurs, when looking into the future by viewing the flight of birds, the drift of clouds or the general position of things such as the entrails of slaughtered animals regarded a tendency toward the left as an indication of coming misfortune.

Plato and Aristotle added another significant explanation. Traditionally the left was identified with the West, a custom still maintained on all maps. But as it was the side of the setting sun as well, the left also was seen as the departure of good fortune. Vanishing light and absence of strength combined in making the left doubly evil and vulnerable.

The superstitious person who has accidentally spilled salt will take immediate remedial action to cancel out any unfortunate aftereffect by throwing a pinch of salt over his left shoulder.

There are significant reasons why he does so. As the result of the "upsetting" incident, the superstitious person believes the devil is about to pounce on him. But being a most cunning creature, the devil will do so not only from the rear where he cannot be seen, but also from the left or the weaker side.

Salt is loathsome to the devil. It is linked with God and his power and was used in the divine ritual. It signified all that was incorruptible and immortal. A substance used as a preservative would be inimical to any evil force out to destroy. Hence to hit the devil in the eye with a pinch of salt would not only temporarily blind him but make him turn tail at once with his mission unaccomplished.

"Sinister" considerations continue to prevail in other spheres of life. People are warned not to get out of bed on the left side. By doing so, they will start the day wrong, entering immediately the realm and power of the "evil one." To walk into a house with the left foot first has been regarded an ill omen and makes the superstitious carefully watch their step.

The ominous origin of the "sinister" left created the irrational prejudice against left-handed people. That they preferred, or even were compelled, to use their left hand when "normal" men would use their right, was seen as an indication of their having some link with malevolent forces and, most likely, with the devil himself.

## IRON BARS

In the world of magic, iron is the most effective guard against the devil. And it is this belief that contributed to the good-luck connotation of the horseshoe. It must be realized, however, that the horseshoe does not attract good luck but repels the devil.

The ability of iron to ward off the devil has its roots in remote history and man's early powers of observation. First there were the meteors that struck the earth and were seen as heavenly missiles. Everything connected with their "supernatural" appearance combined to make the meteors carriers of divine and occult power: their fiery streak on their passage downward from the heavens, their mysterious arrival and the discovery of these ancient meteors embedded in the ground.

Man soon learned to make good use of the salvaged meteoric iron. With the aid of the sacred fire, he forged his tools and weapons from it. He saw in the iron a divine and magically mysterious gift especially sent to him from above. Most of all, that it had come from outer space, then identified with heaven or the seat of God, made the devil loathe it.

Always ready to attribute the still inexplicable to supernatural causes, man soon credited iron as the divine element against which those serving the devil were powerless.

The stone-wielding natives of many a country had no chance against the superior power of iron weapons which, in man's primitive way of thinking, they ascribed not to the metal itself but to its magic. On the other hand, the victorious foe seemed invulnerable by protecting himself with shields and armor made of iron. This also was thought to be due not to the hardness of the metal but to its mystic force. Early warriors cleverly used it to increase the terror of their enemy, and their own reputation of being unassailable and immune from attack, by spreading the notion of the magic power of the iron.

Numerous customs can be traced to this belief in the magic potency of iron. The first-century Roman author Pliny recorded how the idea had taken root in his time. People removed nails from coffins to stick them into the lintel of their bedrooms, to "lay" spirits who might haunt them at night. Scots and Irishmen used iron to ward off attacks by fairies. Christian families believed that by putting an iron poker across the cradle of an unbaptized child, they would protect the infant against the power of the devil.

## TERROR AT NIGHT FOR THE HEALTHY

For thousands of years man has believed that the earth was crowded with evil forces, demons of the most varied kind and rank. Minor devils, closely associated with the forces of the dark, were said to be particularly active and effective during night hours. It was then that man was least protected and would more easily fall prey to the spirits. Even the Bible suggests this occult belief. In the 91st Psalm the faithful are reminded not to be afraid of "the terror at night" (verse 5), and this phrase certainly was not meant in a figurative sense originally.

As those cunning demons operated at night, they cleverly chose those least prepared as their victims—those who were asleep. That was the reason why people closed their windows at night. To keep them open was asking for trouble. It was tantamount to an invitation to evil spirits to come in.

The fear of such intrusion was aggravated by another conviction connected with the occult. It was believed that during sleep a man's soul left his body to go wandering. This concept was fostered by dreams in which a person seemed to travel to distant sites. When, on awakening next morning, he found himself "back" at home, he was sure that as no one could travel so vast a distance in so short a time, it must have been his spirit that had undertaken the trip. Therefore, he reasoned, while the spirit had been away, his body must have been lying in bed like an empty shell, unprotected and awaiting any evil spirit to enter and take possession of it. This made man all the more anxious to watch out the moment darkness came, and when he went to sleep, all windows were tightly shuttered.

## TERROR AT NIGHT FOR THE SICK

### Flowers in the Hospital

If healthy people were exposed to dangers during darkness and forced to take due precautions, it followed that at night anyone sick was even more vulnerable to attacks by evil spirits. Already weakened, the patient offered a minimum of resistance to intruders who would take advantage of his condition.

Aware that entry during the night would be difficult with the windows shut, the fairy spirits used a devious means to gain access to the room prior to "closing time" and before the sun had set when they were still powerless.

Friends visiting a patient would show concern and cheer him up by bringing flowers. The visitors did not realize that their gifts carried harmful and dangerous entities. For flowers, according to ancient belief, were not only beautiful plants but could serve as a hiding place for spirits anxious to get to the weak.

Once night had come and the lights were out, the spirits would pounce on the sick person, attempting to take possession of him and to inflict all the harm they could. That is why all flowers were removed from a sickroom before nightfall. The usual explanation given—that this was done because the flowers would use up vital oxygen during the darkness—is not only fallacious but a rationalization of the original occult belief in fairies and their potentially lethal attack during the dark of night.

## PULLING DOWN THE SHADES

The mystery of death caused man to adopt a multitude of "mourning" customs. If today they seem outmoded, they still express respect to the departed and reflect the grief suffered by the relatives.

Often such interpretation is also a rationalization. In reality, the lament is a defense mechanism. Its true purpose is to protect the survivors from malevolent agencies closely linked with the death.

This applies to the custom of lowering the shades in the house where a death has occurred. It was not done to convey the mood of gloom or to symbolize the darkness of the shadow of death that enveloped the home. On the contrary, mourners were alarmed that the body, now deprived of its soul, was ready for reoccupation and that some evil force might enter the empty shell.

More frightening was a Chinese belief that by a chain reaction a dreadful metamorphosis could take place. Within the body remained a lower soul, so the Chinese thought, so far inactive and too weak to achieve anything. Should a ray of sun or moonlight reach the soul, the immobile body or corpse would be transformed into a fearful vampire. To avoid this, the shades were drawn.

## BURIED AT CROSSROADS

Until quite recently, suicides and executed criminals were refused burial in consecrated ground. Their actions were regarded so heinous and contrary to God's will that he would not welcome them in territory set aside in his name. To entomb in the very soil dedicated to God a man who had defied the divine prerogative was tantamount to sacrilege.

This led to the custom of burying recalcitrants far away from the cemetery—at crossroads. The choice of the spot was motivated and reinforced by an even more significant tradition. From antiquity, crossroads were regarded as belonging to the devil, which made them an appropriate meeting place for witches.

Consequently, to the pious Christians the crossroad became the most debased and abandoned site, the focus of pagan abomination and hence the best place for putting away those who had denied God his right to give and take life.

The fact that crossroads were the traditional sites for witches goes back thousands of years, to the ancient Greeks and Romans. In their mythology, crossroads were dedicated to the moon goddess Artemis-Diana, identified and often confused with Hecate. As the divinity of witchcraft, she was invoked in magic rites and associated with the uncanny and the world of ghosts. Statues to both goddesses were put up by the Greeks and Romans wherever three or more roads met. Frequently the figure had three faces and occasionally three bodies. Such a site was almost preselected for the witches to gather and was seen as an area reserved for the dead.

In the Pacific, much later, Bali natives regarded the crossroad as the location of evil spirits, placing their offerings to the demons at that spot. And in certain parts of Scandinavia, bonfires were lit at crossroads on St. John's Eve to drive away the dark forces of trolls and other demons which were thought to be abroad on that night and to be especially active at those junctions.

Thus, the crossroads, especially sacred in pagan worship, became the obvious meeting place of those engaged in the black arts. This, in turn, made the crossroads an abominable place to Christians, who chose them as the resting place for those who had become disqualified from any claim to Christian burial.

When people no longer realized the origin of the choice of the crossroad another explanation was advanced. It suggested that the locale was chosen to confuse the earthbound soul of the buried dead and to make it difficult for the soul to find its way back "home," where in its desperate loneliness and abandonment, it would start haunting the living. This fear led to a gruesome custom practiced for a long period. Suicides and executed criminals were not only buried at crossroads, but a stake was driven through their hearts to fix them permanently to the spot.

Crossroads also have come to give us all that is "trivial." This commonplace word literally recalls (from the Latin *tri* for "three" and *via* for "way") the meeting of "three ways."

## THE LUCKY CAUL

The caul is the membrane, the amniotic sac that surrounds the fetus in the mother's womb and contains the fluid that acts as a ''shock absorber'' to shield the yet unborn child against hurt and injury. Shortly prior to birth, this ''skin pocket'' bursts, releasing the water and making it possible for the child to be born. The membrane itself is expelled later as part of the afterbirth.

Occasionally, however, the caul clings to the child's head, as a lucky omen. The ''happy hood'' was once treasured and prized highly. Anyone able to say that he was born with a caul on his head was also saying he was particularly favored and would never die by drowning.

The reason the caul became such a powerful talisman is obvious. As it had once acted as protection to the fetus in the womb, so it would continue for the mature person. Which is why those going to sea used it as a charm against being shipwrecked and perishing in the water.

The caul adopted the role of the lifesaver. In some parts of the world, it was thought to bestow second sight on its owner or to make him immune from a sorcerer's attack.

To be born with a caul was such a rare occurrence that it gave the caul even more supernatural significance. The popular belief that witches used cauls in their black magic made it all the more essential never to lose it.

But the magic of the caul was not restricted to those born with it; it could be transferred to others. Some people, primarily sailors who lived in constant fear of drowning, would pay the maximum to acquire it. To advertise a ''caul for sale'' was not an unusual custom.

## PULLING THE WISHBONE

Who has not at one time or another shared in the custom of pulling a wishbone?

The procedure is simple. Two people grasp either end of the *furcula*, the name of this forked bone of the chicken, by hooking the little finger around one side. Each pulls his way till the bone snaps in two. Because of the bone's structure, the breaking point is never the exact center, and one person is bound to obtain the larger piece.

Whoever does will have good luck. More generally, he or she will have any wish silently made at that moment fulfilled.

Pulling the wishbone is a children's game. Whenever there is chicken on the dinner table, the children expect to try their luck. Who then would guess that this innocent custom can be traced back into antiquity and to serious concern about sex?

The cock and the hen played a significant role in the history of man. The birds were associated with mysterious forces beyond human understanding. The primitive mind took note of the conspicuous way in which the rooster made itself heard on occasions vital to man. He saw in it not a natural occurrence of daily living but something closely connected with the supernatural. The cock's crow announced the coming of dawn and with it the passing of night and the happy ending of the period associated with demonic rule. The cock was indeed a strong ally of the forces of light in their constant fight against the powers of darkness.

The clucking of a hen proclaimed the laying of an egg, the start of new life. Hence the hen was a symbol of fertility.

As such, the bird assumed sacred status and its bones were believed to have innate magical powers beyond their natural functions.

It was not a haphazard selection that the furcula became the wishbone, but a deliberate choice. Although it is located below the neck of the bird, this forked breastbone of combined clavicles strikingly resembles the human groin, the place of the male and female genitals, the very source of fertility, and the assurance of the continuation of life. Consequently the wishbone became a focus of generation: to give birth to luck and good fortune.

## THE UNLUCKY COLOR GREEN

All over the world green is considered the most luscious color. It is the hue of growing things, and hence became the symbol of fertility. Nothing gave man greater joy than the beauty of green plants and leaves so prevalent in nature at its best. It was the promise of nourishment for cattle and man and symbolic of many increases.

But man must have wondered what actually created the color that reappeared annually when the sun had reached a certain position.

Unable to find a rational answer, man imagined that little green imps, elves or pixies, living beneath the soil, gave freely of their color to all growing things. This was their responsibility, the particular task allotted to them, and a privilege they jealously guarded. Anyone daring to don their green color did so without their permission and arrogated a right which was not his.

Later historical happenings linked with fairy lore reinforced the superstition rooted in natural causes. It is told that the autochthonous inhabitants of Britain donned foliage as their camouflage in their fight against the Celtic invaders.

The Celts believed the camouflage was the true color of their foes and because of their aggressive action, the color soon became associated with misfortune in the form of loss of goods and life.

Once the superstition spread to other countries, many people shunned wearing green, believing the color to invite bad luck.

## "Wearing of the Green"

The Irish are renowned for being superstitious. How then can it be explained that, of all people, they did not steer clear of wearing green?

There is a basis for the miraculous change in the significance of green in Irish eyes; it is linked with religion. It shows how faith can conquer notions however deeply rooted they are.

Well known is St. Patrick's choice of the shamrock as the Irish symbol. He chose it wisely and with a spiritual purpose. In his attempt to convert the people to the Christian faith, he was anxious to teach them the difficult doctrine of the trinity. And this he did by means of an illustration from nature. God had implanted the trinity, so he taught, even in their very soil: in the shamrock. And it was its color which gave the Emerald Isle green as its distinctive hue.

In their religious fervor, the Irish forgot the unlucky past of green and were prepared to ignore its bad side. Proudly they "wear the green" of their shamrock emblem.

## Green and Sex

The association of the color green with the fertility of nature inevitably linked it with sex.

Medieval churchmen made it a symbol of immorality. To say of a girl that she "wore a green gown" was tantamount to saying that she had lost her virginity. This applied especially to the "permissive" period of the May (spring) celebrations.

## The Greenroom

Superstition flourishes most profusely among those people whose occupation makes them face a life of danger and uncertainty. That is why sailors and miners are so superstitious, and, equally, actors. No one, for example, can predict whether a new play will prove a roaring success or a dismal failure.

Actors are therefore careful to observe certain rules lest they offend mischievous spirits always ready to spoil their performance. And no doubt they were well aware of the curse attached to green.

Oddly enough though, during intermissions of a play actors traditionally retire to what is generally known as the greenroom. It is always painted and decorated in that color.

This paradoxical attitude may have one of a number of reasons which may be based more on theater lore than on fact.

Van den Hoff, in his *Leaves from an Actor's Notebook*, advanced the theory that the greenroom received its name because its upholstery, seats, divan and carpet were all green.

Another, though generally refuted theory is that it had been the storeroom for green cloths used in productions of tragedies.

A third view links the greenroom with actors' need for recuperation from the glaring lights to which they were exposed on the stage. Though little realized by spectators enjoying the well-lit faces onstage, the spotlight is a tremendous strain on the actors. And it was thought that a room decorated in green would enable the actors to relax and rest their eyes during breaks. The physiological need was strong enough to expel all other psychological considerations of green as an unlucky color.

There is yet another illustration of how the greenroom came to be.

The Dorset Garden Theatre was one of the early—seventeenth-century—London playhouses. It so happened that the room in which the actors prepared themselves for their appearances onstage was painted green. When eventually the Dorset Garden was superseded by the Drury Lane Theatre, actors remembered and missed their green "makeup" room.

Frequently they voiced the wish to have something like it in the new establishment. The management duly obliged and provided them with a replica of the original greenroom. As in so many aspects, the world-renowned Drury Lane Theatre set the fashion. Other theaters would have looked inferior had they not adopted the example. Accordingly, they, too, included a greenroom in the backstage amenities.

Since those times the color of the greenroom has not changed and though many an actor would not wear anything green on his person, he would nevertheless feel much at ease and regain his composure when relaxing in the room thus colored and named.

## CLERGYMEN ARE BAD (TO) SAILORS

Sailors once regarded it unlucky for a priest, or any man of the cloth, to join their ship, believing he could bring them only misfortune.

The unhappy tradition goes back to the Bible in which we learn how Jonah, one of the twelve minor prophets, tries to shirk his duty to visit Nineveh in the East by joining a boat sailing from Joppa (Jaffa) toward the West. In fact, the boat's destination was Tarshish in the southwest of Spain, at the extreme other end of the Mediterranean. It was surely the farthest Jonah could voyage in the known world in the opposite direction to that in which he was supposed to go.

To catch up with the fugitive, to punish him, and to force his hand, God raised a storm. This greatly endangered the ship, which would have been wrecked with all hands lost, had not the sailors thrown Jonah overboard (which they did at his own request). The moment they did so, the storm abated and they continued their voyage safely.

This biblical example gave sailors every reason not to want clergymen boarding their ship. They would only create extra hazard to the perilous livelihood of the ship's crew.

A later tradition intensified this apprehension. It was a foregone conclusion that the devil hated clergymen. After all, a servant of God was by nature his archenemy. To get hold of a parson and drown him would be his chief joy. To do so he would be prepared to join a ship where, surrounded by the sea, the man of God was as good as caught and unable to escape from his clutches.

Sailors had enough trouble without inviting the presence of the devil by permitting a clergyman to be on board. Once the devil had disposed of the parson, his original prey, he might well embark on other mischievous schemes.

There is also a suggestion that out of deference to and fear of the ancient, pagan sea gods, a parson was kept away. After all, who really knew whether these gods had actually been swept off the ocean. If they were still present, they would resent a clergyman as their natural foe.

## WOMEN NOT WELCOMED

A sailor is said to have a wife in every port. Once on firm land, he soon finds his way to her dwelling and, surely, would not miss her loving embrace. But at sea he views a woman as "taboo."

Those experienced with the havoc one female can cause among an all-male company would recognize good common sense in the superstition. A ship's crew could raise a hurricane of jealousy in competing for her favors and the morale (and morals) on board ship would be wrecked.

The real origin of the superstition, however, is much more deeply rooted in the world of the occult. Sailors feared that the potential female passenger might in reality be a witch, and to have such a creature on board might prove disastrous. This apprehension caused their phobia toward and rejection of an otherwise so welcome female in their midst.

## WIDDERSHINS

The power of the sun was recognized in the dawn of man. Its light gave life and its warmth was essential to the growing of crops. Mysteriously traveling across the sky, the sun was worshiped as the supreme god by just about every race in every climate, a fact we still commemorate each week by calling its very first day in the sun's honor.

The oldest monuments in existence, no matter where—at Stonehenge in Britain, at Machu Picchu in Peru or at Tenochtitlan in Mexico—were erected to pay homage to the sun and in acknowledgment of man's dependence on this celestial body.

That people still worship God by looking up and equate heaven with the sky is partially founded on this early worship of this brightest star.

No wonder that primitive man was thrown into panic whenever an eclipse occurred. The life-giving god, so he thought, was about to be devoured by an evil beast. But whatever its cause, an eclipse was deemed to forecast bad tidings for the earth and man. Therefore man employed every possible magic and brought offerings to rescue the god or inveigle him to return and shine again.

Man's concern with the sun was not reserved only for such exceptional and dramatic moments. It occupied his mind throughout his life and became the source of numerous customs and self-imposed restrictions. Modern society continues to observe them to a large degree, though not necessarily realizing their primitive, magic roots.

It was recognized that the sun never stood still. The only exceptions applied to those moments when miraculously divine power stopped the progress of time to help man. The book of Joshua thus tells how God had done so to give the Israelites sufficient time to win the battle against the Amorite army (Josh. 10:12-14).

To human observers the sun has always seemed to take its regular course from the east to the west, from dawn to dusk. This daily solar trip has been perpetuated in everyday speech and geographical terms. We still say that the sun "rises" and "sets." The splendor of the Orient mystically resulted from the rising (Latin, *oriens*) sun. Colloquially, to die is "to go west."

Just as it seemed to be in man's power to impede or help the sun on its way, so the sun for its part was believed to be able to help man in his progress. If he followed its direction he was assured success. To go "against the stream," on the other hand, would doom his efforts and curse them from the outset and must be avoided at all costs.

The direction contrary to the apparent course of the sun became known as "widdershins." The term is still used among people of the northern districts of England and in Scotland. From the Old English, combining the words for "against" (*vithr*) and "movement" (*sinni*), it means "backward." To do anything widdershins would be foolish, as it was unlucky. For anyone to adopt that direction would cause as much horror as if the hands of a clock would suddenly start turning backwards.

That is why, from the very beginning, man carefully emulated the sun's example in his most varied activities. Earliest football games were fertility rites, engaged in to foster the strength of the solar body, symbolized by the round ball, and therefore had to be played from east to west. A housewife in the Northern Hemisphere would stir the food on the stove "clockwise"—the way the sun was imagined to travel. Likewise at a meal observant Moslems would pass the dishes in the way the sun went. Should strangers unaware of the tradition pass the food counterclockwise, no Moslem would accept it, declining the dish politely.

The magic of the sun has thus dominated the world. It has done so not only in caring for the harvest and in bringing about each new day, but also in its influence on the choices man would make that would determine the pattern of his life.

## THE WITCHY ORIGIN OF THE ROYAL GARTER

Well-known is the generally unaccepted story of how, after having successfully challenged the French crown, King Edward III in 1349 had established the much coveted Order of the Garter. This badge of chivalry was to be reserved for persons of only the highest distinction.

At a royal ball, so goes the tale, the Countess of Salisbury's garter had slipped and fallen to the ground, greatly embarrassing the lady. As a true gentleman, the king himself stooped, picked it up and, making light of the incident, put it on his own leg. But lest bystanders might misinterpret his action (or start gossiping about the unfortunate slip later on), he had remarked very audibly—and possibly for no one to misunderstand the implied threat—that "May he be shamed who thinks ill of it."

The king felt that the occasion merited to be remembered in perpetuity. And for this reason he had created the noble Order of Chivalry. Its very motto recalled the words he had uttered at the time. *"Honi soit qui mal y pense."*

In spite of its frequent repetition, however, the story is hardly convincing. Fourteenth-century ladies, even those attending royal functions, were not so finicky or modest that the mere loss of a garter would have caused them to blush or feel uncomfortable. The reason for all the commotion lay in a completely different area, a theory first advanced by Margaret Murray.

At the time, a garter was not simply an article of clothing used to hold up stockings. It was also said to be the distinguishing badge of a witch which she secretly wore. To lose it publicly and thereby to give away her allegiance to the devil was thus not just a cause of embarrassment but of acute danger (and more so if it concerned a noble lady). Recognized as a witch, even her status would not protect her. The countess' very life was threatened.

Suddenly a delightful social occasion had turned into a most frightening situation. By the king making light of it, he protected the lady's honor and saved her life.

By picking up the garment in the sight of all and donning it himself, he intended to reveal that certainly it was worn by the countess as an innocuous piece of finery and not as the ominous badge of a witch. However, just in case there might be anyone daring still to think otherwise and to link the garter with the world of the occult, he loudly remarked, ''May he be shamed who thinks ill of it''—by interpreting the garter the witchy way. His words were uttered not in a jocular vein but constituted an actual royal threat.

A king tackling occult power at a royal ball was the real background of the Order of Chivalry, still so greatly cherished.

# CHAPTER FOUR

# The Occult in Language

## COBALT—HOW A GERMAN DEVIL WENT DOWN INTO THE MINES AND CAME UP AS COBALT

German people were convinced their homes housed a little devil whom they called a *Kobold*.

Various explanations have been given as to the meaning and origin of the name. Some saw in it an early individual's name—Gottbald in Old High German. And just as the English euphemistically called the devil Old Nick, the Germans called him *Kobold*. Others derived the name from words that spoke of the cottage (*Kobe*) being ruled (*walten*, the English "wield") by it. The Kobold would really mean as much as "the governor of the house."

Starting off as a guardian spirit, the Kobold deteriorated into the impish little creature who delighted in pranks. He would upset things, break precious vases, spoil a cake or curdle milk. He might do anything that would cause trouble and annoy the mistress of the house.

Eventually, Germans blamed anything that went wrong, not on natural causes or their own mistakes, but on the gnome or sprite.

Miners who, because of the very circumstance of their dangerous occupation, tended to be superstitious, particularly believed in the impish Kobold.

Time and again, deep down in the earth, they would discover a reddish-gray ore of lustrous sheen. At first there would be no doubt in their minds that they had found something really valuable. But when they tried to smelt it down, this promising-looking element would prove entirely worthless, yielding no metal. Worse still, it seemed to smell of sulfur and made them sick.

The miners were convinced that they had not made a mistake in their initial assumption, and that it had been the Kobold—the demon of the mines—who had changed the precious metal into this base and dangerous substance. The Kobold alone surely was to blame for this evil substitution of a rich discovery with a useless, vitiated substance. And to express their firm belief, they called the find after the demon, and that is how the English word cobalt got its name.

The devilish name stuck and was even retained when Georg Brand, the Swedish chemist, around 1730 discovered the hidden qualities of the metal.

Despite its radioactive healing properties, cobalt (in its name) perpetuates man's early belief that evil spirits were always out to annoy and damage him.


## NICKEL

The fear that the devil was able to creep into anything has possessed men's minds for thousands of years. It has led him to take countless measures to obstruct his entry.

Enlightened men have ridiculed such fear as gross superstition. And yet, the belief gave Old Nick permanent residence not just in chimeras and illusions but in the substantial world of metallurgy and hard cash. He so much ''bewitched'' a metal still used in modern alloys that it is universally known by his German name. Americans acknowledge Old Nick in their five-cent piece, a nickel.

Nick's itinerary leads from tantalizing prospecting operations to the money market, from mining to minting.

It all began in Germany. Miners anxious to find some new source of copper believed they had discovered it in quantity in rich deposits of apparently genuine copper ore which showed the typical reddish-brown color of the metal. But once they began digging up the ore, their early expectations were dashed. When the ore was smelted down, it yielded not a single ounce of copper.

In their frustration, the miners looked for an explanation of the mystery of the ''disappearing'' copper. They had been so sure of its presence. Had they not seen it with their own eyes? Therefore, it could only be the result of the work of mischievous forces, of goblins, dwelling inside the mountain. It was the devil's doing, they were now fully convinced. He had bewitched the copper, so they duly named the substance "the devil's copper" which in German is *Kupfernickel*.

This it remained for many years and, disappointed, people took little notice of the ore that "by the devil's doing" had lost all commercial value. But then, in 1751, Baron Axel Fredric Cronstedt, a Swedish scientist and mathematician, took a new look at it.

There was no doubt to his trained mind that there was no trace of copper in the substance. Instead, and much more exciting, it represented a totally new, so far completely unknown, metal with slightly magnetic properties. And in due course Cronstedt was able to isolate it. Wondering what to call it, he dropped from its name the copper part, the presence of which he had shown to be unjustified. All that was left now was Old Nick—in German, *Nickel*. It did not take long for the new name of the metal to be adopted all over the world.

Soon other metallurgists and scientists discovered its great usefulness as an alloy. Soft copper became hardened by having added to it just a little nickel. Copper coins, which up to that time had a short life expectancy, suddenly could be changed into *hard* cash.

Americans produced the first specimen made with the novel alloy in 1857. This was valued one cent. The presence of nickel, which guaranteed its prolonged life span, made people refer to it colloquially by the German demon's name. But soon, long before modern inflation, the gremlin took possession of the five-cent piece, and the nickel has been associated with that coin ever since.

## CHARISMA

Believers in the occult are convinced that people have an aura. Invisible to all but the psychic, it surrounds and emanates from them and can have a most potent effect. But extraordinary people are endowed with an even more powerful radiation. Like a magic spell, this can exert a supreme influence on large crowds, if not entire nations. And a long forgotten term has been dug up in modern days to describe that very condition and to explain recent events in the world of politics, and its most evil manifestation, demagoguery.

Charisma spoke literally of a divine "favor," a free "gift" or grace, granted by a supernatural power to a specially selected individual.

The present-day popularity of the term may be due to Max Weber, the well-known German sociologist. In his writings he was the first to apply the word in modern days and used it to describe the phenomenon of "charismatic leaders." His phrase caught on and was soon applied to national figures throughout the world whose appeal, for the best or the worst, hypnotized the masses.

Both as a word and a concept, charisma goes back to ancient Greece, where it meant the showing of favor and grace. Personified as the Charites (mythologically the three daughters of Zeus), these Graces (in their Latinized form, *gratiae*) were believed to vouchsafe their free gift to certain favored people. Inspired by them, these people became distinguished by their extraordinary personality which could be expressed by physical beauty, intellectual, artistic and moral stature or the ability to divine the future.

The Apostle Paul, who was deeply influenced by Greek thought, took over its charismatic tradition. Adapting it to the new faith he taught (Rom. 12:6; 1 Cor. 12:4-11), he did so in the sense that the gift—granted by God—was not meant to enrich the person so favored but to enable him to bestow good on others. However, to be thus honored was not the result of personal sanctity, nor was it a reward for good deeds. It was undeserved and unmerited—in the later theological phraseology, "Graces gratuitously given."

Paul enumerated nine different such gifts which included the art of healing, the working of miracles, prophecy and the talent of "speaking with tongues."

Modern religious groups have gone back to Paul's description and definition of the divine Graces. Their members claim to have acquired the ancient gifts in a charismatic renewal and strongly experienced awakening "to the life of the holy spirit within us."


## TO HAVE A HUNCH

At some time or other almost everyone has a hunch and correctly guesses some future event. Rarely does he bother to investigate what gave him this gift of premonition and wonder why it was thus called. And yet, to begin with, the hunch was highly regarded as an extraordinary power closely associated with the occult.

It all started with the hunchback in far-distant days. His peculiar shape made him not an object of pity or derision as one might suppose but a person especially selected by the gods to carry "on him" gifts denied to others. Therefore a hunchback was greatly desired as a valuable asset to one's company.

The comparative rarity of hunchbacks added to their worth. Only the rich and ruling classes could afford to keep them. And since everyone could not acquire a live one, figures representing them were made. As good-luck charms, they were thought to be especially effective against demonic powers and the evil eye.

The Egyptian Pharaohs worshiped as a god the dwarf Bes for the luck-bringing virtues of his hunch. Many Phoenician sailors would not set forth on their trading missions without first having placed the figure of a hunchback god into their ship to guard them. Likewise, ancient Romans, wherever they went, carried hunchback amulets with (and on) them.

The hunchbacks' supposed power to avert evil and thereby to ensure the continuation of good luck may have had various roots.

First of all there was the fundamental awe and fear of what we now call the grotesque, a phenomenon unusual and unaccountable. The very mystery of the odd growth caused other men to look at the baneful being with wonder and reverence. It made them treat any hunchback with deferential respect.

Just as man is attracted by beauty, ugliness repels and horrifies him. The twisted figure of a hunchback thus would act as a most powerful force even against demonic beings. Unable to bear the sight of him, they would turn tail at once. Hence to have a hunchback or his replica nearby would serve as a sure means to keep demons far away.

Jokes are made not for fun alone. They can have serious results and serve to defuse a tense situation. More so, uncontrollable laughter can shake a man so much that he forgets everything else and often becomes unable to continue a job he has already begun. It was thought that the image of a hunchback produced so much hilarity in anyone, including those who belonged to the occult world, that, seeing him, all they could do was to laugh. This completely nullified their original intention to inflict harm.

Hunchbacks were bogies of a unique kind. They did not paralyze people by fear but rather they made them break forth in such fits of laughter so that they forgot all about their original, possibly adverse mission. Hunchbacks were like a divine gift. That is the initial reason for their presence at royal courts. Kings engaged them not only as resident jesters. Their main purpose was to be a living human mascot, employed to protect His Royal Highness and those near and dear to him.

People are no longer in awe of hunchbacks. We now know the scientific, medical explanation of their spinal deformity. Nevertheless, his ancient magic has not died, and belief in the hunchback's supernatural gifts survives in numerous people. Some men afflicted with a hunch learned how to capitalize on their misfortune and man's ancient and still subconscious belief in their psychic power. Stationing themselves outside gambling casinos, for instance, for a price they allow visitors to touch them for luck.

And even that is not the end of the story. The hunchback's imagined link with the spirit world through his hump caused the hunch to become "detached" from the rest of his body and to be abstracted. Ever since, it has found a separate existence in man's life and vocabulary. Every time we have "a hunch," our flash of insight and glimpse into the future are derived from the original hunchback.

## THE GLAMOUR OF GRAMMAR— KNOWLEDGE IS (MAGIC) POWER

The unknown is always the mysterious. For a considerable period of time and into the Middle Ages, reading and writing was a dark, hidden secret to the illiterate, and known to only a few. And these, originally mainly priests, wisely kept the knowledge to themselves. With it they could wield power and keep the masses under control. In the eyes of all others, the secrets of their mastery of language endowed them with magical, supernatural gifts.

For many centuries in Europe, Latin was the chosen language, the means of the exchange of ideas among those guarding this monopoly. Those who mastered the tongue were not only revered but looked upon by the untutored with great awe. Their power of words seemed to have given them occult power over the lives of the people as well. By their knowledge, so the masses believed, they were indeed able to cast spells, work magic and be adept in witchcraft.

To master any language properly implies the knowledge of its grammar. The very term "grammar" described such "enchanted" gifts of the realm of the occult. And it was by a small change of one consonant, a not uncommon accident in speech, that "grammar" gave birth to "glamour," initially spelled *glamer*. All that had happened was that an *l* had taken the place of the *r*.

The original meaning of the "new" word truly reflected all the awe shown to those learned, instructed men who by their wisdom could use a tongue of the remote past to make thoughts live, to cast spells and "charm" people.

What glamour girl or Hollywood star would ever guess that in their tempting description in a PR release was buried not only a belief in black magic, but also what the average person regards as the most boring part of learning any language—its dry-as-dust grammar.

The "enchantment" they give thus goes much deeper than their apparently only skin-deep beauty. Originally it was meant to be "bewitching." The entry of "glamour" into the modern vocabulary is due to the Scots and, among them, to one of their great sons, the novelist Sir Walter Scott.


## HEX

To bewitch a person is to (put a) hex (on) him. Hex is what remains of the German witch—*die Hexe*. She always appears as a female.

She has left her mark as well in the very sign called "hex," used by the Pennsylvania Dutch. Mostly farmers, they marked their barns with the symbol, intending it to be "a painted prayer." This, they were convinced, would keep at bay evil spirits out to harm their buildings and cattle. Another theory suggests that this painted charm may have received its name because frequently it took the form of a six-pointed star, known as the *hex*agram. And hex, coming from the Greek, stood for the figure 6.

The German *Hexe* shared a common root with the English hag. This is now exclusively used in a contemptuous sense and speaks of an old and ugly woman, whereas, originally, "hag" described a witch and a sorceress.

Going back to an Old English word for "hedge"—*haga*—the hag in her evil-seeking pursuit was imagined, if not actually being airborne, to ride hedges.

# FROM THE ESCAPEGOAT TO THE SCAPEGOAT

Most people will agree that to make a person a scapegoat is an evil practice. But few indeed would guess that what we now regard as a metaphor was initially very real and that the scapegoat itself belonged to the realm of the devil.

The first scapegoat was not an abstract creature but a live goat. Our modern idiom continues to reflect the original belief in the force of evil and recalls man's early preoccupation with how to tackle it and to rid himself of its threats and consequences.

The scapegoat has its birthplace in the Bible—in the sixteenth chapter of Leviticus. The date of its birth is the tenth day of the Hebrew month Tishri, the most sacred of all days in the Jewish year—the Day of Atonement, Yom Kippur.

A ritual was then solemnized which, fortunately, has been discontinued for two thousand years, definitely ever since the destruction of the Temple in A.D. 70.

It started with a peculiar kind of lottery drawn by the high priest. Two choice young goats were provided and placed at the entrance to the sanctuary. (At first this was the portable tent of meeting, used by the Israelites on their way from Egypt to the Promised Land, the prototype of the later Temple.) The high priest then cast lots by means of two inscribed stones. One of these lots doomed the goat which, as a sin offering, would be sacrificed to God on the altar and was therefore specifically marked, "For Yahveh." The second goat was destined to be sent out alive into the wilderness—"For Azazel."

By laying his hands on the latter animal's head, the high priest transferred to this goat—not just symbolically, it was thought, but actually—all the community's transgressions and sins.

This done, the goat now "laden with the sins" was led to the edge of the desert, to be released there and to escape. By doing so, it took with it the burden of the people's sins it now carried vicariously.

It was generally assumed that the goat had its neck broken or was cast down a steep cliff. The reason is obvious. If the animal was not dead, the people feared it might turn around and return to the people the very sins they were happy to have disposed of by its departure.

The escape goat was made to take on man's sins to suffer for them. Escape goat eventually was shortened to scapegoat. And ever since, scapegoats all over the world are burdened with the blame for whatever others have done.

## Azazel

Who was Azazel to whom the goat was actually sent or was meant to escape to? The name Azazel occurs only in one passage in the entire Bible (Lev. 16:8, 10, 26) and in no other literature of the world.

Those anxious to maintain the belief in an originally strict monotheism even in the very early stages of the Hebrew religion have tried laboriously to see in Azazel no extraordinary or supernatural being. They presumed that Azazel was merely a geographical site, the name of some inaccessible, mountainous rocky region in the desert to which the goat was sent.

For this same reason others have suggested that Azazel was not even a proper name but the odd combination of two common words. These portrayed the "rugged" (*azaz*) and "hard" (*el*) nature of the mountain in the wilderness from which the goat was to be cast down.

The Greek and Latin translations of the Bible explained the name of Azazel as the fusion of a Hebrew and an Aramaic word, describing the animal as "the goat (*ayz*) which goes (*azal*)" into the desert. This differentiated it from the goat that stayed on to be sacrificed on the altar.

However, none of these various attempts to explain the true nature of Azazel seems satisfactory. Each in its turn was motivated by the wish to exclude any suggestion of the existence of any other power worshiped beside God. But even in the Bible the world of the occult is represented.

Possibly Azazel was the name of a powerful desert demon, a being of the satyr family, probably a goat deity, to its worshipers a being as real as God himself. The source of evil and its personification, it was therefore the most appropriate figure to which to dispatch and banish all evil that had become attached to the people during the year. By this ritual all the sins were returned to their original and rightful owner.

Azazel, representing the dark side of life, the forces of evil and night, was the original counterpart to God, the ruler of light and of all that was good. This would reflect the once powerful Zoroastrian view of the innate dualism in life. The two contending forces of good and evil, light and darkness, as this Persian faith taught, were coexistent in the universe, each fighting for supremacy.

That is how, in later traditions and significantly so in the apocryphal book of Enoch, Azazel was described as the leader of the fallen angels and the author of all sin. He had taught man the art of warfare and with it the making of every type of weapon. Women, on the other hand, had learned from him the art of seduction: how to entice the male by painting their faces, dyeing their hair, artificially shaping their eyebrows and driving him to distraction by perfume.

Azazel was in reality Satan, the great adversary of goodness. He was the first to corrupt man's style of life and its quality by revealing to him the secrets of witchcraft. The goat was offered Azazel as a bribe. It was hoped that in accepting it he might be prompted to act as a friend and in silent connivance refrain from accusing men before God of the sins they had committed.

Finally, there might well be a connection between the Hebrew Azazel and Aziz, a god worshiped by the ancient Canaanites in the very territory the Israelites came to occupy.

## Transference Of Sin

The entire idea of a scapegoat, however, extends far beyond Azazel's realm which was limited to a certain location, possibly situated in the Sinai wilderness.

The primitive mind believed that it was possible to transfer evil of many kinds onto another being, or even an inanimate object. Just as a man can shift a load of wood from his own back onto that of another (a man's or an animal's), so ancient man reasoned, he could do likewise with the guilt, the sickness or the evil that "burdened" him.

This general principle was applied all over the world. Only the individual way in which this was done differed in the various cultures. Often an animal or a bird served as the "scapegoat." It was let loose or let fly, driven off by pelting it with stones, cast into a river or down a cliff, ritually slaughtered or burned to ashes.

Preceding the Hebrews by hundreds of years, the example of an actual scapegoat was known in the civilization of the Hittites and

Babylonians. At the time of a plague, Hittites ceremoniously sent a goat, symbolically laden with the dreaded disease, into enemy territory. They believed that it would carry with it the pestilence. In this way a dual purpose was simultaneously achieved. It would take away the scourge from them and give it to their foe, thereby eventually destroying him. In Akitu, the Babylonian celebration of the New Year, a goat, too, took the place of man and was sacrificed to the goddess of the abyss.

Incas used a black llama to take away their sicknesses. Another South American Indian tribe appointed the guinea pig as its scapegoat. Similarly, Moroccans kept a wild boar in their stables. They thought it would attract and divert from their precious steeds the evil spirits out to do them harm.

In Britain, Shropshire people beat a cat to expiate them for their sins. The Bible demanded (Lev. 14:7) that a man who had been cured from leprosy had to release in a field a bird dipped in the blood of its slaughtered fellow. It was imagined that it would take the place of the afflicted person, taking with it his dreadful disease.

Orthodox Jews to this very day observe a similar practice on the day before Yom Kippur. Symbolically they transfer their sins to a fowl, the *Kapporah Hühnchen*, as it is called in Hebrew-Yiddish phraseology. Prior to killing the bird, they swing it around above their head three times and while doing so recite a formula, saying, "This is my substitute, my vicarious offering and atonement." The chicken, so they imagine, suffers for their sins and thereby shields them from the punishment which really should be meted out to them.

In some people's mythologies, the search for a scapegoat went beyond the animal kingdom. They believed that their own god offered himself as sacrifice for their sins. He died for them—vicariously—just as is told, in the Christian faith, of Jesus Christ. They duly represented and even dramatized the event in a solemn ritual which became a central part of their religion.

Human beings also died as scapegoats. In Greece, this role was accorded such honor and privilege that men volunteered for it. Nothing seemed more meritorious than to give their own life for the sake of others and by doing so rid them of any feeling of guilt or possession of evil.

The scapegoat covers a tremendous territory. It extends from the desert of Sinai to everyday modern speech and from the practice of gruesome rituals to noble human self-sacrifice. It includes the story of a god dying for man's guilt and the occult belief in the devil.

With its roots so far back in man's history, it is strange to realize that the word "scapegoat" was first coined as late as 1530 when William Tyndale translated the Hebrew Bible into English. It was his attempt to render adequately the mysterious Azazel as it appears in the book of Leviticus. In his version, Tyndale spoke of "the goote on which the lotte fell to scape."

## "TO SLEEP LIKE A TOP" OR "A LOG"

Witches seem to have crept into the most unexpected places. People completely at rest and so much at ease that nothing would rouse them, are said "to sleep like a top" or "a log." Who would ever guess that this now-so-common phrase was truly bewitched?

The usual explanation links the phrase with the well-known toy which was enjoyed in the nurseries of ancient Mesopotamian culture. Gyrating on its tip at tremendous speed, its very movement is so imperceptible that the top really looks as if it were at a standstill. And according to this interpretation, those sound asleep would be as much at rest as apparently the spinning top.

At the very least this popular explanation is very farfetched. Why, of all things, choose a toy to describe those who are completely "out"? Was it meant to say that a person "sleeping like a top" in reality was all wound and churned up and only shamming rest and repose? But the "answer" becomes more unreal if it is remembered that the spinning top stays in its illusionary state of immobility for only a very short time—not enough even for forty winks. It does not take long for it to start wobbling and then to fall over. Therefore, this traditional explanation makes no sense and can easily be discarded.

An alternate theory traces the simile to France and "recognizes" in the top the English transliteration of the French word for a "mole"— *taupe*.

This might seem a logical answer. The mole spends much of its time—unobserved—underground. People might easily imagine that it does so to make sure of sleeping comfortably, long and sound, undisturbed by all the noises overhead.

Nevertheless this "genealogy," like that of the spinning toy, easily falls to the ground and is just as odd. Why should the English have chosen the French word for mole to express their sound sleep? Was their own species of that furry creature not good enough or perhaps less restful?

It could be feasible (and there are other examples of the kind) that the English literally adopted a popular French saying. But the Gallic equivalent description of a person who is sound asleep does not speak of a mole at all. The French say that he or she sleeps "like a wooden shoe" which certainly makes much more sense.

However, new complications arise. The French word for a "wooden shoe" is *sabot* which, indeed, is responsible for all international *sabotage*. And very surprisingly, *sabot* was used by the French as well to describe a wooden top. But then again it must be asked why the French "wooden shoe" (even if holding a wooden top) on crossing the English Channel should have changed its name and be translated into the English tongue to be rendered "top."

Might not top actually have come out of the log? To sleep "like a log" seems more logical. Just like the French wooden shoe, once put down it was truly at rest and, if heavy enough, could not easily be moved. And it was in connection with this very log that the occult took over the quest for a right and sensible explanation. An apparently down-to-earth article served as a most useful cover-up for those engaged with the supernatural.

It was told that witches when leaving for a nightly tryst went out of their way to make their absence from home inconspicuous and unnoticed. Anyone who found their bed unoccupied would become suspicious and start asking questions. To avoid this, the witch placed a log in her bed. At times, to make the deception look still more realistic, she would top the log with a nightcap. Whoever then looked at her bed in the dim light would think that she was fast asleep, so soundly she did not stir once.

Very much aware of the lurking danger from those who were witch-hunting, the woman took an additional precautionary measure to make absolutely sure that her dummy body would do its duty and work well as her sleeping representative. She would use for the log wood from trees witches regarded as endowed with occult power, such as the hawthorn and the elder. A log that came from such a magic source would surely not give away the show by delivering to her foes the very person who looked after the supernatural to which both were so deeply attached.

A witch had to be careful at all times. Consequently when meeting one of her own kind and wanting to discuss a coven she had attended the previous night, she had to do so with great caution. If overheard, she would endanger herself and her group. For this reason she would say that last night she had slept "like a log." This said everything to those in the know.

Eventually the phrase was adopted as a telling password among witches. However, when the outside world somehow got hold of it, all the magic went out of the log and it lost its original function as a secret sign.

Discarded by witches, it was taken over by the world at large. And if we now happily sleep "like a log" or "a top," we do so unperturbedly, and are truly unconscious of the occult root from which the log grew.

# CHAPTER FIVE

# Weird Creatures

## FAIRIES

Belief in fairies seems very childish to modern man. Fairy tales are good for nurseries and even there have been replaced by stories of Superman and creatures from outer space. Little do we realize the important role fairies have played in the early life of man and how they continue to exert a notable influence.

Most likely fairies were not as unsubstantial and ethereal as now believed. To begin with, they were not bearers of luck. One theory asserts they were the original Stone Age inhabitants of large parts of Britain. When the Celts, a race of much taller stature and equipped with better armor, invaded their country from Europe around 500 B.C., the indigenous fairies refused to submit. They withdrew into the dense forests where they settled, eking out a living as best they could. However, they did not give up the battle. They waged a kind of "guerilla warfare," attacking the invaders in insidious ways.

It was not easy to trace them. To make their detection more difficult, they lived underground and even employed camouflage by donning the green foliage and color of their surroundings. This explains the myth of the "little green men": the product not of a vivid imagination but of a dire experience.

Members of the conquered race, the original Britons, often raided their foes' homes during the night not only to harass them but to supplement their sparse rations. Thus the frightened people wisely left bowls of cream and oatmeal outside their dwellings. These rations had disappeared by next morning, indicating that the forest spirits had accepted their goodwill offering and would not harm them. If spurned, the fairies would become most spiteful and wreak vengeance.

Faint memories of specific aspects of the displaced people have survived: their numerous acts of retribution and the many ways in which they tried to ensure their survival in a hostile environment. Certainly they must have fired the imagination of later peoples, and the stories they passed down continued to be embellished in their telling.

However, all that was actually remembered was that these early "little people" were dark skinned, small and possessed outstanding occult powers.

Their tiny weapons were no match for the iron armor of the invaders. Yet their sharp flint arrowheads proved lethal because they were dipped in poison. Bewildered by the devastating effect of these Lilliputian arrows, the invaders attributed it to magic power. Those primitive missiles became known as "elf bolts" because they were believed to be charmed. (It is interesting to note that in German lumbago is called *Hexenschuss*—literally "the shot of a witch!")

Just as present-day aborigines are able to communicate over vast distances without modern technological gadgetry, so were the fairies. This further added to their mystery and the awe in which they were held. They also knew and made ample use of the healing and dangerous properties in plants and minerals. With their aid, they could cure disease, paralyze people or even transport their minds to other dimensions.

In the absence of a natural explanation for all these phenomena, the fairies of old were regarded as a race of supernatural creatures endowed with the power to work magic. To propitiate them was a wise counsel. Even the names by which they were called attempted to flatter them and were chosen with great caution. They became "the good folk," "the hidden people," and "the good neighbors." Some, because of their darker skin, were referred to as "brownies."

The powers of magic attributed to the fairies caused people both to fear and to seek to appease them. But greatly puzzled by them, people also tried to find out who they really were and how they lived.

Mostly invisible, fairies nevertheless shared the existence of man; they would reveal their presence only when they felt so inclined. In their lives time was a relative quantity. People who alleged to have visited them claimed that what had seemed to them such a short while had really been many years. On the other hand, to fairies a single second could be crowded with an immense number of events.

Their abode was underground, just below the surface. In fact, they were responsible for the growth of all verdure, a claim discussed in Chapter Four on the color green.

Others asserted that fairies were homeless souls. They belonged to unbaptized and stillborn children or to pagans. Having been refused entry to the Christian heaven and hell, they were free spirits lingering on in this world, able to flit here, there and everywhere.

Medieval magicians saw in "the little people" creatures that had magically materialized out of the elements of earth, air, fire and water. To raise them and to employ their powers, magicians devised a complex ritual of spells and ceremonies.

Another belief held that fairies were "defrocked" angels. Being less bad than Lucifer and his gang, they had been sentenced to the earth rather than sent straight from heaven into hell.

Finally, the view was held that fairies did not come from the other world but were closely attached to man, dead or alive: they were his astral body, the subtle and tenuous ethereal counterpart of man's physical body that could leave the physical shell during sleep and travel far and wide, experiencing another dimension.

The great variety of traditions and occult assumptions relating to fairies inevitably led to the conviction that they were closely akin to the witch, another survival of the "old religion." Thus, many of the stories and beliefs about them overlap. Witches were said to dance on their Sabbats in the magic circle, just as fairies did in their rings.

The fairy myths may be rooted in the ancient worship of nature. They might well be a take-over of the outlawed old religion which had deified the forces of fertility and which, in the form of nymphs and satyrs, were thought to dwell in the trees, the rivers and the wells. And did not the fairy keep closely in touch with those mysterious forces?

Because of the mischief the fairies were alleged to cause and the consequent fear this aroused, their association with witches and their craft was a strong belief.


## THE LEPRECHAUN

The leprechaun is the most famous of all Irish fairies and gnomes. Stories abound about their knowledge of hidden treasures and their ability to reveal the hiding places to whomever is lucky enough to get hold of the pygmy sprite.

It is, of course, essential to keep the creature constantly in sight. Should one take one's eyes off it, even for a split second, the leprechaun will make its escape and with it would disappear the chance of acquiring a buried crock of gold.

Aware of this means of escape, leprechauns make use of it by duping their captor. Suddenly they might call out: "Your house is on fire!", "Watch out!" or a similar alarming cry. And when their captor then looked away, the leprechaun would have vanished and with it the fortune which had seemed so close.

Many stories have been told of how leprechauns cunningly managed to keep the crock of gold underground. Best known is the tale of the Irishman who had actually succeeded in forcing the fairy to lead him to the site of a buried treasure. But alas, he lacked any tool to dig it up. Wisely, or at least so he thought, he marked the spot by taking off one of his red garters and tying it around the tree that grew next to it. As the leprechaun had done what was required of him, he let him go.

Rushing home to fetch a spade, the man was back in less than three minutes. The leprechaun meanwhile had departed but, prior to vanishing, had put identical red garters around all the other trees growing there. Thus tricked, the man never found the treasure nor did he see the roguish elf again.

The leprechaun's name describes the dwarfish creature very aptly. A combination of Gaelic words, it refers to a "small" (*lu*) "body" (*corp*) which, by way of making it even smaller than it already was, has attached to its end as a suffix the diminutive *an*.

The notion that leprechauns were shoemakers is a fallacy, based on a language misinterpretation. Not versed in the Gaelic tongue, some people imagined that "leprechaun" stood for a "half brogue," fusing the Irish for "half" (*leith*) and "shoe" (*brog*). Brogue described the typically Irish shoe of untanned hide. A leprechaun was so called because usually he made only one shoe, which fitted his little figure all the better into Irish fairyland.

The first mention of the leprechaun links him neither with Irish shoes nor crocks of gold. Anticipating the modern submarine, the story told of how a leprechaun was able to teach man how to travel below the seas invisible from above.

## INCUBI AND SUCCUBI—THE SOURCE OF ALL NIGHT-MARES

People have always been mystified by the unusual, and they are particularly fearful of occurrences and phenomena of an evil nature. Prior to the scientific age, they were convinced everything had to have some cause which, if not natural, lay in the realm of the occult.

Long before Freud, sexual dreams left their mark on the mind of man. He wondered what created them. Equally, the birth of deformed children puzzled him.

Looking for an explanation that made sense to him, he invented an ominous creature which, he thought, visited people during the night and in their sleep made love to them. Therefore any sexual dream was not a chimera but the actual experience of this odd type of ghostly intercourse with its monstrous birth as a possible consequence.

The name given to the lecherous demon reflected this conviction. The spirit visiting a sleeping woman was called *incubus*. From the Latin *incumbere*, it referred to its "lying upon." In the case of man—changing the position—it was the *succubus*—the one who was the "underlier."

To speak of a nightmare man experiences is merely a follow-up of this ominous tradition. It reflects the belief that something truly heavy had taken position on one's chest during sleep. Weighing down the victim, it caused a most frightening sensation of being suffocated, and was remembered with trepidation on awakening.

The "mare" in nightmare has no relation at all to the female horse. It recalls the old Irish queen of elves known as Morrigain which was just another term for incubus. The French, in their usual logical way, called a nightmare "the fiend that tramples" (*cauchemar*). And Chaucer was well justified to express the prayerful wish to God to "Blisse this house fro the nightes-mare."

## JACK-O'-LANTERN AND WILL-O'-THE-WISP

The mysterious and ominous seemed to surround man everywhere, particularly so in the dark of night. A fatal experience known and feared was the sudden appearance of lights that hovered around marshy lands.

Lonely, straying wanderers attracted by them were put into a hypnotic spell. They could not but follow those flickering lights and, misled, eventually found themselves lost in the midst of a swamp from which there was no escape.

Ignorant of their real source, man imagined the lights were the spirits of dead people flitting about, possibly in search of a body they could occupy. Various regions identified them differently. The Russians said they were the souls of stillborn infants. Totally lost, they were floating about in limbo between heaven and hell.

Because those flames appeared like beckoning lamps seeking to guide the straying wanderer, they were called "Jack-o'-lantern" or, more simply, "the friar's lantern." The more highbrow, shunning such rather homely terms, used instead the Latin *ignis fatuus*. This spoke of "the foolish fire" which misguided and deluded man, leading him to certain death.

Best known, however, was another name for the phenomenon, "will-o'-the-wisp." Originally and much more correctly, it referred to "Will with the wisp." Not a friar nor a Jack, William used neither flames nor lantern but a handful of straw, a wisp, to achieve the identical nefarious aim, causing men to lose their way and subsequently their very lives in a bog.

Of these two expressions, will-o'-the-wisp alone survives in everyday language as the term used for any deluding scheme or ephemeral Utopian dream that ends in frustration and calamity.

All those flickering lights and wandering flames, by whichever name they were known, certainly were not spirits, Jacks or Williams. Only man's imaginative mind, when still lacking a rational explanation, could thus see them. Eventually they were recognized as a natural phenomenon. These phosphorescent lights hovering over swamps at night were the result of the spontaneous combustion of gases produced by decaying plants or the decomposition of other organic matter.

With the mystery gone, Jack-o'-lantern's lamp should really have been extinguished. And yet, it is still lit up in countless numbers all over America on one night every year. No longer linked with the marshes, it is now the name of the lamps fashioned out of pumpkins, turnips and potatoes which decorate American homes on Halloween, that great mysterious night of the year.

The custom goes back to the Druids to mark the arrival of winter.

The hollowed-out vegetable with its glowing light within reflects their mysterious ritual.

The Irish believe the Jack-o'-lantern began with Jack, one of their countrymen. He had loved life and all its pleasures, but particularly strong drink. He shunned work and helping other people was not in his line. He was a very stingy person.

His dissolute, selfish life eventually qualified him as a permanent resident among those wicked people whose home was hell.

Jack, however, in spite of his drinking, had his wits about him. Well aware of his rather unpleasant final destiny, he was determined somehow to change his luck, without changing his way of life.

One day, when meeting the devil, Jack enticed him to climb an apple tree to pick for himself the most luscious of its fruits. But the very moment the evil one had taken hold of the apple, Jack traced the sign of the cross on the tree which forced the devil to stay aloft in great distress.

Whatever the price, he had to come to terms with Jack and make him remove the sign that kept him in the tree. Jack promised to erase the cross if in turn the devil would give his word to leave him alone for the rest of his life and, what was even more significant, not to demand his soul after death.

Everything seemed to go Jack's way. There was no longer any need for him to worry, he imagined. But when the day of his death arrived and he was ready to go to heaven, he was duly refused admission. A man of his type certainly had no rightful place there.

What could Jack do now? Just hovering around as a homeless wanderer was out of the question. All that was left for him to do was to go to the very place he had hoped to avoid at all costs. But even hell now had its gates closed to him, since the devil was obliged to keep his word, and never to take Jack into his abode.

Poor Jack was at a total loss. He tried to climb back up from the netherworld. But in the dark and confusion, he could not find his way. Possibly to help him and light up the path from the abyss, the devil threw him one of the glowing coals used to keep the hellfires burning. Jack, who just then was eating a pumpkin (a turnip or a potato other traditions say), got hold of the ember and stuck it inside the vegetable. And ever since he has used this improvised lantern in his ceaseless search all over the world for a place to rest.

Another version of the story tells that Jack made the devil climb the tree just for fun. He had meant it as a practical joke. But, unfortunately, the devil had no sense of humor. And when Jack had been refused admission to heaven for his stinginess, he tried to find accommodation in hell. But the devil had neither forgotten nor forgiven the time when Jack had made him look a fool. Therefore, he did not grant him domicile. And that is why Jack has been left to walk the earth with his lantern. He must do so till the coming of Judgment Day.

## THE WEREWOLF

The belief that a man could be transformed into an animal or the reverse is so widespread and ancient that it has become part of the myths and folklore of many nations. Modern fairy tales speaking of such changes are relics of those very legends and not just a fabrication of imaginative writers.

Equally universal and old is the conviction that some men took on or were forced to assume the shape and nature of the fiercest creature known, and did so because they were particularly gifted, fated or punished.

The type of animal depended on the locality of the myth. In Africa, natives believed in the existence of man-crocodiles, man-leopards and man-hyenas. In South America it was the jaguar and in Turkey, the boar into which people were thought to change.

Europe was overrun by wolves all the way from the Atlantic Coast to the Russian steppes. For centuries, this creature presented a dreadful menace. His ferocious attacks claimed countless victims. (The last wolf was killed in England only during the reign of King Henry VII, in Scotland in 1743 and in Ireland even later. In some parts of Europe wolves are still reported.)

Wolves were a greater danger in winter when their own prey was scarce. Driven by hunger, they invaded human habitations to kill and devour cattle and sheep. If these were insufficient they would attack humans and even carried away children, to feed on them or nourish the cubs with their flesh.

Not surprisingly panic seized entire communities at these times. The strongest of men seemed helpless against the attacks of the famished creatures. To hear the wolves' eerie, drawn-out howl at night or to watch them skillfully hunting in packs added to the terror.

The mystery and the horror were deepened when a man was bitten by a wolf that carried rabies, a disease then unidentified and for which there was no cure. Frothing from the mouth like someone possessed, the victim contracted the dreadful and lethal sickness, himself taking on the dangerous madness, and the animal was assumed to be some sort of supernatural being. Consequently, people came to see in the wolf no longer an ordinary animal but a mysteriously transformed man endowed with dangerous, occult powers.

It did not take long for fact and fiction to mingle and to create in people the conviction of the existence of "werewolves." The word clearly describes the ghastly nature of a "wolf-man," as *were* was the Anglo-Saxon word for "man." The phenomenon became known as lycanthropy, a term that conveys the identical meaning but does so in Greek: *lukos* being the Greek for "wolf" and *anthropos* for "man."

Several important factors contributed to the belief which, however farfetched it may now seem, was very real to those threatened and haunted people.

First, they must have heard some of the ancient myths that spoke of shape-changing and even perhaps of the case of a man who had been transformed into a wolf.

An example from the Classical Age was related by the Roman poet Ovid. Surprisingly, it is linked with Arcadia, which came to be renowned as a haven of rustic bliss. In the story Lycaon, the king of Arcadia, was a cruel tyrant and much evil was committed in his name. Zeus, as chief god, was determined to stop Lycaon from continuing his wicked ways. To confront the brutal ruler, Zeus came down from heaven to call on Lycaon in Arcadia, making no secret of who he was.

The king doubted that his guest was really the supreme divine ruler he alleged himself to be. To test him, he served him a dish made of human flesh for dinner. One account related that he murdered a messenger who had just arrived. Another, more gruesome claim, asserts the flesh came from the body of one of his own sons.

Zeus, beside himself with rage, lost no time in punishing the bloodthirsty tyrant. He destroyed the palace and changed the king into a wolf. One tradition claims that not only the king, but also his remaining sons were changed into wolves. In the transformation Lycaon assumed every lupine feature except in the eyes. These, as in the werewolves of later years, kept their human expression.

No doubt the myth attempted to explain the presence of countless bloodthirsty wolves in Arcadia and their frequent, fearsome attacks on the peacefully grazing flocks of sheep.

Primitive tribes were supported in the belief in werewolves by their own faith, one of the very early forms of religion known as totemism. This taught that each group of men had descended from a specific animal—its totem—which it looked on as its "guardian." Sacred to them, the animal would be protected by the tribe. Identifying themselves with the totem ancestor, they could easily believe that some outstanding member of their race was able to assume the original "shape."

All this was given even more credibility by reports and experiences of children lost or carried away into forests and reared by wolves. When finally found, they had not only adopted lupine traits but actually regarded themselves as wolves. Rudyard Kipling's famous figure of Mowgli in his *Jungle Books* is based on such an experience. The young Indian boy considered the wolves his brothers.

Primitive peoples had vivid dreams largely attributed to their eating habits. Dreams to them seemed most real. Who, after all, could prove to them the difference between the world of imagination and that of fact? Therefore, when recollecting a dream in which they had been a wolf, they believed that this had been so and that on waking they had merely returned to their original human shape.

Fantasy-producing drugs, either taken orally or applied in the form of ointments, caused people to imagine that they were no longer humans but wolves. Thus deluded, they acted exactly as the beast would: they moved on all fours and attacked men and cattle, tearing off their flesh and devouring it raw.

Lycanthropy described this type of mental aberration. People who suffered from it exhibited wolfish traits. This kind of insanity has served as a major explanation of the werewolf phenomenon.

Indian religion further confirmed the possibility of the existence of werewolves. The Hindus' belief in the transmigration of souls and in reincarnation assumed a close kinship between animals and man. Any animal could be possessed by the spirit of a former human, retrogressively passing through such a stage on its journey to the final destination of Nirvana.

Ancient, magic hunting customs were yet another contributory source for the idea. The hunter who impersonated the chased animal by donning its hide and imitating its demeanor not only tried to deceive his prey by appearing like one of its pack, he actually imagined that he himself had taken on its personality.

In the sixteenth and seventeenth centuries, fear of werewolves grew into a mass hysteria, especially in France. It has been suggested that within a period of less than 150 years, 30,000 cases of werewolves were recorded. No one seemed safe either from attack or from suspicion of being such a creature. And once people started believing this sort of myth, they soon found confirmation of their fears wherever they looked.

The discovery of the mangled body of a child "proved" to them that a werewolf must have slain yet another victim. The mysterious disappearance of people was explained by saying that they had been carried off by the beast. And there were not a few perverted characters who discovered in the werewolf story a useful means by which murders, depraved blood lust, sadism and even cannibalism might be covered up or the blame passed on to an innocent person.

In hard times, when people were starved for meat and in their craving might even live as cannibals, their untutored minds were ready to believe that it was not nutritional deficiency that was the cause of their horrible desire but that they had actually somehow or other, turned into wolves. And if it was pointed out to them that they still looked like human beings, they rationalized their lack of lupine features by saying that their pelt had grown inside out.

Having "established" that werewolves existed—even if only in their minds—people still seriously wondered what it could be that triggered off such a weird and ominous transformation. They thought it was attained either by the individual's own deliberate will or that the state was inflicted by an ill-intentioned outsider. There were different methods of shape shifting.

Most effective was the donning of a girdle made of the skin of a wolf or of a man. On the other hand, those especially endowed could become a werewolf by sheer willpower or, as we would say today, by self-hypnosis.

How to detect wolf people, either in their human or lupine guise, became a significant question. After all, if only for the victim, it was a matter of life and death. With the passing of time and the spread of the epidemic, ever more features were imagined to betray a werewolf disguised as a man or woman. All one reputedly had to know was what symptoms to look for.

Certain unfortunate features immediately caused suspicion. Men who grew hair all over their body (medically now explained as a case of hypertrichosis) were very unlucky. They could not hide their "wolfish" skin. To have converging eyebrows above the bridge of the nose was a distinguishing feature seen as yet another unmistakable werewolf trait.

Incidents of a little-known disease added to the werewolf mania. People who suffered from porphyria would develop horrible blisters the moment they exposed their skin to the sun, and their resultant facial distortion and ugliness made them ready victims of werewolf hysteria.

To rid yourself of a foe in those unhappy times, you merely accused him of being a werewolf. By his alleged pact with the devil he was able completely to disguise all his wolfish features. And once he was in the clutches of the law, he could not win.

There was one sure means by which to verify beyond the shadow of a doubt the true werewolf nature of a person. Any wound inflicted on the person while in his wolf shape would not vanish. It would show up on the identical part of the body once the werewolf had changed back into its human form.

Deep rooted was the conviction that no matter how the wolf traits showed themselves, the devil had his hand in it. Who else would give man the power to transmute and to take on the nature of a wolf? Hence, those afflicted with or merely suspected of lycanthropy lived dangerous lives. In the eyes of the Church, and subsequently of the law, theirs was a heinous crime which only death could atone. Hunting werewolves developed into a fascinating "blood sport."

Those believing in the occult gave their own explanation concerning werewolves: a person's astral body can assume the personality of the wolf while, during the transformation, his physical being stays in a trance.

The werewolf belongs to the world of the occult, but he is also part of the story of man: his power of imagination, his obsessions, fears and gullibility. Two thousand years ago the Roman naturalist Pliny reprimanded those of his countrymen (especially the authors) who were foolish enough to give credence to the occurrence of lycanthropy. There were falsehoods, he wrote, however barefaced, to which people would bear testimony and thereby show their lack of wisdom. And yet, fifteen hundred years later, countless people still fanatically believed in such absurd metamorphosis and hideous transformation.

When Hitler saw the approaching doom of the *Reich*, which he had intended to last for a thousand years, he planned the formation of groups of young fanatics. They were to roam the country and wreak bloody vengeance on the invaders. His scheme came to naught. However, significant was the name he had chosen for those suggested ruthless marauders. They were to be known as "werewolves."

The concept of the werewolf is closely linked to that of the vampire, particularly by the legend claiming that after death the ghost of a lycanthropist becomes a vampire.

## THE VAMPIRE

Vampire, a word of Magyar or Turkish origin describing a "blood sucker," and vampirism, the belief in such bloodthirsty creatures, existed in primitive form as far back as the ancient world. It was in the Middle Ages, however, that, like the werewolf, fear of vampires assumed epidemic proportions.

Several traditions and phenomena combined to create the vampire myth. A primary factor was the belief in the potency of blood.

Blood has always been recognized as a vital substance of life. Observation had taught even primitive races that loss of blood could spell death, and so from the beginning blood was regarded as the source of life and the seat of the soul, a precious fluid of divine nature, endowing vigor and virility. But its very value rendered it highly dangerous.

People looked with awe on blood. The mysteries surrounding it caused numerous and often contradictory practices, either to annul its dangerous properties or to add strength to the human body or the gods.

Primitive races presented blood to their gods which, at times, was the essential part of their solemn sacrifice. Blood would appease the gods' wrath or obtain their goodwill. Some races even drank the blood themselves, especially that of their slain enemies. They imagined that by doing so they absorbed extra vitality. Some were so "bloodthirsty" that they licked the dried blood off the spears with which they had wounded or killed their foes.

In their ancient worship, Hebrews likewise poured the blood of sacrificed animals onto the altar and sprinkled it on its four corners. In the Communion Service, Christians partake of Christ's blood. They do so either symbolically or believing in the miraculous transsubstantiation of the wine.

Other beliefs held that blood shed on the ground could not be left uncovered. A woman's menstrual blood was regarded taboo and anything touched by it became unclean. The Hebrew Bible forbade man to partake of any blood, for "the blood is the life." Jewish dietary legislation, evolved from the biblical law, specified various means to remove every possible trace of blood from meat prior to its consumption. That is why Orthodox Jews came to observe the ritual slaughter of animals when the blood was carefully drained away and to demand that meat, before being cooked, should be further drained of blood by salting and soaking it in water for several hours.

This view on blood also accounts to a large degree for accusations and practices of ritual murder in antiquity and medieval times. Men committed these murders, it was alleged, to gain possession of blood deemed essential for additional powers.

The desire to drink blood might well explain the origin of cannibalism, surviving even today in some persons' atavistic taste for steak tartar or blood-red underdone meat. It may be the reason, too, for the ghoulish privilege of some medieval European executioners to retain for themselves the blood and certain parts of the body of their victims.

Given that some living human beings thirsted for blood, it followed that in the imagination of man, some already dead and thought to be anxious to live again or to reinvigorate their spirits in the beyond should yearn for the magic fluid even more desperately. This was one of the chief factors in the birth of the vampire myth.

It was common superstition that the dead or their spirits left their graves during the hours of night to recharge their body with life-giving force. They did this by sucking the blood of a sleeping human, and, some believed, they could also attain their aim by killing the best of the cattle. These vampires were specifically those dead who could find no rest in their graves. They included all kinds of evil people, suicides and heretics excommunicated by the Church. They desperately needed blood to regenerate their power. That was why, in the dark of night, they would ascend from their graves to search for blood.

Man's limited knowledge of the cause of disease was a potent source of prolonging the vampire myth. It is human nature to take luck for granted and to blame misfortune on others. This is all the more true if communities were struck by some fatal illness that wiped out a great part of the population.

During the plague that ravaged Europe in the fourteenth century, indescribable terror seized whole regions. Thousands of men, women and children were hastily buried at a depth of at least six feet. Houses that had become infected by the Black Death were marked with the sign of a huge red cross and the prayerful inscription: "Lord have mercy on us."

The constant threat that one could be struck down by the scourge at any moment created a climate of hysteria and fear psychosis. With no known cause, it was only natural that everyone looked for a scapegoat. The Jews were blamed and accused of having poisoned the wells, thereby creating the plague, and thousands of them were murdered in consequence.

Because the havoc wrought by the plague was of such awful dimensions that it could not be the outcome of "natural forces" alone, people came to believe it had to be the work of some malevolent supernatural power, and began seeking the cause of the disaster beyond mere human beings. They looked for it in the realm of the occult, and the vampire seemed the most likely creature to blame. Thus an ancient legend that had almost died out at the time gained a new lease on life.

Modern heart transplants have raised the problem of determining at what precise moment life really terminates. When has the doctor the right to pronounce a man dead in order to remove his heart? The stopping of the heartbeat, it is generally now agreed upon, does not spell death. For doctors and theologians the entire question has become a very controversial medical and ethical issue.

Not long ago many people were obsessed by the fear that they might be certified dead when in reality they were still alive. An untranslatable German term calls this condition of being "apparently dead," *scheintod*.

Because of his suspended animation and rigid body, the still live person could appear to be dead and be buried prematurely. He finally dies from asphyxiation. Statistics show that such incidents were not infrequent.

The conditions of catalepsy were of that type, though they are now diagnosed as being of a mental nature. The patient is completely paralyzed and in a trancelike state. His complexion is waxen and he shows no sign of life.

Who then could blame past generations of doctors, still ignorant of these circumstances, to have been totally misled by the symptoms and hence declared such a person dead?

To avoid premature burial a law introduced in European countries instructed undertakers not to inter any corpse before the expiration of three full days. It was a period considered long enough for anyone who was only apparently dead to return to life.

Others, still not satisfied and afraid that they might be buried in a state of cataleptic trance, left in their will the stipulation that their coffins should be provided either with a bell they could sound by means of a rope to attract attention and a vent that would keep the inside of their coffin well ventilated, so that just in case their death was not real, they would be able to survive.

Others even demanded that at death their jugular vein should be severed. This would make quite sure there was no possibility of "resurrection." Odder still, but in the circumstances quite reasonable, was the request by some people to have a bottle of chloroform entombed with them. Should their burial prove premature, they would use it to commit suicide in order to avoid unnecessary suffering, since for them there was no other "exit" provided.

And when sometimes it did happen that people buried prior to their real death came to life again and found themselves incarcerated in the grave or coffin, terror seized them. Hoping to be heard, they screamed for help. Attempting to escape from their underground prison, with superhuman power they tried to lift the lid and the earth above. In frenzied desperation they struggled for life. They tore their shroud and started eating it up. They bit into their own flesh and by doing so made their own blood spurt which covered their body, the shroud and the inside of the casket. And, if interred in a crypt, the coffin was hurled around.

Since man did not know the true cause of the terrible noise and the screams coming out of the grave or vault, he imagined that the person buried must have changed into a vampire creature which raised its voice in lust for blood.

Also, robbers anxious for spoil buried with the dead, or anatomists in quest of a body for dissection, used to exhume corpses. If they found a body that showed terrible signs of convulsion, with part of the shroud in its mouth and blood all over, they believed that this "undead" was indeed not an ordinary mortal but a blood-sucking vampire they had unearthed.

## The Vampire Alibi

The vampire myth—so historians have suggested—served as a welcome alibi for the most obnoxious, dastardly cannibalism and desecration of the recently dead in food-starved European lands.

When famine and pestilence threatened people, they went almost out of their minds. To keep alive and to strengthen their weakened bodies, they were prepared to go to any lengths. And somehow they then remembered the superstitious belief in the life-giving, invigorating properties of human blood. Thus, under the cover of night, they committed atrocious murderous deeds in order to suck the blood from their unfortunate victims.

When daylight came and the remnants of their nefarious act were discovered, they deliberately spread stories of the ancient vampire myth. They suggested that it had all been the work of that bloodthirsty creature which once again was at large, undoubtedly because of the apocalyptic times.

Such rumors, helped these criminals greatly. Those who could have made every effort to solve the abominable crime and would have succeeded if they had, did not dare to do so. They were afraid that if they pursued the matter, the fearful being might strike them as well.

The traces of the murder were thus cleverly covered up, but that was not the end of the matter. Gullible people soon took fiction for fact and gave yet another lease on life to the ancient fantasy. As it were, the vampire legend was now truly fed on the blood of people.

Human misfits and psychotic killers adopted the vampire custom and came to present a real threat to society. Theirs was not the world of the occult, however, but of mental and sexual aberration. They even confessed that they were in need of blood as others were in need of alcohol. Their place, therefore, is restricted to medical textbooks.

## Burying the Vampire

Men, always on the lookout for danger, often wondered whether the person they met was "real" and good or, perhaps during times of vampire fever, merely a disguised creature of that kind. Anyone somehow "different" had to be careful. Fear of vampires produced an almost inexhaustible variety of precautions.

In some countries the branch of the juniper tree was kept for protection. If not actually able to keep out the bloodthirsty creature, it nevertheless would render it ineffective.

The vampire myth accounts as well for many deeply ingrained superstitions and burial customs. Their original purpose was not so much to honor the dead as to protect the bereaved.

Primitive people gashed their own bodies at the death of a kinsman not as a sign of grief but because they were motivated by vampire fear. They hoped that the freely flowing blood would feed the thirst of the spirit of the departed and be accepted as a free-will offering for the nourishment of the soul of the dead person. Thus completely satiated, it would not return later to suck the blood out of the body of the living.

Relatives would cover the mirrors in the house of death lest the spirit should see its reflection and stay on. They never stopped watching the corpse which was eventually carried out by a special door reserved for the dead and often subsequently bricked up.

The corpse was then interred deep in the ground, in a coffin with the lid firmly screwed down and with a heavy stone placed above. All this was done not out of reverence and piety but to avoid at all costs the return of the dead or his ghost. Once a vampire had risen, the damage was done.

The bodies of those most likely to transform themselves into a vampire were duly fixed to the bottom of the grave by driving a stake through the heart. This was not merely a physical "nailing down" of the body but a magic rite.

Much thought was given to the choice of the wood for the stake and the choice depended on local traditions as to its mystical qualities. It could be maple, hawthorn or aspen. Aspen was especially chosen because of its sacred association in the Christian faith. The cross on which Christ had been crucified was said to have been made from the timber of the aspen tree, and that was the explanation of its mysterious tremble. This was caused, it was said, by memories of the cruel execution in a never-dying sense of horror and shame.

The legs and feet of the dead were often fettered and, when the shackling was deemed insufficient, limbs and at times even the head were severed.

Sometimes the deceased was buried far away from his erstwhile home, thereby attempting to make his return if not impossible, most unlikely and difficult. It might well be that the choice of churchyards for burial grounds was based on the identical fear. The vicinity of the house of God doubly consecrated the ground and, therefore, would keep the dead in their place and the living unmolested.

To protect themselves further from becoming involuntary blood donors, the bereaved changed their clothes, particularly their color. It was done as a disguise lest their dear departed might recognize them. In some cases, the bereft actually donned masks and, on returning from the burial, never looked back at the grave, and took a devious route home.

## THE BANSHEE

Death has haunted man through the ages. Recognizing in it the all-powerful "final master and lord," people assumed that it would not arrive unannounced but would make its imminent arrival known.

The way death did so could take various forms. Most common were premonitions, when men and women felt that the angel of death was hovering around, ready to claim them. Queer apparitions of one's ethereal double (called by the untranslatable German *Doppelgänger*) and mysterious knocks on window or door were significant forebodings. They were either imagined by a vivid fantasy or clearly revealed to those endowed with the gift of clairvoyance. In Irish and Scottish lore the harbinger of death took the form of the mystical and mysterious banshee.

When Britain was preparing herself to withstand massive air-raid attacks during World War II, considerable thought was given to an efficient warning system. The final choice of signals worried some of those in authority. They were afraid that the wailing sound of the air-raid siren would remind the superstitious Irish of the wailing of a banshee.

The banshee has been a herald of death to Irish people for countless centuries. In the paradox of Irish lore, however, in spite of its foreboding mission, the banshee was not an old hag but the surviving spirit of a woman or a wraithlike woman of beautiful appearance. She was part of the rich folklore of their nation.

As a word from the Gaelic, the banshee spoke of a "woman of the fairies," linking the two words *bean* and *sidhe*.

Her special task was executed in various ways. She might appear "in person" to convey the message of doom by her presence. Or, invisible, she would make her voice heard in a mournful tune—like the melancholy moaning of the wind. Again, she might disclose the bad news to the family of the person about to die. Often she would sound her warning notes under the very window of the person whose death warrant had been signed.

Among the Irish and Scottish people, the banshee was not completely an "unattached" female figure. According to the belief of many, she had a special tie with certain families with whose fate she was deeply concerned. It was to them particularly (and according to some tradition, exclusively) that she appeared when death was about to strike one of their members.

Actually, only the truly noble, of ancient and pure descent, were said to "own" such a fairy. Once again, in the paradoxical way of the Irish, this very belief led to acrimonious social distinction even when it related to the coming of death. In spite of the ominous message she carried, to be visited by the banshee was regarded an honor.

Any bereavement without her prior warning was a sure indication of that family's lack of distinction. A banshee's association with the clan would last as long as the family lived and certainly never depended on the state of its wealth. Even if a member had fallen on bad times, the banshee would stay on as a loyal "friend" to the end.

An Irish elegy records with glee how once "upstart" merchants were misled at the Irish port of Dingle. At the time, this belonged to the noble Knights of Kerry. When one of their order was about to die, the banshee gave due warning in her mournful song which could be heard all over the seaport.

Not knowing the reason, the merchants mistakenly believed that the message was addressed to one of them and consequently were thrown into panic. But, sarcastically, a good friend comforted them, putting their minds at ease and them in their places. They had no need to worry, he explained, as certainly the voice of the banshee could never be meant for them.

Since the banshee was a close friend, it was suggested that her wailing was really meant not to distress but to help. Her song was like a tender call, almost an encouragement to the dying. It was telling him that his ancestral group was anxiously awaiting him on the other side to join it in happy reunion. The call equally was intended to comfort those left behind.

On the other hand, it was also believed that a banshee who for some reason had become hostile to a family announced the forthcoming death in a totally different tune. A shrill and howling sound then, it almost voiced joyous anticipation and delight about the loss and grief to come.

The banshee, whether heard in dread of doom or in comforting reconciliation, linked the occult with the aristocratic world. This fairy cherished true values and not cheap money.

## THE ZOMBIE

Zombie is used as a slang word today to describe a person lacking intelligence and vitality which makes him little more than a living corpse. He is without initiative and so lethargic that one would hardly know that he is alive. To speak of anyone in this way certainly is not kind. But for those acquainted with the origin of the term, a sinister meaning is added which makes the already offensive description truly vile.

Zombies belong to the world of voodoo. They are actually dead people who have been reanimated by the occult power of the voodoo sorcerer-priests. How they achieved the feat has been variously explained. Some claim that they did so by means of a powerful spell. Others have suggested that they attained their aim by the injection of a life-giving drug into the corpse.

Of course there was a reason behind such resuscitation. It might be quite innocuous. To gain cheap labor, for instance, an automated robot could be produced which would execute any duty at the sorcerer-priest's command and without payment. On the other hand, the sorcerer might employ his zombie for certain nefarious missions. He could be used as a remote-controlled human missile to harm or even kill a foe.

The choice of name further explained the miraculous reanimation. Zombie is a term derived from the Congolese dialect in which it described a fetish. It was applied to African nature spirits and deities, but specifically to the snake god still worshiped in voodoo ceremonies. A zombie thus is called by the name of the spirit, the new occupant that had taken possession of the dead body and thereby changed it into a living tool. However, still completely without mind, feeling or will of its own, the zombie is at the beck and call of its priestly master. It is the perfect slave.

It follows that no one would wish to see a beloved family member who had passed away end up as a zombie. Therefore, the bereaved take every precaution to avoid their deceased becoming "possessed."

It was generally believed that only a body still fully "intact" could be used as a zombie. Hence the surviving family anxiously watched their newly buried dead and almost joyously welcomed the moment when he began to decompose. Now the corpse becomes unfit to serve as a prospective zombie.

Additional measures taken gave Haitian burial customs a rather macabre note. So that the dead could not answer a sorcerer's call to rise, his mouth was sewn up. Others felt that only a second death would avoid any misappropriation of a body, so they inflicted death on the deceased for the second time. They did so in different ways, including the strangling of the corpse or injecting a deadly poison into it.

The birth of the zombie has also been explained in a most sinister way. It was asserted that all that was told and believed about him was fabrication, a criminal's convenient cover-up. Zombies did exist, but they never were what others claimed them to be—magically or miraculously resurrected dead bodies. They were living men, but so heavily drugged that with time they had lost all personality and all responsive awareness of reality. Mindlessly they obeyed the commands of their evil manipulator. They had become mere instruments in the pursuit of his schemes.

People, therefore, were not as terrified of coming across a zombie as they were of being made one themselves. The inclusion of a certain clause in the Haitian legal code was designed to combat and prevent such zombie-producing manipulation. The section made it a serious offense to bring about a comatose state in any person in order to exploit such a victim by employing him as an unpaid worker or, worse still, ultimately to dispose of the apparently dead by burying him alive.

Yet another dangerous possibility of turning into a zombie suggests itself. Voodoo worship is capable of producing in some participants a state of such ecstatic derangement that, no longer master of their senses, they lapse into a cataleptic condition. And being unable ever to return to normalcy they become and remain half-witted zombies.

## LILITH—THE FIRST EVE

Modern medicine and scientific knowledge have vastly reduced the incidents of death among women during the last months of pregnancy, the hazards of childbirth and infant mortality. And if such deaths do occur nowadays, their medical reason or the unfortunate circumstances that led to them are recognized. But centuries ago, such tragic events were frequent and a logical explanation was not always at hand. Therefore, people who experienced or even merely apprehended such tragedy "reasoned" that not natural causes but some adverse influence, some malevolent spirit, was to blame.

That is how all early cultures invented fearsome figures who threatened mothers-to-be and their progeny. The child-stealing witch was a common figure in ancient days. She would use any foul means and all her wits to attain her aim. But no witch gained greater notoriety than Lilith, the evil demon of the night.

It may surprise many biblical scholars to learn that Adam had two wives. To make the claim more convincing, the legend added significant personal data. Eve was not Adam's first spouse, it said; she was preceded by Lilith. And when Eve ousted her, she was determined to wreak vengeance by seeking the death of Eve's children and all those who, throughout the ages, would descend from them.

Little realized is that after having told of Eve's expulsion from Paradise (in consequence of her and Adam having eaten of the forbidden fruit), the Bible remains silent about her fate. Nothing more is recorded in Scripture about what else she did or what became of her. And Eve had no further influence over Adam or any man. But this was not the case with Lilith. She survived in the minds of people and became a power greatly feared throughout the world.

The early chapters of Genesis relating the story of Adam and Eve make no mention of Lilith at all. In fact, her name appears only once in the entire Bible. The passage in Isaiah (34:14) tells how—together with beasts of prey and spirits—she would take her place in laying waste the land on the day of doom. The identical verse has also been interpreted to mean that Lilith would dwell in the devastated palace of wicked Edom, Jacob's brother.

It is interesting to note that the later translations of the Hebrew Bible do not give Lilith's actual name, as it appears in the original. Various and misleading aliases are substituted.

The Vulgate, the Bible's first translation into Latin, called Lilith Lamia, surprisingly introducing a Greek mythical character into Hebrew tradition. According to Greek legend Lamia was a beautiful Lybian queen who became Zeus' mistress. Zeus's wife, Hera, consumed with jealousy, killed all but one of the children born out of the illicit union. Lamia was anxious to take her revenge. But unable to do so on Hera herself, she was determined to destroy anyone's child wherever opportunity offered itself. After all, Zeus as chief god would sadly feel the loss of any and every child.

The English translations of the relevant passage make Lilith an identifiable individual. The authorized (King James) version changes Lilith into "a screech owl." The later revised version makes her "a night-monster." Certainly, even in the minds of theologians, Lilith rang her changes "nominally."

## Lilith in Folklore

Though Lilith came to play an ever more important part in postbiblical Jewish tradition, she was not indigenously Hebrew at all. She was merely an "adopted" woman, originating—like so many other early Hebrew concepts and mythological figures—in ancient Mesopotamia, where she was autonomous. Sumerian demonology believed in the existence of a winged female who strangled children and also appeared in storms on the desert. Even her name is not Hebrew but Babylonian. Its frequent erroneous derivation from Hebrew is explained by the fact that Lilith, as the name of the nocturnal demon sounded very much like the Hebrew *laylah* for "night."

Lilith came to occupy a prominent place in the folklore of the Jews. It was imagined that, ever since her displacement by Eve, Lilith had become an inveterate adversary of all pregnant women and their progeny. To guard both, every precaution had to be taken magically.

Being the first woman, Lilith, like Adam, had been created from the dust of the earth and not, like Eve, out of one of Adam's ribs. Therefore, she had been his equal much more than Eve ever would be. She had come to Adam first in his sleep and made love to him in his dream. The children born subsequently had not been ordinary human beings like Cain and Abel, but rather were demons and spirits who thus came to enter and populate the world.

But one day Adam and Lilith had been engaged in a heated argument about their equal rights. Lilith objected to taking a subsidiary position especially in the methods of their lovemaking. Greatly agitated by their first quarrel, she had uttered God's ineffable name. By doing so she had acquired supernatural power which gave her the ability to become airborne. And so she flew away from her husband fast and far.

Adam was greatly distressed, as he could not find her. He asked God's help to locate his missing spouse and bring her back. The Almighty in turn entrusted three of his angels (Snwy, Snsnwy and Smnglf) with the search mission.

With their angelic power and vision they succeeded in tracing and catching up with the runaway wife just as she was flying over the Red Sea. She refused to listen to them, however, and to rejoin Adam. She informed the divinely appointed messengers that should Adam ever marry another woman she would do her utmost to kill any children resulting from such union. If she could not do so on the first generation, she would transfer her vengeance to the descendants of those children, which meant all future generations. After all, these would still be the offspring of "that woman"!

Such terrible threats, the angels realized, demanded immediate action. They could not afford to lose time by reporting back to God to ask for further instructions, thereby giving Lilith a chance to get on with her nefarious future mission.

Taking advantage of the predicament of her position just then above the sea, they tried to drown her. It was a clever move, since Lilith, realizing the peril in which she found herself, was prepared to reconsider and modify her resolution.

To save her own life, she agreed on a compromise which rather cunningly involved the three angels. She promised never to enter a home that displayed their names. That is why amulets used by anxious parents in the East to this day call on these angels' assistance in the protection of their home and children.

## Her Evil Pursuit

With the passing of years, Lilith's power—in the minds of people—continued to grow. At first she was said to be dangerous to boys only up to the eighth day after birth when, by the act of circumcision, they were initiated into the covenant Abraham made with God. Girls were unprotected up to twenty days. Then the danger period was prolonged to forty days in the case of boys and sixty days for girls.

If an infant smiled or laughed during sleep, this was not thought to show happiness or to be the result of a pleasant dream, but was regarded as a sign of danger: Lilith was playing with the sleeping child and hence it was essential to wake it up at once, thereby saving it from Lilith's clutches, for the monster was getting ready to smother the guileless infant.

In her evil pursuits, Lilith did not confine her nefarious activities to young mothers and their babes. From earliest days, she was also known as the great seductress of men. Of ravishing beauty and endowed with glorious long black hair worn loose, she was said to have only one flaw which could give away her identity: she had claws instead of feet. This feature was rather appropriate to her constant endeavors, like a bird of prey, to pounce on men and not let go of them.

Clay tablets excavated in Mesopotamia and stemming from ancient Sumer and the year 2000 B.C. portrayed her figure in exactly that shape. And her image hardly ever changed through the millennia. In medieval France she was still recognized as "the queen with the bird's feet."

It was also claimed that she copulated with men usually during their sleep. This was the cause of erotic, wet dreams. And from the ejaculated sperm were born countless demons.

No wonder that Lilith was called all kinds of names. These included, in the Zohar, for instance, "the harlot," "the dark one" and "the wicked one."

Lilith, it was further alleged, often appeared in disguise and, to attain her objective, impersonated both the highest and the lowest characters. To gain entrance to King Solomon, for example, she had transformed herself into one of the two prostitutes who had approached the king for judgment in the motherhood trial. On the other hand, the queen of Sheba had not actually been the royal personage she had pretended to be but yet another of Lilith's protean impersonations. Her wickedness had been so great that she was even regarded as a fitting counterpart to Satan, if not his wife.

## Countermeasures

Lilith had been a fearsome creature who has left her mark throughout history. She did so not only on literature, folklore and millennia-old artifacts, but also on the lives of young families throughout the world. Especially at that most vulnerable time of pregnancy and childbirth, gullible women and their families have let themselves be haunted with fear. They would take every precaution to keep this vindictive demon away from their kith and kin and out of their home. Thus they would "fortify" the four walls of the room in which mother or child slept with specially written amulets. They placed magic "scripts" above the head and under the pillow of a woman in labor. These became known by the Yiddish term *Tzetl*, derived from the German *Zettel*, meaning "a slip of paper," "a note" or "a written ticket."

Lilith became a renowned figure in the entire world of the occult and not just among Jews. Even Goethe recognized her significance. She appears in the *Walpurgisnacht* scene of his *Faust* together with the warlocks and witches.

The English painter and poet Dante Gabriel Rossetti (1828-1882) further developed the legend. In his poem "Eden Bower" he claimed that Lilith had actually been the serpent in Paradise. To wreak vengeance on Adam's "human wife," she had urged Eve to eat of the forbidden fruit and to conceive Cain—the brother and future murderer of Abel. In her jealousy, she wished no member of the human family ever to be happy. Thus she cursed the world by bringing about the first fratricide.

## THE ROBOT

Man's greatest ambitions have never changed. His constant aim and dream have been to find the elixir of life that would give him perpetual youth and the ability to change base metal into gold. Last but not least, he wanted to create for himself a "new man" who would always be at his service and command.

Homunculus was "the little man" whom, particularly during the sixteenth and seventeenth centuries, alchemists sought to form. (Homunculus uses the Latin *homo* for "man.") Their plan was to create the diminutive creature not by sexual union but by "mixing" semen and blood in their flask. It would have indeed been the first test-tube baby! The idea was especially popularized by the Swiss physician-rebel Paracelsus.

Of course, the ultimate object was the creation of a fully automated being, a human computer par excellence—a robot. This modern description of such a mechanical creature was coined by Karel Capek, Czech dramatist and journalist and one of the pioneers of twentieth-century science fiction. He introduced it in his play, *R.U.R. (Rossum's Universal Robots)*, in 1920. He derived the name from the old Czech word *robotnik* for "slave" and "forced laborer." In his drama a gang of such man-made monsters eventually rose against their own creators.

Capek himself had only updated an idea first written about by Mary Wollstonecraft Shelley, wife of the poet Percy Bysshe Shelley. In her novel, published in 1818 and entitled *Frankenstein, or the Modern Prometheus*, she described the work of a young Swiss student who dabbled in the supernatural. While attending the university, Frankenstein had succeeded in constructing an artificial human from material he obtained from tombs and dissecting rooms, endowing it with life by means of galvanism. However, it proved a veritable monster. When Frankenstein refused to make a mate for it, the creature, frantic with its unsatisfied cravings, committed the most atrocious crimes. It murdered the bride of Frankenstein and his dearest friend.

Unfortunately, for reasons unknown, Mary Shelley had not given the monster a name. People, not very conversant with her book, soon transferred the name of the student, Frankenstein, to the unnamed monster, who, ever since has been wrongly referred to as Frankenstein. Frankenstein thus became a real misnomer for any powerful agent causing havoc, suffering and destruction.

## The Golem—the Most Famous Robot

Homunculus, Frankenstein and robot, all can be traced back to the golem—the most famous of all automata designed by man. Whether it ever really existed has been the subject of controversy. There were those who were convinced that it had been merely the product of a fertile imagination. However, others fervently believed that the golem had been a living creature—the first computerized pseudo-human being.

The name of the golem is a Hebrew word which occurs in the Bible only once—in the 139th Psalm. There God is depicted as the omnipotent and omniscient being who knew man already in the form of a "golem" (verse 16). Translators and interpreters of the Bible wondered what the word in this context meant. The usual explanation given suggests that God's knowledge of man preceded his birth. He knew every individual in his unfinished state, as "unformed substance," in short, as an embryo.

In postbiblical literature, then, the golem was used as a term to describe anything that was unfinished and incomplete, in the process of being made. Thus, a needle still without its eye was called a golem. So was an unmarried woman. Without a mate her life was still unfulfilled and she was "incomplete." Even Adam, prior to being endowed with a soul, had also been a golem.

But this was not the end in the evolution of the golem as a significant term and phenomenon. As the years passed, it took on an altogether new meaning. No longer used to designate something unfinished and imperfect, golem became the description of an artificially created human figure. By a magic ritual, dead matter was infused with the force of life and the ability to mechanically obey any orders given.

It was told how initiates in the occult had molded a human figure out of virgin soil. While circling it "as in a dream," they had uttered magical formulas consisting of a powerful combination of Hebrew letters and God's hidden name. And after having done so numerous times, the figure had suddenly come to life and risen as a golem.

Anticipating later practices of black magic, it was said that those who made the golem could cause it to disintegrate again. They would do so by walking around it in a counterclockwise direction and, reversing the magic spell, recite it backward.

Yet another method alleged to have been used to animate the figure was to inscribe its forehead with the Hebrew word for "truth"—*emet*. From Talmudic times, this had been regarded as "the seal of God," and Jewish mystics appropriated it for their working of magic in secret rites.

If for any reason it was thought advisable, or became essential again to take the life out of this type of golem, all that had to be done was to remove the first letter from *emet*. By this simple elimination of the one letter, the Hebrew word for "truth"—*emet*—was changed into the Hebrew word for "death"—*met*. Simultaneously this magically changed the golem into a formless, lifeless clod of clay.

There was yet another method believed to achieve such transformation of a lifeless doll into an animate being. A piece of parchment or paper was inscribed with the magical formula and then slipped either under the tongue or into the head of the figure. And, obviously, its removal would instantly switch off its life-force and immobilize the golem.

However, there was always the danger that, in case of emergency, it would not be easy to get hold of the golem. It was imagined that he could assume superhuman strength and resist any attempt to remove his source of energy.

### The Magic Code

A great part of *The Book of Creation*, one of the earliest and main works of Jewish Kabbalah, is devoted to the magic power of letters. It taught that these were not elements of common speech and writing alone. If properly used and manipulated they could have a supernatural effect and achieve miraculous feats. Just as nowadays those who know the right combination of numbers can open the door of a safe, so those in possession of the right combination of letters could unlock the doors of the occult and bring to life inanimate matter.

Most effective of all was the knowledge and application of God's secretly guarded names, of which there were many. The Kabbalist, initiated into their secret, would write down the magic code. And the moment he had placed it inside the manlike but soulless figure, it would quicken to become his obedient servant. Endowed with superhuman strength but bereft of speech and individual reasoning, the golem could be sent on any mission if duly "programmed."

The golem became a favorite theme of legend, particularly among German Jews, in the fifteenth century to be more popularized far and wide in the centuries that followed. All the cases reported, whether apocryphal or real, can be divided into three categories.

First of all, there was the golem who was said to have been created as man's mechanical tool and laborsaving device. Meticulously he executed all the tasks allotted to him. He worked hard for six days every week but on the seventh, like any human, he was given his Sabbath rest. With the magic formula then removed, his source of energy was turned off.

The second type of golem was designed with the opposite purpose in mind. When all other men hallowed the Sabbath by abstaining from work, he was to carry out essential duties. He was especially useful on cold winter nights when he lit the fires and lamps and heated the ovens in the Jewish homes to illumine and heat them and warm up the food.

But no times seemed more in need of a golem than those of insecurity, when entire communities were threatened by extermination. The third kind of golem then served as a secret gatherer of information and an automated defense weapon. He informed his owners of lurking dangers and with his enormous strength struck down the foe.

And yet, this wonderful and fantastic magic anticipation of the modern robot and computerized, remote-controlled "missile" had its inbuilt danger. If unrestrained or out of control, it could wreak havoc of fearful dimensions. And this is exactly what is supposed to have happened in almost every case when by magical power occultists had created such golem.

### The Golem of Prague

Most famous of all is the golem of Prague. Though there is no historical evidence whatsoever, tradition attributes its creation to Judah Loew, the city's chief rabbi, no doubt because of his well-known preoccupation with the occult. A sixteenth-century world-renowned scholar, Rabbi Judah was a friend of the astronomer Tycho Brahe. In 1592 he had an audience with the Holy Roman Emperor

Rudolf II. No records exist as to the purpose of their meeting or the subject of their conversation. However, it is generally assumed that their common interest in alchemy brought them together.

It is told that the golem of Prague, like others of its kind elsewhere, conscientiously executed the community's menial duties under the rabbi's directions. But his chief purpose was to act as its guardian, as once again the Jews' very lives were in danger.

On the eve of every Sabbath, so the legend goes, Rabbi Loew removed the magic formula. But then it happened that on one Friday he forgot to do so. And soon the golem, totally uncontrolled, was roaming the streets.

Desperately, the rabbi tried to find him before he could do any damage or desecrate the Sabbath which was about to commence. Eventually he caught up with him at the entrance to the synagogue. The moment the rabbi had taken away the potent script, the golem collapsed and disintegrated.

Visitors to Prague's ancient synagogue are shown odd debris stored in its attic, and the guide explains that this was all that was left of the once famous golem.

Fact or fiction, the golem became so well known that it served as a theme for modern orchestrations, ballads, operas and films.

Though most of the golem legends stem from the sixteenth and seventeenth centuries, their similarity to modern robots make them very much up to date. This applies both to their artificially produced enormous potential power and also to their inbuilt danger to destroy the very people and society who in their wisdom and genius gave birth to them.

# CHAPTER SIX

# The Devil

## POWERS OF EVIL

Man has always been aware and afraid of evil forces. No matter where and when he lived, he felt threatened and experienced suffering and misfortune. It did not take him long to ask about their origin. Somehow, he felt, there had to be a powerful source of all the evil that befell him and his people. Thus, all over the world, man came to personify evil. The way he did so differed according to cultures and periods.

Evil was identified as an independent force that had existed from the very beginning and was a rival to good and to God. It was explained as a being that, once perfect itself, had become depraved.

Evil was regarded as either something apart from man or innate in him. There were some who saw in evil a mere illusion, the deprivation of good. To others, however, life seemed to prove that only evil was real and that all good was spurious and imaginary. Hence they deified evil as the supreme power.

All of history was looked upon as a perpetual struggle against the forces of evil. Man's choice was to ally himself either with ''the light'' or ''the darkness.'' And the way in which Judeo-Christian civilization evolved its concept of evil and its personification is linked with preceding Egyptian, Babylonian and Persian myths. Taking over some of their features, it strongly reacted to others. The final result was the figure of Satan, which has its own story to tell.

## HOW SATAN CAME INTO THE WORLD

Satan is a Hebrew word which, like hallelujah and jubilee, has been adopted universally. But through the years ''Satan'' has experienced a metamorphosis second to none.

To begin with, Satan was not a devil at all nor a fallen angel. He was a contrary sort, someone who objected, obstructed or, at worst, acted as a kind of prosecuting counsel and was His Divine Majesty's most loyal opposition.

When personified, Satan was merely a human "son of God" (Job 1:6), and even when he was "elevated" to a divine task, he still belonged—and faithfully so—to God's "staff." Throughout the Hebrew Bible he never appears as God's rival or antagonist.

Various examples can be quoted of the early use of the word Satan as a verb describing different types of obstructive actions.

When the Philistine princes objected to David's offer to join them as allies in their fight against the rest of the Israelites, it was because the princes were afraid that, once the battle had started, David and his followers might turn "adversary" (*Satan*) and attack their forces from the rear (1 Sam. 29:4).

Only once does "Satan" appear in the Pentateuch in a supernatural sense. It is in connection with God's attempt by means of an angel to stop Balaam, the pagan priest, from his mission to curse the Israelites. Even then the purpose of "obstruction" was to avoid and not to create evil, to act as a servant and not as an adversary of God (Num. 22:22, 23).

Only when, during the Babylonian exile, Judaism had come into contact with Persian dualism, did Satan undergo a personality change. At the time, Zoroastrianism had become a powerful force in the East, teaching that not one God but two independent forces ruled this world: the powers of light *and* of darkness, of good *and* of evil.

The great unknown prophet of the Jews at that time (usually referred to as Deutero-Isaiah) raised his voice against such personification of evil. God, he proclaimed, had created both light and darkness. He alone was the Lord of both good and evil.

Nevertheless, the philosophy coming from the East did not fail to exert an influence on the Hebrew mind, and Satan was now seen by Jews as a power in his own right. Though still subordinate to God, his intentions were malevolent and to harm man was his delight.

The prologue to the book of Job (which inspired Goethe in writing the prologue to *Faust*) tells how Satan wandered all over the world to locate sin and sinners, to make them pay for their evil ways. And where God saw only good, as was in the case of Job, Satan cynically suggested that the man's "pious" attitude was mere opportunism. Satan maintained that Job, in his loss and pain, did not defy and deny God only because of self-interest, and his wish to have and keep God's favor.

At this stage, Satan had stepped on the slippery downward path. And it did not take long for him to deteriorate further in man's imagination. He no longer occupied his time with seeking out evil but produced it himself. And it was at this dramatic moment in Satan's "career" that Judaism drew the line beyond which it did not permit him officially to advance.

In spite of it, outside the synagogue, Satan continued to gain ground and to leave his conspicuous traces in Jewish belief. He came to personify all that was evil and dark.

This view is reflected in parts of the apocryphal books which, though excluded from the canon of Jewish Scriptures, were nevertheless preserved in some versions of the Christian Bible. But it was also expressed—though only occasionally so—in rabbinical tradition contained in the Midrash, the Talmud, mystical writings and in Hebrew commentaries.

Satan was thus identified with the serpent in Paradise. It was said that he had made God test Abraham's loyalty by asking him to sacrifice Isaac, his beloved son. Likewise, when during Moses' absence on Mount Sinai, the Israelites had gone astray and worshiped the golden calf, they had done so at Satan's instigation.

Belief in Satan even left its mark in Jewish liturgy. When on the New Year the ram's horn is sounded, this was done to frighten Satan so that he would forget to accuse the sinners before the divine judgment seat. The nightly prayer for peaceful rest includes a petition which asks God to "remove from us the enemy, sickness . . . and Satan."

It was in the young Christian faith that Satan found a new role and a prominent place. In the New Testament his power and influence were acknowledged. He became the anti-Christ and was seen as the embodiment of the cause of all evil. Satan was described as "the prince of darkness," "that old serpent" which deceived the whole world (Rev. 12:9). It was he who tempted Jesus in the wilderness (Matt. 4:1-11).

Satan was seen as a "fallen angel," and his demotion was due to his pride and jealousy. When God created man in his divine likeness, one of the angels had felt deeply grieved and envious. How could the Almighty give man such dignity, when, after all, man was created only out of the dust of the earth. Leading a rebellion against God, he and those who followed him had been thrust out of heaven down into hell. There, Satan, the fallen angel, had dwelt with his retinue ever since.

Refused residence in the Jewish faith, Satan had found a home in Christian belief. There he was a force to be reckoned with, for in its conquest of the Western world, Christianity spread its belief in Satan. No wonder he became a powerful influence in the minds, lives, folklore and even the judicial system of so-called Christian nations.

Millions of people came to believe in the existence of Satan during the last two millennia. And tragically, the very Jews from whom Christianity had first adopted the belief in Satan became its victims. The Gospels already had referred to them when they had refused to accept the divinity of Christ as "the synagogue of Satan." The medieval Church took up this vilification and used it to classify Jews as "the spawn of Satan." It did so not just metaphorically but to justify the denial of rights to the Jewish people, their brutal persecution and murder. It is one of the sad "religious" roots of anti-Semitism.

## SATAN'S ALIAS—THE DEVIL

As anyone whose intentions are evil, Satan adopted many guises and aliases. If he could not force entry with one name, he did so with another. Of all his names, that of the devil became the best known, although its beginnings are uncertain and undetermined.

Most likely is the blasphemous claim that the devil shares his beginning with the Latin word *deus*, for God. Both words come from the Sanskrit *deva* which means the "shining one."

Gypsies in their Indo-European rooted Romany tongue actually call their deity *duvel*.

Later on, knowledge of Greek discovered in the devil the "slanderer" (*diabolos*) who in his "diabolic" way "threw" (*ballein*—which also gave us "ballistics") "across" (*dia*) mischievous gossip.

When, in the third century B.C., Jews translated their Bible into Greek, the Septuagint, they rendered "Satan" as *diabolos*. Adopted generally, with slight alterations, diabolos then changed his appearance to become the devil.

## LUCIFER

Lucifer is the Latin for "light-bearer"—*lux ferre*—and thus as its root implies, a most deceptive sort of devil. In fact, it is a misappropriation of a beautiful ancient description of the morning star, sneaking into the world of religion and the occult because the Fathers of the Church took a powerful metaphor too literally.

To call the most evil force by such a beautiful name, however, had yet another, self-protecting reason. Lucifer was used for Satan as a euphemism with the purpose not to offend or—by uttering his real name—to summon this most diabolic of creatures.

The name Lucifer recalled the famous passage of the Hebrew prophet Isaiah, originally applied to the Babylonian king who boasted of his invincibility. In powerful dramatic language, Isaiah compared the king to a power-drunk potentate who bragged he would ascend to heaven to make himself equal to God; instead, the potentate was plunged into the uttermost recesses of the pit where he was eaten by worms. In poetical grandeur, the prophet likened the king's apparent invincible glory to that of Venus, the morning star. Shining brightly, it could do so only for a brief period, then would quickly disappear before the rising sun. "Take up this proverb against the King of Babylon, and say . . . How art thou fallen from Heaven, O Lucifer, son of the morning" (Isa. 14:12).

The prophet's imagery might have been inspired as well by a meteor streaking from the sky to vanish from sight.

Going back even further, it can be assumed that Isaiah, if not actually aware of, was influenced by an ancient Babylonian astral myth which, in a different form, later reappeared in Greek legend. This told of the expulsion of the morning star from its heavenly sphere in punishment for its insolence and overbearing pride. At the time, Babylonians saw in the stars not inanimate spatial bodies but living celestial beings. In spite of their heavenly status, they were very much like men, possessed by lust, envy, ambitions and aspirations for power.

By its brilliancy most of all, the morning star asserted that it was entitled and destined to take precedence over all others and to be given the loftiest seat among the star gods. But the supreme power ruling the Babylonian pantheon had resented its arrogant demand and hurled the star down from heaven into the dark abyss.

The Greeks, on the other hand, had Phaëthon. He was one of the sons of Helios, the sun god. For a long time, however, he had been kept ignorant of this fact. When learning who his father was, Phaëthon had approached him at once, to ask some special favor which he felt was now due to him. Helios could not deny his paternity and granted his son's request. He did so rather generously by leaving the choice of gift to Phaëthon himself.

Phaëthon had asked permission to guide his father's chariot across the skies for just one day. As promised in advance, his wish was granted. However, he proved himself far too inexperienced and weak to master the fiery horses which pulled the sun god's chariot. Boisterously enjoying their newly gained freedom under so unskilled a driver, the horses, now completely out of control, threatened to set the world and Olympus on fire. To avoid such catastrophe, Zeus immediately took steps and with a thunderbolt killed Phaëthon who fell into the Eridanus River in a fiery blaze.

When the Hebrew text of the Bible was translated into Latin (the Vulgate), Isaiah's "morning star" was rendered "Lucifer, son of the morning." And the authorized (King James) version adopted this translation. A passage in the Gospels then misled St. Jerome to change the original epithet which described the pride and vain glory of the Babylonian king into a synonym for the devil.

The Gospel of St. Luke (10:18) tells of seventy men who had gone out into the world to preach Jesus' message of the kingdom of God. On their return to the master, they had informed him with great joy they were able to subdue not only humans but demons with his name.

In his reply, Jesus is said to have related that he had watched Satan falling out of the sky "like lightning." And it was this juxtaposition of Satan and lightning that prompted St. Jerome and the Fathers of the Church to identify this lightning from heaven with Satan, the archrebel.

The view that Satan had "come down" from his celestial abode in punishment for his diabolical pride predestined Lucifer for the new application.

Lucifer thus came to stay and to haunt man, and to lead him into many types of confusion. The very vanity said to have been the cause of his downfall became so generally accepted that an English proverb (first documented in *Political Poems* published in 1394) could speak of men "as proud as Lucifer."

It is a matter of conjecture how it came that Lucifer's name experienced an odd kind of revival in modern times. He who was seen as the power of darkness was then used actually to light it up! Was it a temporary decline of his power in the minds of men, rebellion against the archrebel or a symbol of the new "enlightenment" that prompted in 1831 the manufacturer of the newly invented phosphorous friction light to market his novel match as Lucifer? Thus, he took from the devil a name the devil himself had stolen from the morning star.

Etymologists have tried in the case of the phosphorous Lucifer match to cut out the devil altogether. As a true light-bringer, the match, they say, received its name straight from the original morning star and not from the evil Lucifer.

## BEELZEBUB

Confusion reigns wherever the devil appears. This applies to Beelzebub, yet another of his disguises. At first glance, the meaning of his name seems clear to any student of Hebrew. As *Baal Zebub*, he is "the lord of flies." He was first mentioned in 2 Kings 1:3 as a god whom the Philistines worshiped in Ekron, the most northerly of their five principal cities.

King Ahaziah had suffered grave injuries from a fall. Anxious to know his fate, he sent messengers to the shrine of Baal Zebub to inquire whether he would recover from the accident. Elijah reprimanded him for doing so, for it was blasphemous for a Hebrew to acknowledge pagan wisdom.

To have a special deity ascribed to flies might not be farfetched, but in this case, it is likely the "fly" is mere fiction and has been put in its divine place ironically. The Israelites, wanting to make fun of the pagan god and to stress his insignificance, compared him with the dirty insect, which had by then been recognized as the cause of fatal epidemics.

Scholars have wondered what the real and original name of the god was. Using newly discovered inscriptions and a Greek translation of the Bible, they have translated it as Baal Zebul. And correspondingly, another ancient tradition shows that the Hebrews referred to the pagan deity of that name as Baal Zebel, the god of filth and dung.

The true meaning of zebul is still uncertain. According to some it spoke of the heavenly "mansion." This was reason enough for the Israelites to feel greatly affronted, because to them, only their God alone was worthy to occupy that exalted house.

No matter what its literal meaning, Beelzebub became an obscenity for the Jew.

What really happened was that by the change of name the Hebrews had tried to emphasize that like a fly the pagan lord was insignificant compared with the majesty of the true God who was the Lord of all. And the Hebrew Bible's slanted view was then accepted by Jesus and, fully developed, became in the Gospels a completely new concept. They now identified the "fly god" with the evil force. They made him the "prince of devils," if not Satan himself (Mark 3:23). At the time, both Jews and Christians shared the view that all pagan gods were really demons. And ever since, Beelzebub (or Beelzebul) has appeared as Satan himself or, at least, as in Milton's *Paradise Lost* (I, 79) nearest to him in crime and rank.

## MEPHISTOPHELES

Mephistopheles is a comparative newcomer in the world of the diabolical. We know all about the place and date of his birth but are still mystified by the meaning of his synthetic name.

He first appeared in a German book dealing with Dr. Faustus in 1587, though with a slightly different spelling, as Mephostophiles. He was an evil spirit to whom Faust had sold his soul in exchange for the enjoyment of this world. He was then a vicious itinerant magician who, by his devilish art, created mischief wherever he went.

Marlowe (in 1588) and Goethe (in 1808) used the legend in their great dramas. When Goethe in his prologue fo *Faust* incorporated the famous first chapter of Job, in which Satan was given divine permission to test Job's loyalty, he gave Satan the name Mephistopheles.

Mephistopheles' name probably defines his very character as the prince of darkness. Joining the Greek words for "friend" (*philos*) and "light" (*phos*) with the Greek negative (*me*), Mephistopheles proclaimed himself as the one "not loving light."

It was through Goethe's renown and the success of his *Faust* that Mephistopheles, the medieval legendary figure, gained world fame in such large measure that for many years Mephistopheles shared the status, if not actually took the place, of Satan.

## THE DEVIL'S NICKNAMES

### Old Nick

There were probably a variety of reasons for the nicknames bestowed on the devil. They extend the gamut from the pretense of real intimacy to the expression of outright contempt. Accordingly, their purpose differs greatly as well.

The name may have been coined and used to hurt or show sham affection, to infuriate or to cajole, to fool or to buy safety. To many, the devil was so familiar a figure that he was called by all kinds of names. Most of them convey fear and awe. But there are exceptions. These apply particularly to the rather chummy sounding Old Nick which was first documented in seventeenth-century literature. But the genealogy of Old Nick is not so straight and simple and various theories exist as to its origin.

First is the suggestion that the choice of the nickname tried to stress one's own lack of fear of the devil. It was used to refer to him almost in a jocular vein and to make people (and not least the devil himself) imagine that one was on most intimate terms with the Evil One.

Nick, just like Tom, Dick and Harry, was a very common and popular personal name and possibly therefore chosen almost at random. Also, if one showed apparent friendliness toward the devil, he might be fooled and flattered. This would gain one his goodwill—if such ever exists—or at least keep him from doing harm.

Nowadays everyone—no matter the age—likes to be regarded as young and to be so called gives special happiness. But once upon a time it was the opposite. Age spelled maturity and to refer to anyone as "old" and to preface his name so expressed fond regard and respect. Thus to speak of Old Nick made doubly sure that the devil might return the compliment and treat one as a real pal.

Fascinating in itself is the spuriousness of a widely held opinion that Old Nick really "honors" the memory of Niccolò Machiavelli, the famous Italian author, statesman and political philosopher. It all goes back to *The Prince*, his major work. Written in 1513, it became the blueprint of all future ruthless dictatorships.

With the purpose to create and maintain a united Italian nation, the book sanctioned, in fact recommended, that for a ruler to stay in power he had to apply the most callous and unscrupulous policies. Indeed, because of his "devilish" and cynical political philosophy, "Machiavellian" entered the vocabulary of every tongue as a description of cynical political scheming that paid no attention or respect to ethical and moral principles.

Exactly 150 years later (in 1663) the satirical English poet Samuel Butler wrote a mock heroic poem he entitled "Hudibras." In this he not only recalled Machiavelli but jokingly suggested that his cynical philosophy had given rise—by Anglicizing and shortening the Italian Christian name Niccolò—to the devil's name of Old Nick.

> Nick Machiavel had ne'er a trick
> (Though he gave name to our Old Nick).

With the passing of time however, people no longer realized that Butler's "etymological" claim had been made all in fun. They started to take it seriously. Thus in numerous works Butler's "theory" was quoted as a fact. And, ever since, Old Nick stayed closely linked with Niccolò Machiavelli.

A theory that has very little support traces Old Nick to a Scandinavian source. He had come from northern water spirits, which were known as *nickers*, a word also contained in the German *Nixes* and *Nickel*. It would be a rather odd choice to remind the devil, so much at home in hot regions of burning fire, of the very element that extinguishes flames. The Anglo-Saxon root *naec* for "to kill" has been quoted, too, as the real father of Old Nick which would make him a murderer from the outset.

Even more farfetched—both logically and chronologically—is the claim that links Old Nick with jovial Santa Claus. This, of course, was a mere popularization of his real name St. Nicholas, fourth-century archbishop of Myra in Asia Minor. Through numerous legends he became the patron saint of countries, cities and occupations. Pawnbrokers, merchants, sailors and bakers petitioned him, but especially children, who at Christmastime anxiously waited for his gifts.

But little known and possibly purposely ignored is the fact that even thieves adopted Old Nick as their saint and looked for his help. Their appropriation goes back to an early association which actually should have made thieves shun Santa Claus. It was told that once after a successful plunder a gang of thieves were forced by St. Nicholas to restore the stolen goods to their rightful owner and to become honest men.

Eventually the real purpose and circumstances of the ancient contact was forgotten and thieves remembered only that "once upon a time" there had been some very effective relationship between them and Nicholas. Surely they could continue to count on his help. And this erroneously arrived at belief made them adopt the saint as their patron, stealing his good name as it were, and misleading the world into seeing in Old Nick the devil.

On the other hand, people might have only been making use of Nicholas' shortened name while they really were not thinking of the saint at all. They merely wanted to create the impression that they were speaking of him when, in reality, they were discussing the devil. It was all a subtle safety measure against the Evil One, they being certain that Old Nick would not mind their taking advantage of his good name in a life-saving emergency or as an insurance against the devil's machinations.

### Old Harry

Closely related to Old Nick is Old Harry, yet another of the devil's nicknames. It, too, was used to create the impression of familiarity and in order either to coax the devil to be pleasant or make light of him and his power. After all, anyone you could call by his first name, and so common a name at that, would do you no harm.

Others, however, rather suspicious and frightened of such a nonchalant attitude and overawed by the devil's wickedness, derived the innocuous Harry from camouflaged horror. Harry, they said, really referred to the devil's *harry*ing work which constantly harassed and worried men.

Touching more neutral ground, a third explanation is that by its sound the name Harry recalls the devil's hairy aspect—his body was overgrown with hair.

Of course, identifying the devil by his hairy nature had its dangerous implications during witch hunts. Innocent men who prided themselves on their excessively hairy growth came under suspicion. Just as nowadays the wrong notion prevails that extra hair indicates manliness and virility, so in former days it was misinterpreted to reveal a person's true devilish nature.

## LOOKING AT THE DEVIL

### Horns and Tails

Why did horns, a tail and cloven hooves become characteristic features of the devil's physique? Surprisingly, they belonged to one of the most ancient descriptions of a demon. A mythological text, stemming from the ancient Syrian city of Ugarit, tells how El, the chief god, was once terrified almost to death by the appearance of a demon with "two horns and a tail."

A prehistoric cave drawing discovered in France shows the figure of a man represented as a stag with antlers of enormous size! Horned gods were part of the mythology of the dream-distant past. And no doubt the horned figure, so universal and ancient, was a fertility symbol. A Greek god sprouting horns (as did stags, bulls and goats) became the prototype of the later conception of the Christian devil.

All "panic" started with this god—and so did the devil's horns and his tail. They are the gift of Pan.

## PAN, THE GOAT GOD

The Greeks worshiped Pan as their god of flocks, herds, pastures and fields. As he himself was very amorous, he was in charge of reproduction, and his chief business was to make the flocks fertile. As man depended on his flocks for food and clothing, he realized the world could not exist without Pan.

Pan's shape was mainly that of a goat—and for obvious reasons. A goat could traverse all the territory in Pan's domain. He could dart around fields and through herds of cattle. Even more so, the goat was renowned for its lustful nature and fecundity.

Man, always deeply concerned with fertility—that of his field, his cattle and himself—acknowledged the supremacy of the goat god and his reliance on its goodwill. Thus he paid the god the homage he so much deserved, hoping that in return Pan would reward him with extra powers of reproduction.

In its fervor and determination to get rid of the "old god," so deeply rooted in nature, the Church used the goat god's features as part of the image by which the devil was portrayed.

He now grew the goat's horns, and its tail and its cloven hooves. And since Christianity abhorred the physical as unworthy of man, it depicted the devil as lascivious a creature as the goat.

The goat had other characteristics that made him the ideal embodiment of the devil. Its black hair was the color of sin. No doubt it was this consideration that made the Israelites of the Bible select a black animal for a scapegoat to carry away the sins of the people.

Its two horns symbolized the fundamental philosophy of devil worship. This denied God's claim for supremacy as the omnipotent power in the world. It reasserted the Gnostic teaching that just as there were two horns of identical size and strength, so were the forces of evil equal to the forces of God. Moreover, often when God failed, the devil would prove successful.

## Panic

There was another side to Pan recalled to the present day.

Pan loved to have his special fun and do so at the expense of others, mostly by scaring people. He might suddenly dart out of a thicket and by his unexpected appearance and hideous features would frighten passersby. Pan's dominion expanded far and wide, embracing the whole of nature. (*Pan* is the Greek for "all," which accounts for the term pantheism to describe the belief in the identity of God and *all* nature.) When people were alone in a dark forest and heard eerie sounds, they were unnerved. They immediately assumed that the weird noises came from Pan, who also delighted in rattling men by emitting a scream. The alarm it created was called "panic," after the god.

## A TELLING GESTURE

An interesting phenomenon of language is how in its description of certain institutions or individuals, it chooses as their name one of their conspicuous characteristics. Thus in its vocabulary "a part" stands for "the whole." That is how, for instance, "the crown" is used for the king and "the stage" for the theater. This was followed when the devil's horns, as his outstanding feature, became symbolic of him.

When, during the Middle Ages, the persecution and murder of Jews was "justified" by seeing in them the devil, they were said actually to grow horns. And that Jews covered their heads, a practice then conscientiously followed at all times and not just during prayer at synagogue, was thus explained as a clever ruse to hide the very feature that would give them away.

On the other hand, the horned hand became a recognized sign of the occultist. He could easily make it by turning down the middle fingers and the thumb and keeping raised both the index and little fingers. Held up against the light, the gesture was thought to deprive the devil of his power.

## HOW HORNS BECAME THE SYMBOL OF POWER

From the dawn of history, horns were symbolic of power. Primitive man had learned to respect and fear the horns used by beasts in attack and defense. They expressed the brute force that has ruled the world for so long.

Horns and antlers have always served animals to impress others of their own kind. Making them look so majestic, they displayed their superiority. Hence, horns assumed also the quality of a status symbol.

That is why in the various parts of the world, in Minoan, Mycenaean, Mesopotamian and Egyptian cultures man came to worship horned animal gods—the bison, the ram and the bull. Their awe-inspiring majesty made them fearsome creatures which seemed possessed by supernatural power.

And when the horns detached themselves from the original animal (by shedding) they became the property of the gods that replaced them—both in myth and statuary. A divine symbol now, priests and medicine men adopted the horns for their own headdresses.

Horns were also attached to the corners of altars. Their role then was not of ornamentation but of potent magic. Possibly, this is a vestige of former totemistic rites in which man worshiped the beast as his ancestor.

Until the destruction of the Temple in Jerusalem in A.D. 70, the hornlike projections of its altar were regarded so sacred that their power overruled that of the law. From the days of the Israelites, a fugitive criminal was safe from apprehension the very moment he grasped the altar horns. The horns were also sprinkled with sacrificial blood at rites or priestly initiations or sin offerings of animals.

It did not take long for secular powers to adopt the horns from the ecclesiastics. To frighten their foe and to show their own invincible power, rulers and warriors crowned their helmets with them.

This explains why Alexander the Great was called "the two-horned," and may also account for Michelangelo's *Horned Moses* which has puzzled so many people. Generally, the odd feature has been explained as the result of a mistranslation of the Hebrew Bible into the Latin Vulgate which the great sculptor used as his source. However, it is very likely that Michelangelo purposely used the horns to highlight Moses' majestic spiritual power.

## MORE NICKNAMES

It was this fusion of belief in the power of horned animals and the legends of Pan and his lust that caused the devil to be called Horny or Auld Horn. His love of copulation explains why sexually aroused people are referred to in slang as "horny."

The way the devil grew his horns presents a vivid example of how powerful propaganda can be. In its campaign of vilification of the old god and his pagan cult, the Church succeeded in turning a former highly respected badge of honor and majesty into a symbol of disrepute and shame.

And then the wheel turned full circle. When Satanism flourished, those who worshiped the devil instead of the Judeo-Christian God adopted the very features that had previously been ascribed to him by those who maliciously wished to discredit him. The hymns they sang in the devil's praise were bawdy ballads and lewd songs. The practice of sexual license became a significant part of the services held in his honor. The priest in charge took over the role of the devil and with it his sexual function.

Often noted was the fact that the priest's penis was ice cold, of tremendous size and hurt the female partner. Probably no man impersonating the devil in this "service" could perform the numerous copulations allegedly taking place in one session. It was therefore assumed that in reality he used an artificial penis. This would explain its size and the sensations of coldness and pain.

## POSSESSED BY THE DEVIL

There have always been people who seemed to act oddly. They mystified others who looked upon them with awe, wonder and consternation. What made a person so strange and so different?, they anxiously asked.

The "odd man out" might be a figure of supernatural power. He was god-possessed and hence particularly venerable. Therefore, he was treated with respect and reverence, if not actually worshiped.

Going to the other extreme, people imagined that a demonic force, an evil spirit had entered the person. Unable or unwilling to leave him, it had created his "character change" and all the weird and often frightening phenomena accompanying it.

Man learned early to differentiate between his physical body and indwelling spirit. Dreams especially, most vivid among primitive races, convinced him of the reality of the duality of his being. Though his body certainly was confined to the here and now, his spirit could move about both horizontally, in space, and vertically, in time. How else could he explain that during his sleep he met far-off friends, talked to people long dead or visited places so distant that in the ordinary way it would take him many days to get there?

More ominously, strange, evil spirits could enter the body and, taking possession of it, bring about a personality change.

The Hebrew Bible thus explains King Saul's melancholia. It was caused, it says, because an "evil spirit" had entered the king which, luckily, young David was able to drive out by his magic playing of the harp (1 Sam. 16:14-23).

A man suffering from hysteria, schizophrenia or epileptic fits was thought to be possessed by an evil spirit. Lacking the medical knowledge of later days, it was the only way people could account for the bizarre gestures, strange speech, frothing at the mouth and distorted features or convulsions. It was not physical or mental sickness, according to their minds, but the demons possessing the unfortunate victim.

Such "possession," however, seemed to interfere with, if not to threaten, the very life of the group. It was felt that something had to be done to cure the victim so afflicted, not for his own sake alone but for the sake of all others who were exposed to his destructive influence.

The assumption that terrible trouble could be caused by the evil spirit that had entered the body led to the logical conclusion that only its expulsion would restore the person to his former natural self and the group to its equilibrium.

The problem was who could achieve this goal and by what measures? From earliest days, the "wise men," the wizards and magicians, were regarded as qualified and spiritually powerful enough to undertake this dangerous mission. The way they went about it varied among different cultures and became known as demon expulsion or "exorcism."

## EXORCISM

The Greek term exorcism refers to one of its chief features, the use of a sacred "oath"—*orkos* in Greek. The exorcist thus "swore" the evil spirit "out" (*ex*) of a man. He did so by the use of magic incantations and the ineffable miracle-working name of the godhead. Earliest texts of these incantations were recovered on clay vessels in the Middle East and stem from Babylonian times.

In his *Antiquities of the Jews* (VII, 2) Josephus, who lived at the beginning of the Christian Era, gave a detailed account of an exorcism he had watched with the emperor Vespasian and a large group of soldiers.

Josephus described the exorcist, who was called Eleazar, as an expert in "releasing people that were demon-possessed." He drew out the evil spirit from the victim through his nostrils by means of a ring and magical roots. The moment he had become separated, Eleazar adjured him "to return into this person no more," accompanying his oath with incantations.

To impress still skeptical onlookers and publicly to prove that the demon was now actually "abroad," he called on him to overturn a water-filled basin he had placed for this purpose at some distance. When this happened, Eleazar's skill and wisdom had become manifest to all.

A renowned scholar of the time, Rabbi Yochanan ben Zakkai told of a different type of exorcism in which the evil spirit was evicted from his unwilling host by use of smoke produced by the burning of specified magical herbs. Once again, to make sure that his departure was permanent, water was sprinkled on him.

Just as modern doctors try to cure disease in diverse ways and at times apply an experimental method of trial and error, so did exorcists thousands of years ago. The early "therapy" alternated between cajoling or coercing the spirit to depart.

Members of the Essene sect, most active at Jesus' time, were especially gifted in helping those "possessed" and bringing about their cure. No doubt they are responsible for similar stories in the New Testament in which the demons are referred to as "unclean spirits."

Jesus' casting out of demons is a recurring theme. The Gospels (Mark 6 and 7) tell how he gave his twelve disciples the power to expel the demons by the use of his name and cure their victims. Best known is the story of the Gadarene swine. Jesus, meeting a violent madman, helps free him of the "unclean spirits" that occupied him. Dispossessed of their chosen home, the spirits entered a herd of swine which stampeded down a cliff to drown in a lake.

Nothing was thought to produce better results in exorcism than the magical use of the divine name. This tradition came to play a significant role in Chasidism, the mystical Jewish movement that developed in the eighteenth century and was preoccupied with the occult. The "pious" (*Chasidim*) consulted in cases of "possession" were known as "Master of the Divine Name." In Hebrew this is *baal shem tov* which in abbreviated form, joining the initials of the three words, created the new name of the founder of Chasidism—Besht.

Throughout Christianity, the practice of casting out evil spirits was done by calling on the name of God and Christ. The Roman Catholic Church even built a special ceremonial around it, the *Rituale Romanum*.

Exorcism still forms a part of the rite of baptism by the use of salt. Though referred to now as "the salt of wisdom" and explained as the symbol of heavenly nourishment, its earliest application was as a devil repellent.

Possession might be the result of what modern medicine diagnoses as "psychosomatic causes." In such cases, any treatment sooner or later would assure some success. The speed of its cure and how long this lasts depends on individual circumstances and the patient's mind and attitude.

## THE DYBBUK

At death only the body was thought to perish. The soul or spirit survived. But now man was concerned with the disembodied soul's destiny. Where was it to go?

Mystic thought, beginning perhaps in ancient India, evolved the idea of the transmigration of souls. Only those sufficiently purified could reenter heaven or merge into Nirvana. But often too contaminated with earthly pollution, burdened by sin and a waste of life's opportunities, they could not proceed. They had to work their passage back by passing through other beings. They had to reenter at some lower rung of life's ladder, and stage by stage, step by step, move upward. This belief in the transmigration of souls, well known in the East, became a popular notion in seventeenth-century Central and Eastern European Jewish mysticism.

In their homelessness, the spirits of sinful dead people that could not find rest changed into demons. Laden with unpardoned guilt and not admitted into the heavenly realm, they sought refuge in some person. They tried to force entry into some living body, to attach themselves to its soul, but they could meet with resistance, because only certain categories of people were vulnerable to such a homeless "denuded spirit"—those who had committed some secret sin. But once the spirit had taken hold of such a person, it was not easy to dislodge it, and it acted as a source of further evil. Methods of exorcism were devised entailing a meticulous ritual that could be performed only by those highly proficient in this art.

If successful, the exorcist obtained a double result. First of all, he liberated the invaded person from the malignancy that had brought him or her untold harm, from his "evil pregnancy" as one of the Jewish authorities termed the "demon."

Simultaneously, however, he sent the luckless soul back on its lonely way either to continue slowly working its passage by transmigrations to its eventual bliss or, if beyond such redemption, to go straight to hell and thus no longer be able to threaten the living.

This is the background and very root of the phenomenon that came to be known as the "dybbuk." This implied that an evil spirit had entered a human being and cleaving to his soul, possessed him.

The term dybbuk does not appear in the Bible, the Gospels, the Talmud nor the Kabbalah. It first appeared in seventeenth-century Middle and Eastern Europe. But even then dybbuk was not a proper name. It was a Hebrew phrase that spoke of the "cleaving of an evil spirit" (dybbuk me-ru'ach ra'ah) to the soul of another being. But people got tired of using the long string of words and began to refer to this occult phenomenon by its first word—dybbuk.

With the passing of time it was forgotten that dybbuk was a form of the verb "to cleave," and it was personified and given a life of its own. Suddenly the word dybbuk was used for the actual name of the spirit whose action was described in the phrase. That is the bizarre birth of the dybbuk.

It was inevitable that the dramatic possibilities of possession and exorcism should attract writers who saw promising material in the phenomenon. *The Dybbuk* gained world fame for S. An-ski, a pseudonym for the Russian-born Yiddish author and folklorist Solomon Z. Rapaport. Produced in numerous languages, the play was also set to music and later was made into a successful film. Its theme, thus popularized, captured people's imagination and revived in almost every country the ancient traditions about demon possession.

When the occult came to preoccupy present-day society, a new Christian version was written on "possession." William Peter Blatty's novel, *The Exorcist*, became a best seller almost overnight.

## THE DEVIL'S MARK

Passports nowadays record distinctive marks of an individual as an identification aid. But thousands of years before the introduction of this modern practice, many people were distinguished from their fellows—for good or ill—by being "branded" in some way.

Cain's mark is the earliest such example from the Bible. Whatever Cain's mark was, it served to identify and to protect him as his brother's murderer.

A slave who refused to accept his automatic release in the seventh year and thereby showed contempt for freedom was permanently marked. He had his ear pierced with an awl at the doorjamb, the threshold of his master's house. We recall this practice whenever we use the word "earmark." Now a mere metaphor, in biblical times it was applied literally to the man who did not treasure his liberty.

Tattoos were etched into a sailor's skin not for adornment but to ward off the demons of the sea and, if, unfortunately, he drowned, to make identification of his body easier.

Adolf Hitler, too, made use of the ancient method, indelibly and permanently to identify both those serving him and those he was determined to humiliate and exterminate. His S.S. guards were tattooed in the armpit and his concentration camp victims branded on their wrists.

In odd anticipation of such diabolic application, a devil worshiper himself was said to be "marked." The devil's brand could take on two meanings. It could serve as a sign of shame or be regarded as a proud distinction of a servant dedicated to the forces of evil.

It was firmly believed that the devil bestowed his insignia on those who joined his ranks. The initiation of witches as servants of the devil included their being branded with his mark.

However, since it concerned the realm of darkness, the "decoration" was kept secret as well. Often it was stamped on the most private and concealed part of the anatomy. It might be hidden under the pubic hair, in the anus, under the eyelid or in the armpit. As a clever way of camouflage, this devil's mark could also be disguised to appear as a benign and quite common blemish of the skin, such as a birthmark, a pimple or a mole. Even a mere discoloration of the skin might be taken as irrefutable evidence of that person's allegiance to the powers of darkness.

The belief that at the time of initiation of his disciple the devil put his mark on him gave witch hunters the excuse to prosecute and condemn practically anyone, as there is hardly an unblemished human body.

One of the first procedures in the examination of a man or woman alleged to be a witch was to shave the entire body to remove any cover-up. If the examiner failed to uncover any mark, he did not give up his search. He devised a fiendish new scheme to convict those he wished to brand as a witch. He spread the word that at times the devil's mark (surely an indication of a witch) could be completely invisible. It could still be discovered, however, because the "spot" would prove insensitive to pain and if pierced would not bleed. Hence all one had to do was to examine a suspect's entire body by systematically pricking his skin with large needles. The moment the person gave no indication of pain or did not bleed, the purpose had been achieved.

Being a "pricker" became a new occupation at the time of devil hysteria. Since he was paid a good fee for each "mark" he discovered, the pricker left no part of the body untouched till in his cruel, sadistic and lustful quest, he had "caught" his quarry. All this was done in the name of religion!

A simple, real or imagined mark thus belongs not only to the occult world, but has in very fact diabolically branded man in his most evil and wicked genius.

## "THE DEVIL TO PAY"

When we say we'll "have the devil to pay," we recall early traditions that referred to such hellish debt. To gain an object or enjoy a pleasure, people were believed to have made a bargain with the devil. He would procure their desire at the price of their soul. If ever they regretted the deal or tried to cancel it, they would have to pay the devil an amount almost impossible for them to raise.

However, to link this phrase with this tradition may be misleading. Witchcraft might be so well camouflaged that its presence and practice would not be recognized or even suspected. But there are cases in which its "apparent" presence is not real. And this could well apply to the payment of the devil here. The origin of the phrase much more likely belongs to the realm of nautical life and its specialized terminology.

The devil on a ship does not refer to the Evil One but very prosaically and technically to a seam in her hulk which is most difficult to reach. And even the "payment" in this connection does not mean money at all. In its nautical sense it describes the laborious procedure of tipping the ship onto her side, careening and smearing her with tar to make her waterproof.

The two types of "payment" are both derived from Latin but come from two totally different sources. The monetary reward is rooted in the Latin word (and wish) to "appease" and "pacify" (*pacare*). The caulking version of "pay" applied to the nautical "devil" is rooted in the Latin description of "pitch" (*picem*). The complete and accurate quotation says "the devil to pay and no pitch hot."

## TALK OF THE DEVIL, AND OTHER MEANINGFUL EUPHEMISMS

The power of speech has always been recognized and respected, and has filled people with awe. It made them carefully watch their words. Much more heeded still was the evocative power of speech when it concerned the forces of the occult. Merely to voice their names could summon them, so it was firmly believed.

This conviction is one of the fundamental bases of the birth of euphemisms which have become part of everyday speech. From the Greek, euphemism literally means to "speak well" and "favorably" of a person, object or situation. Actually, it refers to the substitution of their real but dangerous or indelicate description by a word or name that sounded inoffensive, agreeable and was totally different. At times it expressed the exact opposite of the tabooed term it replaced.

Euphemisms were not used originally to avoid giving offense to easily shocked minds. Their chief objective was to protect people from a curse, an evil spirit, a sickness or even death. To mention them by their actual name would invite their presence, thus possibly causing misfortune.

There are numerous euphemisms used in the Bible. Some of them are still applied in everyday speech, particularly those which refer to death. Death was personified and to speak of it actually summoned his presence and was bound to precipitate the very event feared: the severing of the thread of life.

Enoch who had walked with God, "was no more, for God *took* him" (Gen. 5:24). King David told his son Solomon that he was about to "go the way of all the earth" (1 Kings 2:2). Suffering Job spoke of the few years left to him before he would "take the road from which I shall not return" (Job 16:22).

It was the identical reason that prompted the Greeks to call the "spirits of vengeance" (the *Erinyes*), *Eumenides*: "the kindly ones." They did so not to flatter the monstrous creatures and thereby possibly gain their goodwill or to make them change their minds. By not mentioning their real name, the malevolent spirits would be unaware of being discussed and therefore be kept away. To voice their names would "call them up."

If nowadays we jokingly use the phrase "speak of the devil" (and all it implies), it has the same ominous meaning. By the evocative power of speech it was believed that by mentioning the devil's name, he would be conjured up.

## THE GENEALOGY OF THE DEMON

Belief in the existence of evil spirits has dominated the mind of man much longer and more deeply than belief in benevolent forces, and understandably so. The countless frustrations, losses and sufferings man experienced must have created in him feelings of dread and awe from early times, even though he was accustomed to a rough and cruel life. So ever since prehistoric days man has sought the cause of his misfortune and blamed demons. To stop them and thereby make life livable, he used any means possible.

He might try to pay them off with gifts and sacrifices by giving them "protection money." Or he contrived and applied magical spells and charms to keep the malevolent powers under his control.

It was the latter that, instead of turning his back on demons, led man to make every effort to engage them for his own nefarious purposes. Demonology is almost contradictory. On the one hand it speaks of the rule by devils and on the other, of their being employed in black magic.

The very description of the "demon" and the way with time the word changed in meaning shows how man's evil intention or self-interest can besmirch or calumniate even the best of names. To start with, a "demon" was not necessarily evil at all. Frequently, he was highly respected as a divine and protective spirit. He could be a guardian angel, for instance.

In Greek, the "demon" (*daimon*) originally referred to a divine power that "imparted" fate and destiny. It was a good genius and a source of spiritual inspiration. Socrates claimed that a *daimon* was the guide in his thoughts and philosophy who warned him whenever he was about to make a wrong decision. Commentators differed in the way they interpreted the sense in which Socrates used the term. Some said that he saw in the *daimon* the voice of his conscience. Others felt that he used the term for the supernatural experiences he underwent in his cataleptic trances. Nevertheless they all agree that the *daimon* Socrates knew was of a beneficent nature.

For centuries the demon occupied a respected place. His crisis and change of personality came with the advent of the Christian faith. Christians adopted the well-known name but began to use it exclusively for "unclean spirits." Ever since, demons have been satellites of Satan, whether in the form of fallen angels, decried pagan gods or, generally, spirits of evil.

All the former positive values of the "demon" were now completely forgotten. The final blow was struck by King James VI of Scotland (James I of England). He gave the royal approval for the diabolic connotation of all demons when in 1597 he created out of the demon the term demonology, using it as the title of his treatise on witchcraft.

## IMPS

Imps are really pleasant little devils. Whether you believe in them or not, they can teach a lot. Their ancestry, far removed from the supernatural, was most natural, found in the realm of botany.

The ancient Romans had developed the art of grafting fruit trees. To produce a new variant of a species, the shoot of one plant was transferred to another by inserting it in a groove especially cut for that purpose. In Latin such a "transplant" was referred to by the verb *imputare*. It was from this root that the word imp traveled far and fast into the languages of European nations.

Imp came to describe a scion, a sprout, a sapling or an offshoot—either of plants or of humans. That is how Thomas Cromwell used the word when in his last letter to King Henry VIII he spoke of "that most noble imp, the prince's grace, your most dear son."

In German, on the other hand, there is a word that derives from the original meaning of a kind of graft, though no longer on plants but on humans. *Impfen* means to "vaccinate," as it were the grafting of a vaccine into the body.

But among Anglo-Saxons the imp experienced a common social phenomenon. We are judged by the company we keep. For good or ill, it colors us. That is exactly what happened to the imp. This little fellow, once grown on trees in gardens, when on its own was to become so weak that he could not help but acquire the reputation of his fellow traveler in the world of language. During times which were possessed by thoughts of the devil, people frequently referred to those serving him as "his children," the "scions of Satan" or his "imps."

Another explanation is that its devilish label was first bestowed on the imp by an early generation gap. Obstreperous youngsters so annoyed their elders by the trouble they caused that they in their wrath came to call them imps of the devil.

Thus no matter by which avenue, slowly but inexorably a once innocuous botanical term assumed its demonic attribute. And yet, like an echo of the old days, imps retain something of their former pristine nature even in their mischief-making.

## THE EVIL EYE

In referring to a person's hate-filled glance, we might say that "if looks could kill," and would mean it merely as a figure of speech. But there was a time when people were convinced that looks did kill. It all goes back to the ancient days when man believed in the existence and the powerful effect of the "evil eye."

The eye has always fascinated man. Of all his senses it was the most powerful and could embrace an enormous vista ranging from the nearest object to the far-distant horizon. And merely by closing his lids, man could in a flash curtain off everything outside yet still "see"—with his inner eye—an entire world of its own.

There were many additional features of the eye which gave it truly "magical" qualities. The color of the iris mystified man. He guessed that there must be some reason beyond his ken why it varied between people. And if it so happened that the two eyes of the same person were of a different hue or he had a squint, he was destined for suspicion. There was even more magic in the way in which the pupil could grow or contract in size which to ancient man appeared as a supernatural phenomenon.

Looking another person in the eye, we might often see the reflection of our own image, but in miniature. This was responsible for the very choice of its description which from the Latin *pupilla* referred to a "tiny doll." In Hebrew, likewise, the pupil is known as *eeshon*—"a little man."

The eye was thus seen as the most wondrous part of any man—and even of the gods. Ancient Egyptian myth told how Ptah, the creator of the universe, out of his eye produced all other gods. The sun god Ra gave his powerful eye to the goddess Isis who, treasuring it, used it magically.

The eye, so man learned, was endowed with supreme power. By its vision it could absorb all it saw. But was it not able to do so much more?, man wondered. And soon he imagined that from the eye also emanated mysterious, invisible rays which could influence people and the world for better or worse. There were many experiences man underwent or heard of which confirmed this belief.

Man had been frightened many times by the glaring, luminous eyes of beasts staring at him out of the dark of night. And the terror that seized him then was not without reason. It often preceded the animal's attacking and mauling him. Numerous stories were told of how snakes, for instance, by staring at a victim prior to swallowing it, had completely paralyzed it. We might easily say that, scared stiff by the fear of imminent attack, the threatened creature, out of fright and not through any mystic power of the eye, had been helplessly transfixed to the spot.

Modern, enlightened man still feels uncomfortable when a person stares at him. Usually people can "sense" a gaze aimed at them from behind their back so that they turn around.

No doubt it was experiences of that kind that gave rise to the universal belief in the evil eye.

Almost two thousand years ago, rabbinical scholars in the Holy Land debated what constituted the worst feature in a man. Rabbi Eliezer expressed the view that in his opinion it was an "evil eye." Symbolically, later generations took it to refer to jealousy and ill will. At its foundation, however, still lingered the old superstition and fear of the actual existence of an evil eye.

"Magic eyes" now open doors, but for thousands of years they have closed minds and made people shudder. The Hebrew Bible (in Prov. 23:6) warns man not to eat the bread nor desire the dainty meats of him "who has an evil eye." The Gospels, while calling the eye "the lamp of the body" went on to say that, if the eye was bad, the whole body was "full of darkness" (Matt. 6:22-23). Greek legend spoke of the curse of Medusa. Anyone looking at her severed head, and no doubt her eyes, was turned into stone.

*The Witches' Hammerer* (*Malleus Maleficarum*), the infamous guidebook for witchhunters, first published in Germany in 1486, reflected the common belief that certain individuals "by a mere look or glance from their eyes" could bewitch even their judges. Numerous men and women were burned to death in medieval Europe because they were accused of possessing the "evil eye" with which they were alleged to have pursued (and often succeeded in) their nefarious missions.

Sickness both in man and in beast often has been diagnosed as the result of an infection caused by the rays focused on the victim by an "evil eye." This early notion actually survives in our calling a sick person "ill." The word ill is the linguistic contraction of the "evil" eye which was thought to be responsible for the loss of good health.

Even today people feel uneasy if they are exposed to a spiteful or venomous glance. They may rationalize their reaction by expressing contempt for the person thus glaring at them. Deep down, however, they are afraid of the "spectator"—or rather his evil eye.

### Being Overlooked

We still do not like being "overlooked," but it is a minor affront compared with its original, opposite meaning. Anyone "overlooked" had become the very focus of attention, though, alas, by the evil eye.

There were a variety of reasons why a certain individual might have been suspected of having an evil eye. The cause may have been a very natural one, simply the way he "looked." A fixed stare, particularly if accompanied by a frown or scowl, has always been interpreted as an aggressive act. On the other hand, a person's presence at some unfortunate event led people to believe that this happening was actually the result of his evil eye. Some of the most famous personalities have thus been "renowned," and subsequently reviled for it.

Among those so maligned were Lord Byron, Napoleon III, Alfonso XIII, king of Spain, and of all people, Pope Pius IX of First Vatican Council fame. Napoleon, well aware of his occult power, used to wear an amulet attached to his watch for his own protection.

The many disasters that accompanied King Alfonso's public appearances prompted Italians to "welcome" him on a state visit in a unique manner no other monarch has ever experienced. They "greeted" him by wildly rattling their keys. This was not meant as applause but was their way of warding off misfortune and the devil who was supposed to be allergic both to iron and noise.

Pope Pius was said to be one of the worst cases of *jettatura*, the Italian word for a man possessed by the power of the evil eye. Anything he blessed was a fiasco and to receive his benediction was regarded as fatal. (He was antimodernist and this reputation was probably given him by his political adversaries.)

## What Makes an Evil Eye?

An obvious question was how a person said to be so "endowed" originally acquired his evil eye. There are various explanations:

It was an heirloom, people said. Like other features, you inherited it from your ancestors. You just could not help having it.

Those believing in the devil saw in the evil eye his special misfortune-producing gift which he had reserved for and bestowed upon his favorites.

There were other magical answers. An eye contained a fiery substance which, like sunrays focused through a piece of glass, could cause destruction.

An angry look did not result from an inner emotion alone, but was activated by a powerful spirit which, emanating from the eye, was able to pounce on the very person that had provoked the wrath, duly to punish him or her with its daggers.

According to another view, a bad person was able to concentrate all the evil in his eye which, overflowing from it, would hit the target dead on.

Like a loaded weapon, the evil eye was always ready for action. It could be triggered off at a moment's notice to damage life and property, to jinx man and his endeavors.

Apart from a hereditary malignancy, an eye could turn evil by reacting to the fortune of others. Good luck was counterproductive if latent evil in an eye caught sight of it. Out of malice and jealousy it would "shoot to kill."

The malevolent effect of the so-called evil eye may not at all be the result of magic or the supernatural. People very susceptible, sensitive to unkindness and believing in the alleged evil influence of the eye, may truly experience it. We know of the power of autosuggestion and how some persons make excellent subjects for hypnosis. Even telepathic abilities of men, it has been claimed, enabled them to exercise "the hostile look" successfully.

## Countermeasures

Believing that exposure to the malignant rays of an evil eye could do untold damage to him, his animals and his crops, man felt the paramount need to guard and protect himself and all he cherished by taking immediate and strong countermeasures.

Possibly no other fear has been so worldwide and the cause of such a multiplicity of defensive precautions to deceive or avoid it as the evil eye. From the simplest measures to quite complicated procedures, there were an imaginative variety of remedies, amulets, charms, spells and gestures.

People wore around their neck a piece of garlic, renowned as a devil repellent. They attached to or sewed into the clothing worn by their children a bag containing bread and salt, or at times put these "God-blessed" ingredients into the child's pocket.

Bracelets, brooches and bangles were worn to avert the glance of the evil eye and thereby avoid the malignancy it could create which would be beyond repair. Sometimes the amulets were suspended between the eyes.

Inevitably magic played a significant part in man's unceasing fight against the demonic evil eye. He confronted the person suspected to be endowed with it with the potent symbol of the devil's horns which he made with the index and small fingers of his hand. It was the application of "like to like" magic.

Many customs, attitudes and expressions common now and regarded as completely innocuous originated in man's dread of the evil eye and his consuming concern to defy and defeat it.

Modern woman might be horrified to realize that the eye shadow she uses was first introduced for reasons that had nothing to do with beauty culture. Darkening her lids was one of the precautions she took against the pernicious influence of an evil eye.

"Blue for boys" seems such an innocent, lovely custom, but it began not as a proud display of his male sex. Very seriously it was put on the still weak infant to protect him from any harm that could be done to him by the evil eye of someone jealous of his masculinity. This, too, was the purpose for (particularly Oriental) people to ornament both children and livestock with strings of blue beads. The divine color of these beads was meant to act as a guard against devilish glances. The colored balls often attached to a baby's crib or carriage go back to this original fear. They provided the infant boy not with an innocuous toy but with a protection against the spell of the evil eye.

Once again, the belief that like can cure or beat like has been applied here as well. It was thought that one could outstare malevolent glances. That is why some specially polished precious stones came to be worn not as ornaments but as magical eyes for protection.

More conspicuous still was the use of huge eyes painted on both sides of the prow of a ship. Certainly they were not decorative either nor a magic means to enhance the vision of the skipper. As outsized eyes they would outshine the death rays of evil eyes.

Latin Americans still use the obscene gesture of "the fig" to avert the influence of the evil eye. The thumb thrust out between the first and second fingers symbolizes the genitals. Their vital generative potency alone was regarded strong enough to overpower the evil glance.

The dread of the evil eye gave man also all his "fascination." To start with, the word expressed the "bewitching" of a person and also the countercharm used, which usually was in the shape of a phallus.

Fascination was the Latin *fascinum* for "penis." The life power of sex would prove more potent than the rays.

People spat, if possible three times, at anyone thought to possess the evil eye. This was not done out of contempt. Spittle used to be regarded as a holy substance, as part of the power of man's soul. And this divine ingredient therefore would be inimical to evil forces.

Horse brasses now are merely part of history and, possibly, exhibits in museums. Once they were thought to be necessary to the animal but not to provide the horse with a shining and attractive ornament. They were to give protection against the evil eye.

A popular pattern used was that of the disc, the shape of the sun renowned for its supernatural power to outshine the forces of darkness. The highly polished brass was meant by its dazzling effect to deflect the injurious glance from the vulnerable animal.

Knots were yet another safeguard. They entangled the evil force and thereby kept it at bay. This is the reason for the buckle once worn on nurses' belts, a custom still observed in some parts of the world.

The nurse's constant proximity to (the spirit of) sickness was her professional hazard. So as not to be infected by its radiation, she needed an extra "shield" that immunized her from being "overlooked."

A peculiar custom at a Jewish wedding occurs at the very end of the ceremony, when the bridegroom breaks a glass, and does so rather noisily. The glass itself originally had to be of value. The material loss and the "racket" were supposed to divert the attention of the potentially evil force from the happiness experienced by the couple at that very moment. Otherwise, the evil spirit might be so roused in its envy that it would be determined to spoil the good luck, and the marriage would never "take." That, too, is the reason why the assembled congregation accompanies the breaking of the glass by shouting loudly *mazel tov*—"good luck."

The less you talked about your good health and the more you hid your good fortune, the safer you were and the surer to keep it.

This is the origin of the understatement. This traditional "trait" was due not to a sense of modesty or to gentlemanly restraint, but to a selfish fear and concern to preserve one's good luck. Speaking too much of one's blessings would rouse the envious agencies of the evil eye. Therefore it was not advisable to praise others or express admiration of them. Such acknowledgment of their merits would be tantamount to endangering them by drawing them to the attention of the evil eye.

That is why people learned to qualify any compliment they paid and the person concerned understood. If they showed no restraint, the recipient did not feel flattered but frightened. He well realized that the "praise" could act adversely. (It is not accidental therefore that in the ancient Hebrew the same word expressed both "blessing" and "curse.")

Those exposed thus would show no gratitude for the "kind" remarks made. Immediately they would appeal to higher powers to help them against the sudden threat (activated by their so-called friend) to their good luck. A common exclamation on such an occasion used to be the Hebrew for "glory be to God," that is, hallelujah. This was not voiced to thank divine power for all the good given. God's name was used as a bogey to frighten off the envious evil forces.

Those lucky enough to have good fortune, whether in wealth, good health, good looks or happiness, were well advised to camouflage it. So as not to lose it, they had to do everything within their power to avoid drawing attention to it which to many would spoil most of the pleasure.

Beautiful children were given ugly names or wrapped in rags. You did not boast of your wealth or advertise it by showy display. And you certainly did not provoke the jealousy of these mysterious powers by talking of any success you might have had.

Jews afraid of the evil eye felt its threat particularly when discussing something happy or someone (especially a child) who was good looking. As a countermeasure they followed the remark at once with a word charm. This consisted of a telling Yiddish-Hebrew phrase that implied "May there be no evil eye!"—*kayn ayn ha'rah*. Slightly mispronounced and shortened, the words are usually rendered *kaynahorah* which sounds very much like *kayn* (the Yiddish for "no") horror.

## ON THE LOOM OF LANGUAGE

The evil eye had its lasting effect on the way we talk. Just as it was responsible for the word "illness" and was said to be activated by jealousy, the evil eye has actually created "envy."

The word is the one case in which jealousy, instead of splitting up a unity, has joined "two into one." Etymologically, "envy" is the combination and contraction of the Latin words for to "look" (*videre*) "against" (*in*) a person. It is the same "ill will" that gave birth to all that is "invidious."

These many customs, taboos and words were not coined or created accidentally. They were devised and designed with deep thought and anxious concern. Each of them was the result of man's constant obsession with the destructive potential of the evil eye.

# CHAPTER SEVEN

# Witches and Witchcraft

## THE ORIGINAL WITCH

People who are convinced that the existence of witches has always been a figment of the mind continue to use the word in modern days, metaphorically, and more particularly so in the political sphere, when they speak of "witch hunts." However, witch-hunting was a loathsome pursuit between the fifteenth and eighteenth centuries. For more than three hundred years many thousands of wretched people were shunned, persecuted, tortured and put to a gruesome death by burning or hanging. One estimate puts their number as high as nine million.

At the very beginning, to be called a "witch" had no evil implication. The Anglo-Saxon root of the word described a "wise" person: *wicca* in the case of a man and *wicce*, of a woman. Witchcraft thus pointed to "the craft of the wise" which could be rendered much more correctly as "wisecraft."

Despite the innocence of their name, witches, nevertheless, were alleged to practice magic, and they were an age-old phenomenon. Their occult skills were part of ancient life and were accepted with awe and fear, or with revulsion. The Hebrew Bible condemned them and commanded that "you shall not allow 'a witch' to live" (Exod. 22:17). By implication this acknowledged their existence and their effective work. They were ostracized because whatever it was they did was seen to contradict, rival and undermine the recognized divine rule.

Odd misconceptions relate to both age and sex of the witch. Generally people came to assume that all witches had to be women and the traditional portrait was that of an old hag with a long pointed nose, sunken cheeks and a hairy lip, riding on a broomstick. In fact, witches may be of either sex, any age and be bewitching in looks.

The many repulsive traits they were said to show are associated with the female aging process. These include excessive hair on the face, a haggard look and a single tooth sticking out. But to attribute these features to the witch was a later development in society's attempt to make people loathe and shun the witch altogether.

## THE MAKING OF A WITCH

Various considerations and circumstances made a man or a woman turn into a witch.

Many "wise" men and women had dedicated their lives to what came to be termed in modern days the "old religion." (The theory that witchcraft was a survival of the ancient pagan cults was powerfully propounded by Professor Margaret A. Murray, Egyptologist, anthropologist and renowned scholar of witchcraft.) The witches served the old fertility gods and practiced their rites with no evil thoughts. To aid man and not to harm him was their aim.

But because they did not accept and follow the established order they were condemned. Unable or unwilling to give up their pursuits and to submit to the ruling authority, they began to practice their way of life clandestinely. This made it and them all the more mysterious and subject to suspicion. In turn, it made them attractive to those who were always drawn to the occult and enjoyed living dangerously.

On the other hand, the very power they came to exert over other lives made them a rival to the Christian faith. They were accused of having chosen the devil as their master and of serving him. In exchange for their souls, they were given magical powers and all the goods of this world. If priests guided man to heaven, witches did so to hell. Pope Innocent VIII in a papal bull of 1484 denounced witchcraft as heresy.

Self-delusion was another factor that led people to imagine themselves to be witches. Without considering what such assertion might cost them in suffering and even life, they were convinced that they belonged to that extraordinary group of people endowed with supernatural gifts. Self-deception can achieve miraculous things, even more so if it is linked with the desire for power over people.

There were also those who shammed witchcraft. They did so in order to be dreaded, to subjugate others and to amass a fortune for themselves. The reputation of having occult power gave them a tremendous hold over the gullible who lived in fear or with unfulfilled, lustful desires.

The field of their activities was wide, and they found many victims ready for the plucking. The Church itself had made men believe in the existence of a realm beyond the senses, and those sham witches traded on it. Why should the supernatural be exclusively reserved for the priests? Thus the sham witches were ready and only too willing—for the asking and a substantial fee—to help people master life and to gain control over the demonic forces with which they allegedly had a special agreement.

Another opinion held that at some periods of dearth, poverty could create a witch, just as it could a prostitute. When penury forced people to go hungry, some women tried to sustain themselves by an odd type of occult blackmail. Claiming to be witches, they threatened neighbors that unless they provided them freely with food, they would be cursed by them, and forced to regret their lack of charity for the rest of their lives.

## A STUDY IN BLACK AND WHITE

The original witches' wisdom has frequently proved beneficial. Living in close contact with nature, they were well acquainted with the healing properties of plants, a knowledge arrived at by trial and error but which has subsequently been applied to cure many ills.

It is thought that digitalis was discovered by a witch. Histories of medicine tell how the drug was first introduced by an eighteenth-century English physician, William Withering. The doctor had heard of a "wise woman" in his district in Shropshire who was renowned for helping people who suffered from heart disease. He obtained a sample of the potion from the woman, and identified powdered foxglove leaves as one of its chief ingredients. He recognized that this product of the foxglove plant gave the witch's brew its remedial properties. And so digitalis became part of man's pharmacopoeia.

The witches' potions, drugs and power of mind over matter cannot surprise modern man who has learned of the hallucinogenic effect of some mushroom varieties, the working of aphrodisiacs, and has found penicillin in the green mold of cheese. But to ancient man all this was "magic."

Apart from the application of such natural sources, no doubt early witches possessed psychic faculties, hypnotic power and the gift of telepathy. Their influence must have grown even more once their authority had been established and people had reason to believe in the efficacy of their practice.

To pass from white or beneficial magic to its counterpart in black magic was not difficult. Once a witch had been recognized as the owner of supernatural, occult talents, evil was not far away. In fact, those who could do so well could produce evil even better.

The frequent occurrence of inexplicable disease and sudden disaster gave impetus to the deterioration of the image of a witch. Unable to account for the many phenomena that haunted and destroyed men's lives, such as paralysis and leprosy, could people be blamed if they discovered in the "wise one" a ready-made scapegoat to whom to ascribe the causes of all the evil experienced, particularly if she or he had made false claims to unusual powers to her or his own advantage in happier times?

It can be assumed that those who used their wisdom to help others would abuse it if it served their purposes, and would have little hesitation to enforce their will by curses.

Soon witches were said to exert their evil influence, and could harm even those far away. Many stories gained currency—based either on fact or fiction—that by manipulating figures representing the intended victim, they could actually inflict on him untold harm.

One example was the waxen image of the person which the witch would melt down over a fire, destroying the real person many miles away. Another favorite figure was the voodoo doll symbolizing the target of attack; sticking pins in the doll would cause the real person magically to suffer pain and damage in the same spots.

Such feats were enlarged in the telling, and that is how the "wise one" of antiquity became the "witch" of black magic, evil spells and other life-destroying activities.

## WITCH HUNTS

When man became possessed by a fear of witches, he applied every means to detect and identify them.

Because he believed they were "branded" and therefore identifiable by the devil's mark, the suspects were carefully examined. Woe to those who bore on their skin some unusual blemish, a hairy growth, a pimple, a mole, a wart or a birthmark. It was claimed that these protuberances were actually nipples through which familiars sucked the witches' blood.

In the words of King James I of England, witchcraft was one of the most "horrible crimes," and so witch trials were greatly promoted by the monarch.

During his reign, the imfamous water ordeal was employed to determine guilt. The suspect was thrown into water. If the victim floated, it was taken as a sure indication he was a witch. The pure water had rejected him! If the body sank, the person on trial had proved his innocence. All that was now needed was to rescue him prior to drowning.

In their worship of the devil and the practice of their craft, witches denied and defied the power of God. Certainly, they did everything to show their contempt. Thus the Church came to regard them as heretics for whom no punishment was too severe.

Constantly threatened, witches made every effort to hide their secret and their allegiance to the Evil One; the Church therefore felt justified to do everything within its power to make them confess. If the suspect passed the floating/sinking test, it was not seen as proof of his not being guilty. On the contrary, it only showed the terrible power of Satan who had aided his servant. The witch would only confess under sufficient stress. Thus the Church sanctioned and practiced in the name of God the most cruel and fiendish tortures. After all, had not the Bible commanded not to suffer a witch to live?

And we can imagine yet another factor that contributed to the persecution of witches. When women became identified with witches, man must have resented their influence. Traditionally a woman was believed to be inferior. And therefore any power she exercised could never be of her own making. She executed Satan's work and bidding. And as the Evil One never did anything for nothing, she had paid for her power by giving her soul to him.

## THE WITCHES' COVEN

In religions, private prayer and congregational worship have always been used in the attempt to commune with God. In the realm of the occult, too, a witch worked either independently or joined with others in "group practice." And just as theologians have advanced strong arguments in favor of communal prayer meetings, so witches were also convinced that by joint endeavor they increased their occult power. But instead of gathering in churches and announcing their meeting far and wide by the ringing of bells, they met clandestinely in the open air. They did so because theirs was a supernatural mission of arcane art, reserved only for the initiates. Their pact with the devil (whether imagined or real) was condemned by the authorities as dangerous and declared illegal. Detection would mean dire punishment, if not death. That is how the witches' coven came into existence and acquired its special features.

The word coven derives from the same root as "covent" of London's famous Covent Garden with its market and opera house. Their common source is the convent. Covent Garden really should be called Convent Garden. In former days its site actually was the garden and burial place attached to the Convent of Westminster. It merely happened that somewhere along the way the convent lost one of its letters and has never reclaimed it.

The word convent itself is pure Roman in ancestry, going back to the Latin *conventus* and, like modern business "conventions," described the "coming together" of men *and* women for some purpose. Eventually the Church appropriated the word. To begin with, it applied it either to the buildings housing a monastic order or the actual community of friars, monks or nuns resident there. Originally, therefore, a convent served as the domicile of either sex. Only in later days was the word restricted and exclusively reserved for houses of nuns. In an even more specialized religious tradition the term was used for the company of Christ's twelve Apostles.

And presumably it was in their constant endeavor to supplant the worship of God by that of the devil and to parody Christian institutions that witches began to call their own gatherings covens.

Coven, then, is an archaic form of the word convent. In its occult connotation the term has been traced back to 1662. It was first used in the confession of Isobel Gowdie, a witch who spoke of "thirteen persons in each coven." Gowdie was depicted both as "an old woman" and "a pretty, red-haired girl," but despite what she looked like, all records agree she was Scottish, and that she was hanged for her "crime." They are also unanimous that her body was burned to ashes to ensure the total and irrevocable destruction of her supernatural, malevolent power.

The institution of the coven goes back to ancient days. Some say it evolved from the Eleusinian mystery cult of the eastern Mediterranean which held secret meetings and restricted the number of those admitted. One claim links the coven with the horned god of the days of Pan worship. Those participants danced within a magic circle, which would hold a maximum number of thirteen people.

Though denied by some, it has been assumed that a coven consisted of exactly thirteen members. The ideal coven was made up of six men and six women presided over by a "devil," or whoever deputized for him. This tradition may be founded in the Scottish girl's confession but remembering the magic significance of that numeral, it is likely to have been chosen as the right quorum. As it has been noted earlier, thirteen would be a number selected to mock Christian sanctity.

The coven referred to a practicing cell of witches, and often was organized in the same manner as political underground movements are. Each member on joining the group was given a new name by which he or she was to be known. Though usually explained as an indication that the witch had assumed a totally new way of life, the practice had a much more vital and obvious reason—to hide the identity of the witch.

Another security rule was that members of a coven were never to know each other's real names or to meet outside the coven. This was a safeguard lest under duress of torture one might reveal the identity of other members. Only the leaders of the different covens were known to each other.

To avoid unnecessary competition or interference, each coven was allotted its own district. It was further stipulated that the distance between the groups had to amount to no less than one league, which is roughly three miles.

Next in importance was the question of how and when to meet.

There were two distinct types of gatherings: the ordinary, regular "business meeting," and the extraordinary assembly which was a celebration. The first became known as the Esbat and the latter the Sabbat.

## THE ESBAT

The Esbat was held at least once a month and, generally, looked after the affairs of the craft. Ideas and news items were exchanged and instructions given. The Esbat also included the performance of certain rites and the working of magic. This varied from coven to coven, and what actually went on there has been subject to much controversy.

The term Esbat most likely is derived from the Old French verb for "to frolic" and "to amuse oneself"—*s'esbattre*. According to the lore, was not one of the main features of the get-together of male and female witches a "frolic," of erotic lasciviousness? Thus, it was believed the name emphasized one of the chief items on the Esbat's agenda. This was not for the mere purpose of "sex," however. Its roots go back to the old religion with its fertility magic. The coitus practiced was meant to influence nature and to ensure that crops and cattle would be fruitful.

## THE SABBAT

A highlight in the witches' lives was their major "conventions," known as Sabbats, grotesque imitation of the Sabbath, the seventh day of the week ordained by the Bible to sanctify God and his work of creation. Would not Satanic forces, dedicated to all that was evil, choose as a name for their assembly that of the day set aside for holiness?

There was yet another factor that favored the adoption of the term. The Sabbath was closely linked with the Jews who had observed it meticulously wherever they dwelt and in all ages. When witchcraft came to obsess people's minds, the Jews experienced one of the most fiendish persecutions by Christian powers who saw in them a personification of the devil. Therefore to adopt and adapt the Jews'

Sabbath as the name for the witches' most evil day seemed an appropriate choice.

The odd spelling of Sabbat has a very simple explanation. The witches took over the name from the French, in which tongue the Sabbath appears as Sabbat.

A further suggestion was that the Sabbat was so named to honor Sabazius, a Thracian god, whose worship was distinguished by the debaucheries and frenzied orgies which came to be linked with the witches' gathering on that occasion.

The date of the celebration varied in different regions. Most favored and common were Candlemas (February 2), Walpurgisnacht (April 30), Lammas (August 1) and Halloween (October 31). The meeting took place during the night, appropriate for the forces of darkness. Usually it commenced at midnight and terminated with the rising of the sun when the witches made haste to get home.

Next in importance to the date and time of any meeting was the choice of the right site. This had to be a secluded spot providing sufficient room for the witches to gather and to perform their rites. Among the favorite meeting places were clearings in the forest or pastures removed as far as possible from settlements.

Finally, there was the question of who of the witches was qualified to be admitted and how many. Ideally the number of males and females should be equal, but if this could not be arranged, the missing "sex" should be made up by incubi in the case of absent males or by succubi in the case of absent females.

Fantasy certainly ran riot, and man's lustful thoughts must have had a field day according to the accounts given of what went on during that night, particularly if these were taken down as evidence in the prosecution of witches.

A more pornographic description of the goings on could not be found in the language, the literature or the practices of our so-called permissive twentieth-century society. Only then it was the Church that undertook the examinations and tests, told the prosecutor what to look for and presided over the trial.

The witches met in their "natural" state—stark naked. They were also said to have paid homage to the devil by kissing each other's posterior. Specially honored was a meeting attended by Lucifer himself, represented frequently by a ram or a man taking its guise.

Apart from the orgy with its countless copulations, the entire ceremony aimed at defiling and mocking sacred Christian tradition. For instance, a holy wafer used at Communion was fed to dogs or soiled by human excrement or by the witches urinating on it.

Altogether the witches' Sabbat was not only out of bounds to all other people but got out of hand, it seemed.

## THE FLYING WITCH

The airborne witch anticipated man's mastery of the air by many centuries. What now is regarded as the result of the genius of science and a beneficent gift was then condemned as a malevolent talent and part of the evil craft of a witch. It is the old story of how a myth can become a reality.

That witches could fly at unimaginable speed through the air became a firmly established belief. No matter for what purpose— whether to join a coven, to attend a Sabbat or just in pursuit of a single evil mission—witches took to the air.

Gullible people asked no further questions. As according to their belief a witch could do anything, they were not surprised she could fly unaided by self-propulsion.

Others, however, looked around for some satisfactory explanation. They reasoned that, in spite of her demonic power, a witch could never become airborne of her own accord. Taking the example of terrestrial traffic, they thus imagined that a witch rode in the air on some creature. This could be a goat, a dog or, preferably, a demon.

But even these natural and supernatural mounts were eventually discarded. Being witches, so people thought, magic was at their disposal. This enabled them to transform a common and inanimate object into a fantastic conveyance. That is how the legend grew, and witches were assumed to ride through the air on cigar-shaped, elongated missiles, three-pronged pitchforks and, eventually, on the streamlined broomstick, the ordinary common or garden birch broom.

Another important question is how did the notion of flying witches come about? Several factors and traditions combined in creating the belief.

First of all, biblical tradition supported the possibility of miraculous flights. Had not Enoch gone up to heaven? Did not everyone know of

Elijah's fiery ascent? Beyond these divine miracles concerned with God's servants, there was equal scriptural "evidence" that the powers of darkness were not subject to gravitational force. Did not the Gospel tell of how Satan had carried Christ to the top of a high mountain?

Witches were regarded as possessing demonic power, so they would be capable of similar feats. The world of demons was at their disposal. They would carry out any task a witch commanded, even to elevate and propel her through the air. When the world was full of witch mania, people suspected their presence everywhere.

People were deeply perturbed when the identical type of misfortune struck at places far distant from each other and yet within the shortest possible interval. They were convinced that one witch was responsible for both disasters, but they also realized that even a witch could never have moved so far and so fast from one place to another by ordinary means. The only explanation was that the witch must have traversed the distance in some supernatural manner—by flying through the air.

In order to increase their power and hold over man, some evil women did not deny the fantastic claim. Others, who were completely innocent victims of mass hysteria and ecclesiastical prosecution, "confessed" their nocturnal flight under torture.

Some of the accused witches themselves, if not actually giving currency to the belief, fostered it. But they did so not to deceive people and to gain dominance, but in good faith. They firmly believed in the truth of their assertion, and what prompted them is linked with the interpretation of dreams and the effect of drugs.

Modern theories about dreams have much to say about "flying dreams." Occasionally, while sleeping, people imagine themselves to be lifted up and to soar into the air. One school of thought explains this peculiar sensation as the attempt of man's unconscious mind to encourage the person to proceed with a task ahead. Long before Freud, Adler and Jung, people had been aware of "flying dreams" in which they found themselves at some site far away. When waking up they were still very conscious of the odd sensation and vividly remembered the content of their dream. They imagined that they must have been "up in the air" and in the far-off place.

But there is an even more significant explanation. So-called witches used to anoint their body with salves made up of ingredients such as aconite and belladonna that had hallucinatory properties. These would have produced in their minds those very flying sensations and a vivid "experience" of something that actually never happened. Using a term of our own drug society, their "trip" had been very real.

A contemporary report supports this view. It tells of a certain Mr. Porter who had watched a witch. After she had taken off her clothes and rubbed her body with an ointment, she had fallen into a trance. He had not moved away but kept her under constant observation from his hidden vantage point. When, eventually, the woman came to again and got dressed, she told Mr. Porter that she had just returned from a flight which had carried her across seas and high mountains to a remote region. She would not believe that she had never moved even one inch from the spot where she fell asleep. She insisted that her drug-induced illusion of the flight had really taken place.

Thus the flight of witches is not such a farfetched myth. Multiple factors—religious thought, fertile imagination, the effect of drugs and dreams—combined to make it a "valid" claim.


## THE WITCH'S BROOMSTICK

The broomstick is a simple object, used for hundreds of years in every home to sweep it clean. But the moment it was attached to a witch, this household item changed into a complex and puzzling article. Did witches really ride it? And why, of all things, did they choose it and not some other, more suitable carrier? How did the entire idea of a witch's broomstick first arise?

The answer to these questions certainly belongs to the lore of witchcraft but also relates to as diverse topics as camouflage, defamation, walking aids and ubiquitous sex.

Anything a woman (or for that matter, a man) did, when assumed to be a witch, immediately was subject to suspicion and strange interpretations.

Broomsticks, in times gone by, served not only to sweep the house and yard but when going out, people (and especially older women) would take their broom with them to help them cross streams or vault over hedges, ditches, and so forth.

Naturally, with the aid of the stick, their progress was much faster. Therefore, in a manner of speaking, they seemed almost to fly on the stick. And it was only a short step to seeing the hag not grasping the stick in her hands but actually straddling and riding on it.

Sticks have always played an important part in magic. Modern magicians would be incomplete without their wand. Like the "pointing finger" out of which the wand evolved, it was thought to be endowed with supernatural power which could work wonders or play havoc. The stick was very much like the mysterious snake (yet another prototype of the wand) that, instead of remaining coiled up, could suddenly become as stiff as a poker and, striking out, inflict a fatal bite.

Witches certainly would need the stick for their type of work, but they lived dangerously and any object in their home that could give them away was carefully hidden. To discover an actual wand there would have led to their inevitable arrest, prosecution, torture and death. Hence a broomstick was the ideal substitute and an obvious and clever choice. It belonged to everyone's household and would never arouse suspicion. Most of all, it was always ready for instant use. Without a moment's notice, a witch could get hold of it, not to sweep the floor but to sweep through the air.

Everyone realized the broomstick itself had no inherent propelling power. This was supplied by the ointment that, prior to the takeoff, the witch rubbed not only on herself but onto the stick as well. And it was this secret mixture that served as the fuel.

All that was told and believed about witches riding a stick was reinforced by the recollection of ancient myths. These told of demigods or other supernatural beings that used to travel through the air miraculously on the back of beasts. And thus carried aloft, they pursued their divine or diabolic mission.

Procreation has its prominent place in the world of the occult with its worship of the forces of nature and its essential fertility. As mentioned earlier, witches have been alleged to indulge in orgies in which intercourse with the Evil One was the culmination in the celebration of their Sabbats and Black Masses. Is it any wonder, then, that the broomstick, so tightly gripped between the witch's legs, was really the phallus of the devil which she enjoyed riding?

The flight itself had its hazards. Both witch and broom could easily be brought down by the ringing of church bells. Witches worked out special routes to avoid passing over churches. Nevertheless, they were always alert during flight to take immediate evasive action should, inadvertently, they pass over an uncharted church. They knew that otherwise they would crash.

During times when people were obsessed with witch hysteria, and afraid of "witchy" air attack, they rang the church bells all night long. It was a noise that lulled them to sleep, sure that this earliest antimissile cover would serve to protect their bodies and souls.


## FAMILIARS

Familiars were the constant and loyal companions of a witch. They were indeed part of her family. But few people would guess the real depth and antiquity of their association and that the witch's "familiar" preserved the original description of "family."

To speak of "family life" nowadays suggests a loving relationship, even though people might complain of its present decline, if not the total lack of it. However, the surprising thing is that there was little love lost in the "family" as it existed at first. There was no affectionate bond at all, only bondage in which one party was completely subservient to the other.

"Family" from the Latin *famulus*, referred not to a blood relation but to a "servant." He was employed in the household, and had to be at its head's beck and call, as was a witch's familiar.

In whichever form, it, he or she justified its existence by doing the bidding of the master as an obedient "familiar"—a servant. In most cases, the order given commanded the familiar to undertake a malicious errand on behalf of the witch. And like any faithful butler, a familiar might even venture to offer wise counsel to its employer.

The first instance of the use of the word in the occult sense was found in Reginald Scot's *Discoverie of Witchcraft*, published in 1584.

There were different types of familiars and each fulfilled a significant role. It was thought that most commonly a familiar took the shape of a cat. This in turn at times created dangerous situations for ordinary people who without cause could be victimized as witches. This applied especially to a woman who for one reason or another was disliked or had annoyed neighbors. The pet she owned or loved was "recognized" as her "familiar" and was taken as irrefutable proof of her being a witch, though she herself had never in her life shown any interest in the occult.

Without any further need of investigation, the pet's presence led to the poor woman's prosecution, condemnation and death. Therefore during periods of hysteria over witches, the keeping of a pet carried an enormous risk.

As familiars were deemed such an essential tool of the trade for a witch, to own one was very important. The question was how to acquire it. A witch might be given her familiar on the occasion of her initiation, and thus it would work for her from the very moment she started operations. When ready to take up her profession, she could do so all the better with a proper "assistant."

On the other hand, there were witches who specialized as experts in the training of familiars. They would supply the most valuable specimens.

As with ordinary pets, if not even more so here, a familiar might take a liking to a certain witch and attach itself to her permanently of its own volition.

Perhaps oddest of all heirlooms is the familiar, which could be left as a legacy.

In the main, however, the familiar was a ghost of which a witch could take possession by going into a trance, offering her own "vacated" body for occupation. And having "moved in," the spirit would henceforth work through the witch. This phenomenon is similar to the claim of a medium that a spirit from the "other world" has entered her body and is speaking through her as her "guide."

If the familiar was a pet, it was well looked after. It was given its own name. To be properly fed it received its own special diet. There was a tradition that to keep a familiar in good working condition, a witch would do well to feed it some drops of her blood or—if she was lactating—of her own milk from time to time.

## THE CAT

To see in the cat a witch's familiar, it has been suggested, was an early case of mistaken identity. The confusion was tied to the broomstick which the witch was alleged to use.

The original "cat" had not been a cat at all—in the feline and purring sense. The cat in a witch's home had actually been the dialect word for the magic broomstick she used for her occult work and transportation.

Everything known of this feline creature "conspired" to make it the ideal representative and vehicle of occult power and thereby the witch's familiar, if not her very impersonation.

That we call a cat "pussy" is really of divine origin. It recalls her deification in ancient Egypt where Pasht (also known as Bast or Bastet) was worshiped as a cat goddess—our word "pussy" being derived from her.

The Egyptian *Book of the Dead* spoke of "the Great Cat who is in Heliopolis." As a feline solar deity, the cat was thought to protect man. Thus cats were regarded by the Egyptians as so sacred that to kill one was a capital offense. At death cats were mummified and buried in cemeteries reserved for them.

## The Cat in Myth

From Egypt the belief in the power of the cat spread everywhere, and the myths and legends of many countries added to its fame and involved it more and more in the world of the occult.

The Greeks were among the first to make the cat a creature that had a special bond with the netherworld and with death. The myth started among the gods and was caused by another of Zeus's dalliances, this time with Alcmene, wife of Amphitryon of Thebes. She had become pregnant by Zeus and was bearing Heracles in her womb. In her fury and envy, Zeus's wife, Hera, was determined if unable to prevent the birth, at least to delay it and thereby to prolong Alcmene's labor pains.

For this purpose Hera stationed the goddess of childbirth, Eileithya, and the Moirai (the Fates) outside the adulteress's home. With their knees together and clasping their hands, by sympathetic magic they kept the child back in the womb for nine days after the delivery had actually been due.

But Alcmene had a faithful servant, Galinthias, who made use of a lie to end her mistress's suffering. Rejoicingly she announced to the divine magicians holding their watch that there was no need for them to go on doing so. Their magic had been unsuccessful, as Alcmene had just given birth to a lusty child.

Apparently frustrated in their effort and deeply disappointed, the goddesses jumped up in surprise. This immediately broke the spell. Alcmene's womb opened and she gave birth to Heracles.

All Hera could do was to give vent to her anger. As her plans had been sabotaged by Galinthias, she was resolved to punish her. To do so she transformed her into a cat which she banished into the underworld. There Galinthias became the priestess of Hecate, the queen of the witches and the goddess of death. And that is why cats remain loyal to witches.

Another Greek tradition tells of how Hecate herself became a cat temporarily and had saved her own life. The incident was related to the monster Typhon's bid to take over the world and rule both heaven and earth. To escape him, Hecate had taken on feline features. But once Zeus had put down the rebellion and slain Typhon, Hecate resumed her original shape.

She never forgot that by taking on the disguise of a cat, she had been able to survive. Cats became her favorite creatures to whom she extended special treatment. They could count on her at all times and in all circumstances. But they could do so particularly in matters that concerned her special sphere of influence: witchcraft and all that is related to the realm of the supernatural.

Norse mythology also contributed in relating the cat to the witch. It pictured Freya, the goddess of marriage, fruitfulness and fertility, as sitting in a chariot that was drawn by cats, probably specially chosen for the task because of their own prolific faculties.

In its conquest of paganism, Christianity branded Freya as a witch. And, as cats had once pulled her along, she pulled the cat with her into darkness. Christians remembering the Norse myth saw in the feline creature an ominous companion of all witches.

This presents yet another of the paradoxes so frequent in life. Without qualms Christian nations continue to honor the goddess Freya every Friday, the day named to pay homage to her. But they decried the cat as an evil being which served the powers of darkness and therefore was a harbinger of bad luck because it had once faithfully worked for that same goddess.

## The Cat in Its Own Right

The cat does not owe its uncanny reputation to myths alone. Personal experiences of people confirmed and reinforced the traditional attitude and the cat's occult stature. The cat truly merits prominent status. Everything known about a cat places it in this choice position.

A cat has always seemed to be "psychic" and endowed with gifts no ordinary being possessed. It seems to "sense" the invisible presence of supernatural forces. Some people believe that its voluntary purring was due to its seeing a ghost. Individuals who are allergic to cats or who suffer from ailurophobia, also "sense" a cat's presence even if they have not seen it. They do so most probably because a cat transmits (by radiation or its aura) some psychic message which precedes its physical arrival.

The night has traditionally been the realm of the devil, under whichever guise he might choose to appear. And the cat is a nocturnal creature. It can see in the dark; its eyes are moonlike; they shine like mysterious green luminaries. And its caterwauling is so eerie. It goes on its hunting expeditions when the shades of night have enveloped the earth. Its arched back, its fur that can bristle and if stroked emits sparks are features that add to its mystery and its assumed occult propensities.

Hardly any other creature is so enigmatic, inscrutable and independent. A cat will do what suits it best and no power on earth can persuade it to change its mind. It has its own apparently "irrational" likes and antipathies.

The cat excels in fecundity. And if witches in their practice really continued the ancient fertility rites, a cat certainly would serve them as the finest aid and symbol, not least by sympathetic and imitative magic.

Cats love to curl up in front of a fire, and the hearth used to be the sacred center of all homes. Once again the feline had chosen the company of a god. The very form the cat assumed lying there was the magic circle and all it implied.

Only a cat is able to speak—silently—with its tail. This has a vocabulary all of its own, so much so that in Greek a cat was literally called "the tail waver." But this very tail also reminded the ancients of the wriggling serpent, so closely linked with the underworld and its dark pursuits.

The cat's proverbial "nine lives" (three times the sacred figure three) is based on its fantastic power of resilience and recuperation. Does not a cat always fall on its feet? It was worshiped as a lunar being, and was not the moon symbolic of constant renewal? Though it wanes, inevitably it will wax again.

Fearsome is the cat's habit and gift to lie in wait motionlessly and for hours on end. Watching its victim apparently so unconcerned, suddenly it will pounce on it and not let it go, as witness its devilish and death-dealing play with a mouse or a bird.

No other animal thus was better suited, almost preselected to be attached to a witch, the priestess of black magic. And as witches were alleged as well to possess the gift of shape changing, cats equally were thought to serve as the most appropriate form for a witch to assume.

There was yet another and significant reason that made a witch choose the cat of all animals. Cats were pets in almost every home. And no one could really ever know for certain whether a specific cat was just the ordinary feline kept to catch mice, or whether it engaged in the dark craft of the occult or was—much more sinister still—a transformed witch!

This explains why in the traditional picture of a witch she retains the cat's claws in her long nails and the cat's green eyes.

## The Black Cat

It is not accidental that of all cats the totally black one is most popularly associated with witches.

Black is the color of the powers of darkness. Without making a sound a black cat could move invisibly through a moonless night, making its mission all the more awesome, weird and puzzling.

In Egypt, where cats had been deified, they were mostly of a sandy color. An all-black cat was a rarity and therefore all the more sinister.

Although merely fiction, the assumption that black cats could see best in the dark added to their notoriety.

Once again legends did their part to increase the occult stature of the black cat. The Greek goddess Hecate and the Scandinavian deity Hel, who were both linked with death, had black cats as their feline aides. No wonder that by this association in the eyes of people, black cats themselves appeared as omens of misfortune and death.

With this background it was not surprising that suspected witches in their torture-induced confessions indicted the black cat. They "admitted" it was not only their most loyal servant, but also that the black cat actually carried within it an evil spirit.

Finally, it was almost a foregone conclusion to use black cats for black magic.

## THE TOAD

Toads are ugly creatures and few people nowadays are attracted by them. But through the ages the toad has played a significant role in the occult. Next to the cat, the toad became the most favored familiar of the witch.

At one time toads were kept as pets. People felt at home with them, just like the cat. And both the feline and the amphibian were beneficial animals. While a cat kept away mice and rats, toads looked after the garden. They fed on the noxious insects and vermin which menaced flowers and plants. This was the real explanation of a superstition among the Ozark hill folk which warned that the killing of a toad would result in cows giving blood instead of milk. The true purpose was to protect the toad from extermination since it filled an essential place in the ecology.

But there was much else that made the toad an object of fear and superstition and gave the amphibian its special supernatural standing. Its very appearance was ominous. It had a warty skin and when touched felt clammy. There was the peculiar manner in which it breathed. And yet . . . out of its ugly, repulsive face shone two jewel-like eyes. This was somehow not in keeping with the rest of the body.

These features would have sufficed to make room for the toad in the supernatural world. It possessed a gift of mysterious quality, however. When agitated, the toad would secrete a substance which, if swallowed, would intoxicate a man and carry him into "another world" of fantastic dimensions.

Peasants became so afraid of the ugly creature that they would not touch it. If they did so, they feared that at the very least they would break out in warts. As contradictory as it may seem, they also applied the ancient magic belief that like could cure like and placed a toad on their warts, convinced they would disappear.

The toad was a creature ignored by ordinary people. Surely it was reserved for those serving the supernatural, and did so for better or worse. And that is how the toad found its right mate or mistress in the witch.

Fancy and fact soon commingled and created a bizarre mixture of tales and practices. Some were recognized as the mere figment of the imagination. Others, though equally false, were cleverly and profitably used by mountebanks to sell their wares. Another notion, apparently the most farfetched of all, has been proved by medical science to be completely correct and has been used in successful scientific experiments.

A rocky knobble between and somewhat higher than its eyes made people believe that the toad carried in its head precious stones. Appropriately called "toadstones," certain "gems" thought to resemble them were marketed as having valuable and magic properties.

It was believed that the stones could be obtained only from a living toad. In fact, the animal could be most cooperative. By its own volition it would eject the stones when placed on a cloth of scarlet, a color it loved.

So-called toadstones were assumed to be an effective antidote for poisons. Swellings, inflammations and pain caused by the sting of a poisonous insect, spider or snake would at once be reduced and relieved by the mere touch of a toadstone. Anyone who had swallowed poison could save his life by taking the stone in powdered form. This would instantly render the poison harmless.

Apart from being a lifesaver, the stones were reputed to be so sensitive to any type of toxic substance that its very proximity would make them change color. That is why toadstones were employed like a Geiger counter or mine detector.

No wonder then that the miracle-working "jewel" became part of coveted amulets which were either suspended from the neck or worn on a ring. Crushed toadstones became a valued ingredient of philters, spells and love potions.

Shakespeare recalled this myth in the famous passage in *As You Like It* (II,1):

> Sweet are the uses of adversity,
> Which like the toad, ugly and venomous,
> Wears yet a precious jewel in his head. . . .

There was the intoxicating effect of the toads' peculiar secretion from their skin glands. The toxic substance was duly identified and given the name of *bufotenine*. This combines the Latin "toad" (*bufo*) and the Greek "tendon" (*ten*). It was also established that the secreted fluid produced elevated blood pressure and was even said to be hallucinogenic. Thus the "wise women" who partook of the elating drug certainly had every reason to feel "high." They were not lying either when they claimed by its aid to obtain extrasensory perception and to have supernatural experiences. Truly, the toad was their most faithful and helpful "servant." They could be genuinely fond of it and grateful for the potent ingredient it provided them for their secret brews.

## The Toady

One of the myths about the toad started with the mysterious substance the toad exuded. While toadstones were seen as lifesavers, the toad itself was regarded as extremely venomous. People believed that if they ate so much as a toad's leg, they would die.

Itinerant quacks soon spied their chance. They made good use of this tall tale to con people into buying remedies they claimed would cure any fatal disease.

To demonstrate the remarkable effect of their concoction, they made their assistant swallow a dead toad—renowned and feared for its lethal nature. And in no time, as everyone expected, the poor young stooge would be writhing in agony. And then, as the climax of the "exhibition," the quack would ask him to take his fabulous panacea. Its miraculous effect would become immediately apparent. The youth's convulsions and contortions ceased in a twinkling. Completely restored to health, he was the "living proof" of the efficacy of the proffered nostrum. Subsequent business was reportedly brisk.

The abuse of the toad in those unethical circumstances eventually transferred its name to the stooge who, for a small consideration, had been prepared to gulp down its ugly dead body. He became known as a toadeater, an epithet which was soon contracted into toady. "Toady" ever since has been used to describe those people who, lacking all self-respect, will show obsequiousness and servility to gain even the slightest favor or advantage.

## WITCHCRAFT AND THE BLACK MASS

Historical judgments have often been made not to present objective truth but, by slanting or actually falsifying events, to justify one's own existence or way of life.

Examples abound. For two thousand years, the Pharisees were never the hypocrites they were accused of being. Their calumniation was due to a deliberate effort by their antagonists to discredit them.

To blame the Jews for the crucifixion of Christ, likewise, did not conform to facts. The Romans executed him and did so not for religious but for political reasons. They clearly did not intend either to please or placate the Jews whose country they had invaded. But the early Christian community, to curry favor with Roman authorities on whose goodwill they depended, had no compunction about blaming the Jews.

Some traditions depicted King Arthur as an evil tyrant, which did not reflect his true character. The notion was created and fostered by Celtic monks in return for the king's robbing of the monasteries for the enrichment of his soldiers.

Typical of the pitfalls in the writing of history was the way in which ecclesiastics (in the Dark Ages the only literate men able to record happenings) dealt with King Arthur's exploits. Because he had shown no friendship to the Church, they either ignored his existence or, if referring to him at all, did so with biased minds, representing him as a man of little valor and even less value.

The identical method was applied by the Church to pagan traditions after its attempt to destroy them root and branch had proved unsuccessful. Realizing its inability to eradicate the old faith, it adopted many of the pagan customs, reinterpreting them the Christological way. That is how the pagan goddess Eostre survives in Easter, and the Roman Saturnalia in the Christmas celebrations.

Christianity, nevertheless, could not absorb all the pagan traditions. Many of paganism's beliefs proved too strong. They threatened the very existence of the young Church which saw in them a powerful subversive force.

Their continued existence intruded dangerously on the territory staked out by the Church. And as all other measures of persuasion— promises of salvation and threats of damnation—had failed, Christianity took the final step. It proclaimed such beliefs and practices as heresies and the work of the devil. Anyone aiding or abetting them was denounced to be in his service and consequently had to be punished and eliminated. To get rid of those who still followed pagan tradition was considered a sacred duty and a hallowed task, undertaken for the sake and in the name of God.

That is why, from the fifteenth century, the practice of the old religion was declared "witchcraft." Contrary to the "established" faith, it was blasphemous and illegal, punishable by death. Those not toeing the official Christian line exposed themselves to prosecution. If they did not confess and present evidence of their devil worship, torture was applied on the luckless victims. And the outcome was a foregone conclusion.

The promised confiscation of all goods owned by the convicted suspect in itself made the authorities or those in their service only too anxious to prove their point. The application of tortures appealed to the basest instinct of man and attracted the sadist whose lust to inflict pain was now sanctified.

But history never stands still. Suddenly, things were reversed. As the Church had ruthlessly used its power to denigrate pagan belief for the sake of self-preservation, so now did those opposed to Christ and dedicated to the devil use their power. Defiantly they applied every means to proclaim and foster their own way of life and pattern of belief.

Instead of serving God and Christ, they worshiped Satan. Fearing his power, by paying homage to him they hoped to gain his favor. And exactly as the Church had done by taking over the old pagan rites, Satanism did now with Christian practice—yet with a significant difference.

It certainly used Christian symbolism and hallowed tradition but did so to mock Christianity. In obscene travesty of everything holy to the Christian faith, it tried to raise and exalt the devil, Christ's archfiend and the "original" god. And that is the background of what came to be known significantly as the Black Mass—the central ritual of Satanism.

To caricature Christian tradition was not Satanism's sole purpose. Its aim went much further. By twisting, distorting and almost literally turning upside down everything that was sacred to Christianity (its symbolism, liturgy and practices), it would be able to render the divine enemy powerless, and thus to destroy God's dominion to replace it by the rule of Satan.

The Black Mass practiced now as part of witchcraft is of recent origin. Some aspects of it are mere fiction. Their description is based not on factual evidence but on fertile imagination prompted by the wish either to sensationalize or defame the diabolical cult.

Books by the Marquis de Sade, for instance, contributed their share in spreading fantastic tales. It was to be expected that the esoteric and arcane nature of the Black Mass gave ample room for statements which could not be disproved and therefore catered all the more to man's love of the erotic, the exotic and the bizarre.

## The Ritual

Every feature of the Black Mass is aimed at parodying Christianity and blaspheming its holy sacrament. The cross was turned upside down; the candles, black; the chalice was filled not with wine but with blood; the host was pierced or at least covered with a dagger and it might be defiled with urine or excrement; prayers were recited in reverse.

The most distinctive part of the service, however, was its sexual quality. A naked woman served as the altar, and the mass was celebrated on her stomach or buttocks. The men and women participating in the worship did so completely naked as well and their copulation was its climax.

But the suggestion that such a mass was planned as a mere orgiastic frenzy, sex for the sake of sex alone, is incorrect. The naked woman taking the place of the altar was meant to symbolize the generative power of nature. The entire liturgy revived the ancient fertility rites which, by sympathetic magic, tried to ensure the fecundity of all growing things: in the soil, in cattle and in men. Even the coitus practiced was seen as an expression of love.

Another school saw in the witches' nudity even less of lustful eroticism. A witch wanted to be as close to nature as possible and therefore deemed it essential to discard anything that could act as a barrier, as clothes would. She also regarded her body as a center of radiation of psychic power which she was ready to release. But this she could never do if her body was enclosed by any garment. There was magic power in nakedness which witches felt made them truly free to let themselves go in ecstasy, just as in the Book of Samuel (1 Sam. 19:24) prophets were said to have done. Not least, by taking off their clothes, witches eliminated all artificial social distinctions. As they desired to be at one with nature, so in their nudity they became equal among themselves.

No doubt, because the pleasures of the flesh played an eminent part in the worship of the devil, it drew congregations to whom traditional religious services had little to offer. The Black Mass became a telling phenomenon of the modern counterculture. More so, it revealed man's attraction to the mysterious and his innate concern with fertility of any kind. In the ritual of the Black Mass he returned to pre-Christian days when, thousands of years ago, his ancestors worshiped the dark forces of nature with all their hearts, their minds and their bodies.

## VOODOO

Truly dramatic is everything that concerns voodoo: the circumstances that created it, its practice, effect and possibly even the origin of its name.

Voodoo was created in the West Indies by African slaves who had been bought from their African kidnappers by slave traders and transported to the Caribbean. In battling for survival, they needed an identity. This they found in a common faith which they molded out of diverse tribal customs.

The term voodoo has had an equally exciting background. One claim is that it goes back to a religious movement founded in Lyons, France, by Pierre Valdez, in the late twelfth century.

Valdez had been deeply agitated and appalled by the extravagant practices of the Church of his time. The splendor and luxurious living were totally un-Christian, he proclaimed. They misrepresented and actually contradicted the original Christian faith. To reestablish it in its pristine state became his mission. Soon he was teaching a religion that included esoteric and occult elements.

His work did not go unheeded. Others joined him in his battle for reform. They called themselves after their leader. But soon their name became corrupted and known as Waldenses or, in French, Vaudois.

As was only to be expected, the Roman Catholic Church vehemently opposed the new sect and decried it as diabolic and outright sorcery. Its efforts to suppress the heresy, however, were counterproductive. The Waldenses gained adherents in far-off regions of France. They did not die out either with Valdez's death. They experienced a revival in the sixteenth century.

In 1677 Spain ceded Haiti to France and soon French missionaries of the Roman Catholic Church went to the island to convert its people.

They were shocked by their primitive cults, the witchcraft they practiced and the spells they cast. The priests identified them with the
heretical sect of the Waldenses and applied their name, in the Creole
dialect, to those Haitians. It did not take long for "Vaudois" to
deteriorate further and to become finally voodoo, a name that has held
on.

Another, perhaps more convincing, derivation of the term voodoo
is traced to one of the West African regions from which the Haitian
slaves had come. There (in Togo and Dahomey) the black race had
worshiped a powerful fetish and guardian spirit called Vodo. And it
was likely they had taken with them from home, as the only possession
they could carry away, their god, which in the West Indies eventually
took on the form of voodoo.

No man can live without some kind of faith, no matter what it is
called. It gives meaning to his existence and integrates him within his
group. However, the coexistence of several beliefs within one region
among people still immature and intolerant may lead to unending
strife, internecine wars and personal unhappiness.

This unfortunate experience threatened the thousands of blacks in
Haiti at the end of the seventeenth century. As slaves they worked the
sugar plantations, and, to prevent them from joining in a rebellion,
they were scattered all over the island by their French masters.

This made the Africans feel completely lost. Lacking any common
worship, having come from different parts of the African continent,
they had no common bond. They were deprived of a shared faith
which could give them a feeling of oneness and, in the eyes of their
cruel employers, a source of hidden strength.

With the passing of time, however, they were able to create a new
type of religion. This combined the various traditions they had
brought from their different homes far back in Africa. Added to it was
a special new fervor born out of the circumstances in which they lived.
They sought their gods' help to end the slavery, poverty and unhappy
and lonely existence which had become their fate.

Meanwhile, the Christian missionaries who had arrived from
France tried their utmost to convert the slaves to their faith which, they
promised, would bring them, if not freedom, the salvation of their
souls. While their efforts were far from successful, some of their
Christian practices were adopted by the blacks. And that is how

voodoo came into being. It joined the newly created synthesis of primitive African rites with West Indian flavor to Roman Catholic symbols and practices. The new religion was a veritable hodgepodge of diverse rites and teachings.

In their worship the Haitian blacks thus called on Christ and their old-time idols, particularly their snake god. Their hymns glorified African gods and the saints of the Church. They prostrated themselves in front of an altar adorned with the images of Christ, Christian saints and pagan deities. They placed on the altar, together with offerings of fruit and of flowers, bottles of drink and clay jars which they believed to contain their ancestral spirits. The voodoo cult included as well the sacrifice of fowls, goats, dogs, pigs and bulls.

The beating of drums at ever-increasing speed accompanied their chants which, the longer they lasted, grew ever louder. And the pounding of the congregants' feet on the earthen floor and the clapping of their hands produced a highly charged atmosphere of ecstasy and delirium.

As the volume and speed of the music and singing increased, the worshipers broke forth into wild dancing, with their eyes rolling, whirling around and around. They writhed in frenzied contortions, in intoxication, eventually reaching a stage of trance.

The climax of the voodoo service was the moment when the adherent imagined that a spirit had taken possession of his body to control it completely. Now, so he believed, Loa, one of the voodoo gods, rode him like a horse. And while he carried this invisible god on his back, so the voodoo worshipers were convinced, he gained supernatural power to prophesy and to cast spells. When, finally, with the frenzy spent and the trance over, the "divine horseman" returned to his former self, he remembered nothing of what he had said or done during his period of "possession."

The traces Roman Catholic tradition has left on voodoo are apparent in many of its features. The drums used at the service are blessed like church bells. Incense is burned and holy water sprinkled with a leafy branch on those gathered in communion with the supernatural.

The ritual is celebrated by a priest (Houngan) or priestess (Mambo) whose ecclesiastical power is great and fearsome. Using black and white magic they can heal people or harm them. They can even cause their death. Going beyond the realm of this earth, they also claim the gift to make the dead rise again from their graves to assume the odd nature and phenomenon of the zombie.

Once voodoo had taken hold of the slaves, they practiced it with increasing fervor. And the more their white masters oppressed them, the stronger their ardor became. Soon the French landowners who had mercilessly exploited the slaves felt threatened by the slaves' newly gained "supernatural" power. Aware of their practice of voodoo with its occult power and working of magic, the Frenchmen became frightened and panicky.

In 1791 the Africans rebelled. They struggled for many years till they won their independence in 1803. They now formed their own state and became the first black race to become independent and change a colony of a foreign power into a proud country of its own.

Voodoo had accomplished this mission. Its practice had helped a race to survive and to achieve its national goal. But voodoo did not die then. On the contrary, with new vigor it continued its hold on African people and did so far beyond the West Indies. It spread to other parts of the world and particularly so into Latin-American countries farther south, which added their own local traditions.

# CHAPTER EIGHT

# In Search of Protection

## SAFEGUARDS

For man, one of the more mysterious and frightening evil forces he faced was what we now identify as "sickness." It attacked a man's body or mind. An invisible and inveterate foe, it struck him without distinction of rank, and often resulted in excruciating pain, weird demeanor, convulsions and, possibly, in death.

Man soon realized that no ordinary remedy or weapon could counteract those hostile powers and render him immune from their malevolence. Only something endowed with extraordinary, supernatural potency could do so. Magic was needed to enable him to withstand, annul or repel the evil and protect his body and mind, his home and his property from attack.

This battle for survival in an evil-infested world led man to create his first safeguards. These could be strictly positive, by adding to the strength of the individual in need of protection. Or they could seek to employ negative, destructive power against the "assailant." Their magic could rest on the defense or go over to the attack.

Man acquired his safeguards from earliest times and did so all over the world. Specimens have been excavated from prehistoric tombs. As they evolved, they developed roughly into three categories: the talisman, the charm and the amulet. Each has its own story to tell.

The talisman was used in a positive sense: to attract good luck generally.

A charm was employed not only to counteract misfortune but to inflict it on others. As distinct from the talisman and the amulet, it frequently was reserved for a particular purpose. A charm, for instance, was worn to protect a woman during her pregnancy, to aid her in childbirth or to prevent a miscarriage. It could likewise help in cases of snake bite. This, of course, limited the efficacy of a charm in its application and duration.

An amulet was credited with the power to act as a passive protector against evil influences that threatened a person, an animal or a home.

Eventually the three types intermingled and were hardly differentiated. Therefore, in modern times, their names are used almost indiscriminately. They certainly share similar traits in their origin and in their purpose to serve as a guard against the malevolent forces of darkness which could play havoc with man's life and luck.

Man's earliest choice of a safeguard was any object that attracted his attention by some conspicuous and unusual feature. This feature was due, so he reasoned, to some particular spirit and occult power it contained and hence would serve him in his quest. It might be a branch, a root or a stone the peculiar shape or quality of which had caught his eye. A stone that strongly reflected the sun or shone in mysterious colors almost asked to be used as an amulet. On the other hand, it might happen that a heavy thunderstorm, having washed away the topsoil, laid bare stones that had been buried for a long time. Yet to the primitive mind they appeared as the very thunderbolts that had just fallen from heaven and, because of their assumed celestial source, must surely be endowed with magic properties. They were God-given amulets.

Anything linked with the deity, by its very nature, was most obnoxious to the devil and therefore could be made to serve as the best of charms.

Thus the deity's name in itself, displayed in whichever way chosen, became a favorite repellent of evil design.

Anything related to divine power would serve to drive away the devil and act as a luck bringer. This explains the frequent use of blue beads for both man and beast. The choice goes back to the days when people actually believed that God dwelt in heaven and that heaven was up in the sky. And because the natural color of the sky was blue, this was regarded as a divine color to which, obviously, the devil or any of his kind were allergic. They just could not bear its sight, and the moment they were confronted with blue, they would surely rush away. Therefore, to wear blue beads would ward off misfortune.

Sex equally was recognized quite early in time as a supreme force against evil. Sex not only created but it sustained life. Replicas of the phallus were stood up or suspended as a guard and protector. They were employed as such in the most diverse circumstances: for the security of a newborn child, the crop, man's cattle, dwellings and city gates.

Ornaments, too, originated as amulets. Bracelets, pendants and brooches were worn not for the sake of adornment but as a shield to repel attacks of invisible mischievous beings. A man who had found stones with holes in their center was convinced of the occult power that dwelt in them. No doubt, the resemblance of the "holey stone" to a woman's private parts that served as the gateway to birth added to its life-giving and luck-bringing qualities. And threading through the hole the first man-made chain (plaited of grass or hair), he suspended the stone as an amulet from the neck of the person to be protected. It was the first charm.

The Bible contains numerous references to the use of amulets. Most of them are obvious. This includes how the patriarch Jacob collected from members of his household divine images and earrings they had treasured, worn or carried with them "for luck," to bury them under a tree. His purpose was to wean them from idolatrous superstition.

But one instance is most intriguing because of the way it has been misinterpreted and is still misunderstood to this very day. It concerns Cain. When he had killed Abel, so Scripture tells (Gen. 4:15), God had marked him with a special sign. This passage led people to speak of "the brand of Cain" and see in it a symbol of punishment and contempt. But however widespread and generally adopted, this view completely misses the point. Cain received the tattoo from God "lest any[one] finding him, should smite him." It was not meant as a token of disgrace but, on the contrary and paradoxically, as a protective charm—to safeguard the murderer's life.

Some general rules apply to amulets, charms and talismans. They were only effective if they came into a man's possession as an unsolicited gift. Asked for or paid for, they would never work.

To intensify their potency, magical formulas were to be written in red ink which was the color of blood. This symbolized and magically took on the form of that vital fluid.

As children and women were weaker than man, they were particularly exposed to misfortune. Therefore their need of protection was greatest. That was the reason why they were showered with every type of safeguard: with countless brooches, pendants, rings and necklaces. They were not an expression of wealth but of fear. The prophet Isaiah was able to list (3:18-24) in his time twenty-four varieties of "ornaments" cherished by "the daughters of Zion."

The ultimate effect of safeguards might well be psychological. It may depend on the power of positive and negative thinking, the influence of mind over matter. Someone strongly believing that an object would bring him good fortune or help him in surmounting adversity, might well be so strengthened in his effort and aim that, indeed, it will affect and actually change his luck.

## THE AMULET

There were varied reasons that prompted man to produce his amulets. The ancient assumption that like cures like is reflected in the phrase "hair of the dog." It was believed that a person bitten by a mad dog could be saved from hydrophobia by someone applying to him "a hair of the dog that bit him." Nowadays this principle is followed in the case of an alcoholic hangover. It was imagined that a man the worse for drink would feel at once his own good self again by having another drink.

The use of the cowrie shell for an amulet goes back to the identical reasoning. Closely resembling the female private parts, it was thought to possess their life-giving power. To wear it would increase one's sexual potency. Placed on graves, the shells would ensure the immortality of the dead buried below.

As varied as was their purpose so was the form amulets could take. They could be a precious stone, a sacred inscription or a magic symbol. They could represent part of the human or animal body: a foot, a hand, a paw or a tail. A flower, a root or an herb could be adopted as an amulet. A five-, six- or seven-pointed star symbol was another magic protection.

## In Judaism

The position in which amulets were placed was often closely related to the specific task allotted to them. Fixed outside a home, obviously an amulet was meant to keep out the devil or any other evil bringer. That is the purpose of the horseshoe, the hex sign and the original meaning of the *mezuzah*, the small scroll Jews still affix to the right-hand doorpost of their homes. Apart from containing a sacred text (a Hebrew quotation from the Bible), the mezuzah carries outside, and very conspicuously so, one of God's powerful names: *shaddai*— "the Almighty."

Yet another type of amulet was a script. To carry a sacred text on one's person has been a universal custom from primitive times. This would make evil forces catching sight of it immediately take to flight.

Jews thus fortified themselves with Hebrew quotations from the Bible. They were written on minute scrolls and placed in two boxes which Jews bound by means of leather straps on the left arm ("opposite the heart") and on the center of the forehead ("between the eyes"). Referred to in Hebrew as *tephillin* (for "prayers"), they were called in Greek *phylacteries*. This term, which the New Testament uses, stems from a root which very appropriately explains their function as a guardian and a protector. Nowadays put on only by Orthodox Jews while saying their weekday morning prayers, originally and at the time of Jesus they were worn throughout the day.

## In Islam

Moslems adopted the Jewish custom but improved on it. In fact, they went to extremes. They used to carry on them not just excerpts from, but an entire copy of, the Koran. They did so not only to have an opportunity of studying its text at all times but to be magically protected by it wherever they went.

They tied the book to their body by means of a cord, known by the Arabic *himalah*. And, according to some authorities, it was this very word from which came the term amulet in the sense we now use it. *Himalah* simply referred to the fact that the book was "bound" to the person or "carried" by him by means of a cord. But by the amulet's "attachment" to the holy book, the Koran's sanctity rubbed off on it and eventually, in people's minds, conferred on it equal efficacy to guard and protect. That is how a mere string, as it were, assumed the new, meaningful and magic role of an amulet.

## Other Etymologies

The very description of the amulet certainly has puzzled men, and the controversy it aroused could only add to its mystery.

One unsubstantiated claim traced the word amulet back to a Greek sacramental vessel known as *amay*.

Often quoted is Pliny's *Natural History*, in which he mentions *amuletum* and gives numerous applications for it. The amuletum could preserve man from trouble, act as an effective prophylactic against sickness and could be taken as a medicine. And, Pliny adds, it could guard man against magic, evil spells and incantations.

Apart from such general prescription, the Roman writer cites individual examples: By planting cyclamen in his garden, anyone could keep evil beings out of his home and render harmless any poisonous drug. And he goes on to relate that it was for this reason that people colloquially came to call the plant *amuletum* in his time. The snout of a wolf fixed on a door would ward off evil. Spitting into the right shoe would immunize its wearer from being hurt by demons. A piece of amber tied to an infant of delicate health would give it extra resistance.

Pliny's mention of the amuletum proves its widespread use in his age. But, he does not supply its etymology. Apparently the Latin root of the word is *amolior*, which meant "driving away," "repelling" (of danger) and the "baffling" (of evil forces). This would account for the amulet being truly "an instrument of defense."

Since many amulets were actually worn on the body, in Hebrew, very appropriately, they were known as *kamea*. This word is derived from a root meaning "to bind" or "to knot." However to see in the English "cameo" an heirloom of the Hebrew *kamea*, as has been frequently done, is incorrect.

## THE TALISMAN

The talisman as a luck bringer has traveled a very long way. The word was introduced into the world by the Arabs. Hence it carries traces of their tongue. *Tilsam* was the Arab description of a "magic charm." This was not of their own creation but merely a takeover from the mystical cult of the Greeks.

Oddly enough, in Greek the root of talisman—the beginning of the word—most literally was the "end." This in Greek is *telos*, which has become part as well of *teleology*, the doctrine of "final" causes.

The *telos* took on the form of *telesma* whenever Greeks referred to the "completion" of a ritual and the "fulfillment" of a consecration. It was their description of an initiation.

This *telesma* was then adopted by the Arabs who gave us the talisman. In its metamorphosis, the talisman became not only an object in its own right but was gifted with supernatural power. Totally changed, it now denoted the numerous types of discs, stones or figures inscribed or embossed with magic letters, words or signs, believed to bestow great benefit on their owner.

A talisman may owe its existence to mere chance. Because an object was carried or worn on one specific auspicious occasion, such as the defeat of an enemy, the birth of a child or cure from a fever, it was deduced that the good fortune, if not actually due to it, was at least linked with it. And from that moment the person in question would not join in a fight, commence a task or set out on a journey without it.


## CHARMS


Everything in life is relative and dependent on the circumstance of time and place. That one person's meat is another's poison is much more than just an adage. Monogamy and polygamy—both have been declared moral and essential, only by different peoples and religions. Whether the black cat that crosses your path presages good or ill fortune, again depends on whether you find yourself in an Anglo-Saxon country or on the European continent.

To be called a charming person nowadays certainly is a compliment. But in the fourteenth century no one would have welcomed being regarded as such, as anyone who was found "charming" could well have been destined to be led to the torture chamber, if not to the gallows or the stake.

Charm was magic power which could "take in" and bewitch people. The very history of the word tells that charm consisted of neither looks nor demeanor. Derived from the Latin *carmen*, charm was a song and specifically referred to the magical chant and incantation used to bewitch people or to render a solemn rite truly effective.

That explains Bizet's choice of *Carmen* as the name of the central figure of his opera he called after her. She was the alluring gypsy girl who knew how to fascinate men so that, forgetting their duty, they would help her escape the forces of law and order.

The story of the *Lorelei*, made famous by Heine's poem and the music to which it was set, tells of such a siren who, from a rock on the right bank of the River Rhine, by her song enchanted and lured boatmen to their death.

But even charms of that type did not last. And eventually the original song or recited formula, too, would solidify and take on the form of an object. The once verbal spell was made permanent by misappropriating the original magic song to designate objects which, worn or carried by people, would ensure their good luck or their protection against evil, disease, defeat or disaster.

The tinkling sound made by the many charms hanging from a woman's bracelet thus is a feeble echo of the early enchanting song. However, by its very noise it is also thought to drive away devils.

### "A Chip Off the Old Block"

Contagious magic has had its specific place also in the realm of charms. Anything that once had been in contact with an object or person endowed with sanctity was imagined to have caught some of its qualities.

Idol worshipers treasured chips of the *Asherah*, the sacred pole and branchless tree trunk they adored as a symbol of vegetation. Even to own one of its splinters would magically bestow on them fertility. Hence the origin of "chip off the old block."

### To "Touch Wood"

To "touch wood" for luck has the identical roots. Originally people touched what they believed to be splinters of the holy oak of the Druids or the cross of Christ. By their close association in either case with a god or savior, they were regarded to have become holy as well and therefore effective in warding off the devil.

## THE HAND

Widespread (perhaps particularly so in North Africa) is the use of the protective hand as an amulet. Its choice was very logical. If threatened, a man instinctively puts his hand in front of his face, and especially in front of his eyes. And what worked in the physical realm would surely be effective, only probably more so, in the world of the occult. It is not surprising, therefore, that the hand played a significant role in ancient magic as a means of warding off evil. It might explain the existence of numerous "hand prints" among primitive wall paintings discovered in caves.

If the hand so used represented that of a renowned figure, its magic potency was multiplied. And most famous of all such hands was that of Mohammed's daughter, Fatima; replicas became popular in all Moslem countries and in regions under Moslem influence.

Yet another hand became a desired object, but in weird circumstances. Its name would never suggest its purpose nor its gruesome origin. "The hand of glory" was highly treasured by thieves. They firmly believed that if they used it their felony would not be discovered. This hand of glory itself was actually that of a hanged criminal, severed from his body at the gallows. It had to be duly processed by being pickled in an earthenware jar with salt, saltpeter and peppers for two weeks, and then dried in the sun.

When ready, the hand became a candleholder. The candle was not the ordinary type: It had to be specially made out of virgin beeswax, a hanged man's kidney tallow and some sesame seed. If burglars used this combination of the ghoulish candle and gruesome hand candlestick while ransacking a property, this ghastly torch would bring them luck, for the light it shed would send the occupants into a deep trance.

## THE MASCOT

In all his sophistication, modern man continues to fear unknown forces that might threaten his safety and life. Without admitting it, he fortifies himself with special guards both in animate and inanimate forms. They are referred to as mascots.

They may decorate the hood of his car or be a special pet for a regiment. Their purpose, however, is not ornamental or the result of animal love. They are present and cared for for the sake of protection of those they serve and by whom they are being looked after so assiduously.

There is a straight line going back from the misinterpreted "winged angel" on the Rolls-Royce and from the goat led by soldiers on the parade ground to the fetish providing assurance and courage to the most primitive tribes. Tracing the line from present to hoary past shows once again how, in spite of all technological progress, man has advanced but little in surmounting his fears and changing his attitudes.

The mascot has its origin in prehistoric times, when masks played an important role in society. Carved or painted, made of wood, bark, animal skin or wickerwork, masks have been used all over the world. They were produced in the weirdest and most striking forms. Their purpose was twofold. From the very beginning they were meant to serve both as a camouflage and as a deterrent. The masks were donned to conceal the identity of the wearer lest evil spirits might recognize him. The grotesque mien of these masks was intended to frighten off any demons that might otherwise inflict on him untold harm.

The sorcerers engaged by individual groups soon realized the important possibilities such a mask presented, and they made use of it. In the sorcerer's dangerous occupation it protected him from the demonic agencies with which he had to deal. But incidentally, its bizarre features enhanced his status and increased his psychological hold on his own people who came to view him with even greater awe. Eventually, the mask became his very badge of office.

*La mascotte* was an Old French word for "the little mask." And it was through its association with the sorcerer who wore it as his tool of trade that he himself was called after it. Even when witch doctors had become a matter of the past, their designation survived in French (Provençal) dialect to describe both the mask and its wearer—the witch and the sorcerer! This is the origin of the modern mascot which survives in the army, on automobiles or in the pockets and purses of men and women who treasure it as a precious possession which they think ensures luck but which originally was seen to keep away misfortune.

The universal application of the mascot was due to one of the strange coincidences with which life abounds.

Even enthusiastic music lovers and those learned in the history of song hardly would know the name of Edmond Audran, who died at the age of sixty-one, at the beginning of this century (in 1901). A church organist in the French city of Marseilles, he also composed comic operas. In the 1880s these were so popular that they had runs of more than four hundred nights. How short-lived is fame!

And yet it was one of the comic operas he had composed in 1879 which gained him immortality, if not in the world of music, then in that of the occult. The central figure in the opera was a character whose extraordinarily good fortune could not be due to mere chance or be the result of ordinary circumstances and the law of averages. It could only have been caused by some supernatural agent. And looking for an appropriate figure and name, Audran picked from the Provençal dialect the "little sorceress"—the original mask: *La Mascotte*.

It was the phenomenal success of the production and its catchy tunes that made a local slang word world famous, and which in the Anglicized "mascot" survives as the name for objects or living beings imagined to bring good luck.

## THE PENTACLE—THE STAR OF THE MAGICIAN

The five-pointed star of the pentacle has always served as a powerful magic sign both to conjure up demons and keep them at bay. Its potency was due mainly to the supreme sanctity of the three triangles making up the sign. The triangle itself was already a mighty symbol because it represented the holy trinity in ancient Egypt, in India and in the Christian faith. Its triplication in the pentacle surely would render it thrice powerful in repelling and dominating evil forces.

This five-pointed star received its name from the Greek *penta* for "five." This figure is well known from its presence in the Pentateuch (the *Five* Books of Moses), the pentathlon (the athletic contest of *five* events), and the modern Pentagon (the *five*-sided headquarters of the U.S. military establishment).

There were additional Greek names for the star as well and each mentioned its five corners. The symbol was also called a *pentagram*, a word derived by adding to the Greek "five" the Greek for "letter"— *gramma*. Its pattern was imagined to be constituted of five times the letter *alpha* (the first letter of the alphabet), joined in five different positions. Hence an alternate description used for the pentacle was *pentalpha*.

It was the actual star shape that added further strength to the magic of the five. After all, a star was a heavenly body, a well-known sign from above.

Descending from the heights of heaven down to earth, the pentacle was also identified with the footprint of supernatural magic-working powers and thus seen as and called "the wizard's foot" and "the Druid's foot."

The fact that it could be drawn in one continuous line without ever lifting pen from paper made the pentacle all the more significant. It came to be called "the endless knot" and was believed to tie up forces that otherwise were beyond control.

## The Star in History

The pentacle played a prominent magic role in man's dream-distant past.

Its design has been found embossed or drawn on pottery excavated from ruins of the ancient Chaldean city of Ur. In Egypt it decorated the statue of the god Anubis, "chief of the divine pavilion" and, not surprisingly, "lord of the necropolis." Druids wore the sign of the pentacle on their sandals.

The Koran called it King Solomon's seal and based this description on a legend. It told how this mighty king, so adept in the world of the occult, used it whenever he dealt with any supernatural forces. He had received the seal as a gift from God. Its five-pointed body was made of iron on one side and on the reverse of brass. Both surfaces carried the ineffable divine name. Whenever Solomon sealed an order that directed, restricted or banned dark, demonic forces, he used the iron side because of the well-known effect of that metal on evil powers. But whenever he directed or activated the powers of light, he sealed his instructions with the brazen surface.

The pentacle always maintained an important place in the realm of the arcane and magic. It was adopted by the Jewish Kabbalah, the Rosicrucians and Freemasonry.

Painted as an emblem on the doors of homes and stables, it was thought to keep out witches. Authors drew it at the head of their manuscripts or displayed it on the first page of their works, believing that it would keep out the devil and thereby bring luck and success to all they had written. Even letters addressed to rulers or friends were prefaced by the symbol.

Magicians engaged in occult work often wore the pentacle on their chest. At times they traced it in the sand in order to stand at its center. They thought they would be protected against hostile interference.

Even the star that is said to have guided the Magi to the manger in Bethlehem was believed to have been five-pointed. Was not the young Christ child to grow into the savior, and by his sacrificial death on the cross, would overcome the powers of evil?

Architects included the pentacle in their design of churches not as a decoration but to serve as a potent magic sign against demonic agencies who might try to enter the sanctuary.

The five points of the star were interpreted as a magic combination of the four elements of life with the supreme spirit of the unseen, that mysterious source of all occult work, as the fifth. Great care had to be taken in the manner the pentacle was drawn and which way its rays were directed, whether one or two of its points projected upward. Potentially the star could serve good or evil. It all depended on which of the two principles it represented. If one of its points was directed upward ("in the ascendant"), good would prevail, because magically it caused the superiority of the spirit. But should the pentacle be reversed and thereby two of its points be uppermost, they would be symbolic of the two-horned goat. The star then would conjure up the powers of darkness, cause the predominance of their malevolent influence, in short, serve Satan and black magic.

By its very shape the pentacle seemed a microcosm—it mirrored the universe, the macrocosm. Many illustrated magical texts show man thus "fixed," with his arms and legs extended sideways within the framework of the five-pointed star.

The pentacle, by its countless traditions, became highly charged with sacred potency which accounts for its multiple application in life throughout the world.

## THE HEXAGRAM—THE STAR OF DAVID

When in 1905, at Capernaum on the shores of the Sea of Galilee, a synagogue was excavated which had been built in the third or fourth century, an astounding discovery was made. Its frieze displayed the six-pointed star, but the star was not set off in any conspicuous way, for next to it were the pentacle and the swastika. No specific Jewish quality was then attached to what has since in recent times come to be known (though erroneously) as the Star of David.

The hexagram, indeed, was a well-known sign in almost every part of the world and occurs as early as the Bronze Age.

In spite of its frequent use later for purely decorative purposes, the hexagram was originally employed as a powerful magic sign. Perhaps as a stylized star, it was thought to transfer from the skies celestial power down to the earth, to serve man in his continuous fight against the forces of darkness.

Certainly, in medieval days its magic use was widespread and took a variety of forms. Alchemists saw in the star a fusion of their two symbols for the antagonistic elements of fire and water. A triangle with its apex pointing upward stood for fire, while reversed, the triangle signified water. The combination of the two represented and magically achieved harmony.

Others recognized in the star the footprint of the demon of the night. They claimed that its display would not only summon the evil spirit but give man the power to subdue it.

The double triangle was also seen as the representation of the universe. The six corners stood for the four points of the compass and the lower and upper regions. The sign therefore contained in essence the entire cosmos. This gave its user supreme magical power. The number of its six points symbolized the perfect figure and thereby rendered the star a potent magical instrument.

In Persia, Zoroastrians used triangles to symbolize the two supreme forces battling with each other for supremacy in the world. The triangle with its apex pointing upward stood for the forces of light and goodness. Darkness and evil—opposing them—were symbolized by a triangle that was reversed, its apex pointed downward. Interlaced, however, the two triangles became the hexagram which fettered, as it were, the world of darkness to the light, leading to the triumph of good over evil, of spirit over matter.

The hexagram has been subject to numerous misconceptions. Even its description has been misleading. In early times, it was referred to as the seal of Solomon, a name which, to add to the confusion, was also applied to the pentacle. Paradoxically, it was not from the Jews but from the Moslems that this name was adopted. The identical legend that accounted for the pentacle was cited for the hexagram. It had been engraved on the seal or ring given by God to Solomon with which to control the demons.

Most commonly, however, the hexagram was called the Star of David. But the original Hebrew—*Magen David*—does not refer to a star at all. Literally, it speaks of the shield of David. And as the shape of the sign certainly does not resemble a warrior's guard, the correct translation of the term points to the original magic potency *shielding* man from supernatural evil agencies.

The shield of David is of rather late coinage. Completely unknown until the fourteenth century, it only appeared then for the first time in a mystical Hebrew manuscript.

Therefore the shield of David (always now wrongly described as the "Star of David") is not an indigenous symbol of Judaism. Many centuries before its adoption as such, Jews had used the *menorah*, the seven-branched candlestick, as their emblem, just as Christians had used the fish prior to their adoption of the cross. It was only in the seventeenth century that the hexagram became a symbol of Judaism. And possibly it came about by one single incident.

In 1354 King Charles IV gave the Jews of Prague the right to have a flag of their own. And they chose for reasons unknown the six-pointed star. From Prague the star's association with the Jews spread all over the world in the centuries that followed.

A suggestion proffered by M. Guedemann (and explained in detail in *The Judaic Heritage* and *The Unknown Sanctuary* and referred to later in this book in the chapter on the Druids) discovers in the Star of David the perpetuation of yet another error. According to Guedemann, the star has no link with the ancient Hebrew king but was part of Celtic magic. Correctly it should be called the star of the Druids who used it in their magic fight against the Drudes, the ghosts of the night. Hence, King David is not connected at all with the symbol now called after him.

The term hexagram, on the other hand, did not, as one might have imagined, obtain its name from the "hex," that bewitching power of magic lore. *Hex* here is the Greek word for "six." Accurately the name thus speaks of the outstanding six points of the two intertwined equilateral triangles.

Rarely has a single sign stood for so many and varied ideas and been subject to so much diversity of opinion and error. But nothing could surpass the tragic paradox of its application in modern days. Used for millennia as a life-preserving, luck-bringing magic sign, the Nazis changed the star into a badge of shame and of horror. They used it to brand millions of Jews destined to suffer most cruel persecution and horrible death.

## THE SWASTIKA

Solicitude for the sun and man's own fate so closely linked with the solar body were responsible for the design of the swastika, one of man's earliest and most universal symbols. There can be no doubt that its very first, prehistoric usage was magical. Representing the wheel of the sun that rolled across the skies, its advance was facilitated by aid of its "feet," those short protrusions at the four ends of its spikes. It was, therefore, of significance to observe their "right" (original) direction. This had to lead "forward"—from East to West and in no circumstances be widdershins.

The swastika was part of a great number of primitive cults. It was employed by pre-Columbian American Indians, by Hindus and by the ancient Chinese. It served as a powerful emblem in Britain from 3000 B.C. to A.D. 300. Archaeologists unearthed ancient Etruscan tombs marked with the swastika, and have found it displayed in Buddhist inscriptions on the rock walls of caves. Just as it is part of the symbolism in the synagogue of Capernaum, so early Christians used it as an emblem on the walls of the catacombs in which they secretly practiced their faith, away from the Roman persecutors.

The term swastika is of Sanskrit derivation which has led to the claim that the sign originated in India or in the vicinity of this ancient cradle of civilization. Fusing the two words for "good" (*su*) and for "being" (*asti*), it was meant to express, and more so to promote, good fortune and luck.

Later on, the Greeks, interpreting the swastika according to their own culture, called it *gammadion*. They did so after their character *gamma*, as they saw in the sign the fourfold combination of this letter.

*Fylfot*, from the Middle English, is yet another but much later and specialized designation of this magic sign of the sun. This term is almost exclusively used by modern antiquarians, who adopted it from their interpretation of its solitary appearance in a fifteenth-century manuscript in the British Museum in London. The context in which it is found led them to believe that it described a swastika-patterned device or ornament which architects used to ''fill [the] foot'' of a stained-glass window.

The frequency of the swastika's occurrence has puzzled modern man and has led to numerous explanations over and above that linking it with the original sun worship.

Professor Max Müller took note of the existence of two types of swastikas: one with its short arms turned to the right, and the other with its arms turned to the left. He suggested that this dualism intended to represent both the vernal and autumnal sun. Each type, in its turn, was employed to ensure the sun's safe passage and return.

Others have attributed a sexual meaning to the symbol. The swastika represented, they said, the sexual union of the male and female and did so by the joining of two bent lines at their center. Therefore it was deemed a potent magic symbol in the promotion of fertility.

Fire, regarded as the gift of the burning sun, was recognized as essential for the preservation and furtherance of life. And the swastika was thought to depict one of the primitive fire-producing devices. Specimens of that type have been dug up in several parts of the world, from Asia Minor to China. These consisted of two short pieces of wood which were joined at their center. Their four ends were bent at right angles with which to anchor the ''cross'' to the ground. The fire was kindled by the friction caused by turning a ''lighting stick'' at the juncture of the rods. And the replica of this primitive ''generator'' of the necessary energy was seen as a magic sign making sure that man would never be bereft of that life-giving force.

The ''crooked cross'' was also explained as the magic ''fixing'' of the divine fire on earth sent down from heaven in the form of two zigzag flashes of forked lightning.

In Scandinavian countries the swastika represented the hammer of Thor, the northern god of thunder and lightning. Each time he wielded his hammer, it created a deafening noise, after having lit up the blackest of nights for a split second. No wonder that it filled the men of those days with mortal fear, prompting them to adapt it to their own occult purposes: to protect man against the personified gigantic evils of disease and disaster, so that these might in their turn also be awestruck by the emblem of Thor's powerful hammer.

The Indian sect of the Jains, on the other hand, interpreted the sign as a symbol of progress. It represented, so they believed, the four significant stages in evolution which led from the lowest protoplasmic existence to the final release of the soul from the body. When in a holy ceremony they traced the swastika on initiates' foreheads as a mark of blessing, they were certain that it would ward off evil.

Eventually, everything about the sun's wheel, the fire and sex was forgotten. But the early vital role the swastika had played in the life of man lingered on in his memory, and it became a general magic sign, a bringer of good fortune and a defense against evil.

In 1920 Hitler took over the sign from the German Baltic Corps which had adopted it as a badge on their helmets while serving in Finland. They in turn had copied it from the Finnish air force which used it as its distinguishing mark. But it was Hitler who changed the ancient sacred and protective symbol into a figure that spelled death-dealing horror.

## THE SIGNET RING

Signet rings combined several features to render them truly potent in man's battle against mischievous forces and to make them a preservative of good luck. They were first worn (around the finger, the arm or near the heart) not as an ornament nor as a sign of dignity or some ever-ready die to validate documents and decrees with a seal. Their original purpose was magic. It was an amulet of supreme power because of the precious material of which it was made, its magic circle and the sacred name or inscription it bore.

## THE ST. CHRISTOPHER MEDAL

Folk etymology has enriched life with many beautiful tales. People felt that behind every famous name there must be a story. To find it, they gave free rein to their fantasy and their made-up explanations often gained wide currency and at times were adopted "religiously."

Moses, for instance, is a typically Egyptian word, meaning "child." It is well known from the names of such renowned Pharaohs as Ramses and Tutmoses. However, the Bible related its choice to the fact that the child was "drawn out" of the waters of the river and therefore claimed that his name was not Egyptian at all but Hebrew!

St. Christopher's medal owes its name and fanciful explanation, its very existence, to imaginative folk etymology. It is believed to ensure safety to those who travel.

Hardly anything is known about St. Christopher, this early member of the Church. The only facts recorded relate that he lived in Asia Minor in the third century, converted from paganism to Christianity and suffered martyrdom by the Romans.

To mark the occasion of his baptism, he was given the new name—Christopher. In the Greek language of his time, this tried to express beautifully that henceforth he "carried Christ"—in his heart.

The very lack of any other information about his life gave room for fantasy. Numerous legends arose that soon surrounded his figure.

Christopher was explained to mean "one who bore Christ" and that he had done so literally and not merely metaphorically.

A giant of a man, he had lived a humble existence on the banks of a river. One night he had heard a child cry for help to cross the water. Without hesitation Christopher answered the call and lifted the lad onto his shoulders to take him to the other side. But the deeper he stepped into the river, the heavier the child seemed to grow. It was as if he was carrying not an infant but the burden of the world. And so it was. The child was Christ himself who was carrying the sins of man. And this occasion had merited the man to receive as his new name that of "Christ bearer."

Frequent repetition of the story made it grow ever more in its wondrous dimensions. It was now told that originally Christopher had been a soldier. His fervent wish was to serve the most powerful master. And to find him, he wandered the world. Eventually he heard of a king whose might was supposed to excel that of any other ruler. Duly he enlisted in his army. Soon, however, Christopher discovered that the alleged invincibility of his lord was not real. The mere mention of Satan frightened him.

Obviously he had to change masters. And as Satan appeared to be so much more powerful, he gave his services to him. But again it did not take long for him to realize that even the Evil One had a chink in his armor. The moment Satan was confronted with the sign of the cross of Christ he squirmed.

At long last the soldier had found his right master. Christ was the mightiest power far and wide and him alone would he serve. To do so, however, he soon was made to understand, he had to devote all his help to men who were God's children. For that reason he settled on the bank of the river at the very spot where pilgrims had to cross it on their way to Jerusalem.

Day and night he stood by with his stout stick to assist if not actually to carry the pilgrims safely across the river. Its waters ran deep and many times prior to his arrival they had claimed a victim. But from the moment Christopher took up his task as a ferryman, no one drowned again.

And then the story continues to lead up to the very climax—the original incident with the Christ child.

Christopher—the "one who bore Christ"—was now adopted as a safeguard to all travelers. He became their patron. Many churches painted his figure as a mural opposite their entrance. Any passerby by merely looking at it would suffer no harm or accident on that day: "After you have seen Christopher you go safely."

Eventually the painting was replaced by a medal. This became a popular amulet, which even ecclesiastical decrees issued during the recent period of updating the Church will have difficulty devaluing. But it all started in the dreamland of man and his wish to explain what was beyond his comprehension and to gain courage and assurance along his dangerous journeys.

# CHAPTER NINE

# Places, Peoples and Seasons

## HELL

In all ages and societies man was convinced that death could not be the end of life. Surely death was merely a gateway to some other existence. The belief only differed as to the form it took.

When the geocentric world image prevailed, the universe was imagined to be constructed in three tiers. The earth stood in the middle for "this life." Above was heaven and below, the netherworld. Just as we continue to speak of "high" and "low" to express "good" and "evil," so ancient man allocated the two regions to the "best" and the "worst." Heaven was the seat of the gods and a haven for the righteous. The netherworld became the realm of the devil, a place of punishment for the unrighteous and therefore "hell."

And however enlightened man becomes and contemptuous of outdated ideas, he has not divorced himself from their legacy. We go on enjoying "heavenly bliss." We continue to be "in seventh heaven." Pious Jews and Christians, when saying their prayers, might look toward the sky—to God in his heaven, as if he really had his abode there!

Correspondingly, people curse others to "go to hell" or try their utmost to "give them hell."

All this is reminiscent of the story told of a fervent unbeliever. He was proclaiming in public his conviction of the nonexistence of a deity. When interrupted by a heckler, who piously tried to defend his faith, he retorted scornfully, "Thank God, I am an atheist!"

Surprisingly, the word "hell" originally meant merely "hidden" and "covered up." Nothing further was suggested by the name. Only when you took off the lid, as it were, did hell reveal all it concealed.

## THE NETHERWORLD

It is wrong to assume the netherworld was originally exclusively for the wicked. In most mythologies it was the abode of everyone who had "passed away" and therefore had not only passed "on," but "down." The differences that evolved were later elaborations as to the kind of existence the newcomers led and their specific terms and conditions of tenancy.

The Egyptian *Book of the Dead* deals particularly with these questions. It expresses the view that the netherworld could prove a very pleasant place. But this depended on the actions taken by those left behind. If they mummified the body of the deceased and, with great care and punctiliousness, made use of spells and special ceremonies, they would indeed ensure that the dead was alive "down below." He would then be able to pursue in the nether regions almost the identical type of existence he had enjoyed up "on top."

On the other hand, the Babylonian residence reserved for the dead was far from inviting or pleasant. Those entering it had to do so without their clothes. They had to pass seven gates. It was a "land of no return," enveloped in darkness. Nevertheless, even in this Babylonian "hell," the fate of the dead could be eased by proper burial and the provision of food and drink by those "above."

## SHEOL

Vague indeed is the early Hebrew concept of the abode prepared for the dead referred to as *Sheol*.

Sheol itself is a very obscure term. Authorities agree it stems from an Assyrian notion, but which one has been subject to controversy. A number of suggestions have been made. They link the Hebrew *Sheol* with Assyrian roots describing a kind of "chamber" (*shilu*), a "hollow" structure or the act of "asking." This would point to Sheol as a court of scrutiny and investigation. Yet another derivation discovered in Sheol the Assyrian "west" (*shillan*). If correct, this would make Sheol the very first example of referring to death as going "west."

With such diversity of interpretation, it is no wonder that English translations have equally given Sheol a great variety of appearances. It has been described as "a pit," "a grave," or—misleadingly—"hell."

Sheol was situated beneath the earth. It offered a dark and gloomy sort of existence in a very inactive, semiconscious state. The residents had lost all concern for life and the ability to feel and to think. They were more shadow than real.

No one was exempted from having to go there once death had struck. However, on special occasions the deceased was given leave and could return to earth temporarily!

Regulations were completely democratic and no one was able to pull strings. There were no class distinctions. Irrespective of the influence they had wielded on earth, or their wealth or poverty there, now only their way of life counted. The good were rewarded and the evil punished.

The Hebrew Sheol must have been in the hands of early "developers." It seemed to have been the only region out of bounds for God. Even the most righteous, confined to its precincts and anxious to contact God, could not do so. He was refused admission. However, soon the view changed. God was thought to be able to assert his power in Sheol as well and to manifest himself even in that dark and dismal netherworld.

## HADES

The Greek Hades has been greatly misunderstood. The original, classical Hades was not a locale but a divine person, one of the twelve Olympian gods.

A son of Kronos, he was the lord of the underworld. Not evil himself, he was the most impartial of judges, determined to punish with unpitying sternness anyone who had done wrong. He took great pride in his "underground" work. Jealously he guarded its population, always concerned to see an increase in its numbers.

A god of his kind was not worshiped by the living. There were no temples and celebrations in his honor. At best, some people offered him black sheep, but while doing so they carefully looked away from the altar. Most men preferred to forget about Hades since, sooner or later and whether they liked it or not, they would come under his rule. At death, their soul was bound to enter what should properly be called "the house of Hades" but erroneously was shortened to Hades.

As in most descriptions of the underworld, in Greek myth, too, detailed accounts of its topographical features and the type of existence it offered were given. Some said that, appropriately, Hades was located in the west—at the going down of the sun. Souls of the buried entered the subterranean district by the River Styx and were ferried across by Charon who charged an obolus for this service which the thoughtful had placed in the corpse's mouth.

There was a strict division between the souls of the righteous and the wicked. Both were allowed to carry on a shadowy type of life, similar to that which they had led "above." The good, however, had the special bonus of gaining entry to the joys of Elysium, the Isles of the Blessed. The wicked were forced to suffer the torments of Tartarus. To make escape impossible, Hades had appointed Cerberus, the fierce, three-headed dog, to be chief warden and guardian of this underground prison.

## GEHINNOM

"Hell " was never included in the fundamental pattern of belief in the Jewish faith. Nevertheless, at times it came to play a significant role. The Jews first assimilated the idea from neighboring nations or, during their exile, from the Babylonians. They then gave it their own personal interpretation and the world of the occult, the *Gehinnom*—a very special term for hell.

When Gehinnom came into being it was solely a geographical site in the south and southwest of Jerusalem. This was known as the "valley of Hinnom" (in Hebrew *ge-Hinnom*). It was then still, in the words of Milton (*Paradise Lost* I, 103), a "pleasant" place.

However, the valley became associated with a horrible cult, dedicated to the god Moloch. To serve him and obtain his favor, parents were said there to have "passed [their] sons and daughters through fire." Child sacrifice was an atrocious religious practice based on ancient mythological tradition. This to the Hebrew mind made the valley a hellish place. It so incensed Jeremiah that he prophesied (19:6) that because of the evil deeds committed there, the murderous place would be renamed "the valley of slaughter."

It has been suggested that in reality children were passed through the fire there not to burn them to death as a sacrifice but to refine their souls in an initiation rite.

Whatever happened, the valley itself, linked with pagan rites, became so notorious that it was regarded as defiled. To show their contempt, the citizens of Jerusalem came to use it as a refuse pit, for the burning of rubbish and animals' carcasses. Gehinnom became the site for executions and for the burial of criminals or of those ritually unclean. That is how the very sound of the name Gehinnom struck horror in the hearts of people. But in the Hebrew Bible it was never used in the actual meaning of hell.

The clouds of smoke rising out of the valley (whether from the burning of children or refuse), seen from afar, intensified the macabre note of Gehinnom and gave it an entirely new dimension. From earliest days it was believed that God or the gods meted out punishment to the souls of sinners by means of fire. And by fusing the ancient tradition with the actual site, Gehinnom eventually became synonymous with the fiery pit in which the wicked dead had to pay for their sinful life.

The Hebrew Bible thus merely gave us the name of Gehinnom and its association with abomination, death and fire. All other details ascribed to it stem from later days. They arose from the writings of the New Testament and from those books the rabbis had excluded from the official canon of Hebrew Scriptures for being uninspired. For this reason, they had concealed them, and they later became known as the Apocrypha, literally, "hidden writings."

In the Gospels, the Hebrew "valley of Hinnom" (Gehinnom) was called Gehenna, from the Greek. From them came the popular idea of what Gehenna meant in all its imagined tribulations and anguish, changing it into the modern hell as the place of eternal punishment.

Although many of the Gospels' vivid and terrifying descriptions of hell were used metaphorically, they were soon taken literally. Thus people came to believe that the souls of the sinner with "weeping and gnashing of teeth" would actually be cast into "outer darkness," into a "lake which burned with fire and brimstone."

Man's imagination ran riot in its description of hell. Speculations as to its extent, location and nature were boundless. The "valley of Hinnom" seemed much too small for a place of its kind and therefore it was now seen merely as one of the gates to hell.

Hell itself was imagined to be of enormous size, located deep down under the ground. Its fires, which burned continuously, were at least sixty times as hot as any fire on earth. Their smell was that of sulfur. Yet, in spite of the ever-burning flames, mysteriously, hell stayed as dark as the darkest of nights.

## A MATTER OF TIME

Authorities were not unanimous as to the duration of punishment for sinners. Some thought that a sinner had no chance of reprieve or parole at all. They saw the world as either white or black. Once a man, by his way of life, had chosen the path to hell, there was no possibility of return. On the other hand, there was the view that generally won the day, that the maximum sentence, even for the worst offenders, could not exceed a period of twelve months of hell. And oddly enough this ancient belief still determines Orthodox Jewish practice in honoring the dead.

Traditionally, this is done by the recital of a prayer known as "Sanctification" or in Aramaic, *Kaddish*. One of the most sacred and revered customs, even the most unobservant Jew continues to practice it. Every service—no matter of which type and on what occasion—concludes with the Kaddish, in which those mourning a beloved, join.

A son "says Kaddish" for his parent for exactly eleven months after the burial and, if he strictly adheres to tradition, does so at the daily services, both in the morning and at night. It seems today such a beautiful and reverential observance that it is hard to believe that it all began as a magic rite very much concerned with the realm of the supernatural.

A legend has been quoted as the origin of the prayer. It told of a strange sequence of dreams experienced by Rabbi Akiba, the renowned second-century Jewish scholar. One night Akiba had seen in his dream the figure of an unhappy-looking man carrying a heavy load of wood. And then, still in the dream, the rabbi had asked him why it was that he suffered. The man explained he was really dead. Because of the sins he had committed on earth, he was condemned to suffer the agonies of hellfire. To increase his punishment, he himself had to carry the wood that was to nourish the flames that burned him.

The man further related he had left behind a son. During his lifetime he had failed in his duties to introduce him even to the elementals of his faith. If Akiba could trace and instruct him to say just one Hebrew prayer, this would quench the fires of hell.

On awakening, Akiba sought out the boy. The moment he found him, he started teaching him one of the most sacred of Jewish prayers —the "Sanctification" (the Kaddish). And the boy recited it with fervor and devotion.

On the following night the father reappeared to Akiba in a second dream. Gratefully he informed the rabbi that the boy's "saying Kaddish" had saved his soul and canceled the remainder of the sentence.

Ever since, every son says Kaddish for his parents, in case their souls need redemption. But as it was thought that for the worst sinner the maximum sentence was a stretch of twelve months in hell, no loving child could ever believe that his father or mother could have been so wicked as to merit the extreme penalty. And to express this trust, Kaddish is said for only eleven months, though mourning lasts for an entire year.

## STONEHENGE

The origin of Stonehenge has mystified countless generations of men. First, there was the stupendous size of its giant boulders. Where did they come from? Dating back four thousand years, they had been transported all the way to the vast expanse of what is now Salisbury Plain in the English county of Wiltshire. Who could have lifted them? What accounts for the choice of the actual site and what were those monoliths meant to represent? The monumental stones formed a circle, a shape that has always been endowed with magic potency. What did the builders—whoever they were—intend to gain by the massive rocks thus arranged?

There was the enigma of its very name. Certainly, it was not the original one. But why was Stonehenge so called? From the Old English, it means "hanging stones." But what was the source of this odd description? Was it because the stones reminded later people of gallows perhaps? Or was it—as in the case of the hanging gardens of Babylon—because the stones or their lintels seemed suspended in the air?

Whose plan was it to put up huge boulders in the solitude of a vast plain? And what was its initial meaning, the driving force and impelling belief that led man, with infinite patience and precise astronomical accuracy but with only the aid of primitive tools, to erect such a structure? And why did he then surround the entire complex with a magical bank and a ditch? Samuel Pepys wrote that only "God knows what their use was."

Another astounding fact was that this unique type of statuary, apart from forming a magic circle, was aligned accurately with certain celestial constellations rather like the entrance passage of the Great Pyramid. These included significant moments in the movement of the sun, the moon and the stars, such as the equinoxes and solstices. On midsummer day, for instance, the sun rose exactly above what is now known as Stonehenge's Helle stone. Only men gifted with extraordinary perception and advanced mathematical and astronomical knowledge could have designed such "settings."

New revelations were constantly made and never ceased to overwhelm men's minds. As late as 1953, an observer saw for the first time carvings of axes and daggers on the surface that had passed unnoticed for thousands of years. He saw them because of the peculiar slant of the light then illuminating the stones at sunset. Undoubtedly, they were symbolic and magic signs.

The awe-inspiring character of Stonehenge, coupled with all the many questions, was bound to rouse man's curiosity and fancy in quest for answers. Through many centuries he has tried to explain this archaeological and architectural wonder.

This circle of stones, one tradition claimed, was a unique monument. It did not honor heroes of the past but was intended as a warning to the present and all future generations never to desecrate the Sabbath. Once upon a time, a group of young girls had amused themselves on this very site by dancing around in a circle. But they had done so on the Sabbath, the sacred day of the week which, instead, they should have observed in prayer and meditation. To punish them, God had turned them into stone!

In other myths, the stones were humans who had been magically petrified for other reasons.

Twelfth-century Geoffrey of Monmouth linked Stonehenge with the Saxon invasion of the country. It had been built, he claimed, to serve as a massive grave and everlasting monument for early Britons who had been brutally murdered by an unnamed Saxon king. The "magic circle" of their entombment, indeed, had become so sacred that many later English kings had been laid to eternal rest within.

There were legends, too, that concerned the actual stones. A typical assertion was that they had come from an African land originally. A race of giants had carried them first to the mysterious island of Erin where they remained until the wizard Merlin enlisted the aid of the devil to steal them from an Irish woman. They were then tied up, and magically flown across to Stonehenge, to the very spot where they have stood since.

Apart from the wealth of myths that centered on Stonehenge, many other explanations have been advanced by students of religion, folklore and history. One claimed that the Romans, while in Britain, had built Stonehenge as a shrine to honor Uranus, their god of heaven. Others believed it had served as a coronation court for Danish kings. It had been a burial place of sacred dimensions, an altar for human sacrifice, the first Druidic temple and, as was suggested by a British astronomer in 1966, an early sort of computer to calculate and chart the movements of the stellar bodies.

It is probable that Druids used Stonehenge to practice their mystic rites thousands of years ago, but they did not build the sanctuary which predated them.

Those versed in the science of comparative religion can recognize in the basic features of Stonehenge certain common phenomena met with in other, ancient structures and monuments of like nature in different parts of the world.

Stones and windows erected in so clever a manner and with such detailed astronomical knowledge that their direction coincided exactly with the position of a star at a definite hour on a certain day were discovered in sacred observatories high up in the Andes in Machu Picchu, the lost city of the Incas, in Bolivia's Tiahuanaco, and at Chichén Itzá at Yucatan in Mexico.

Stones have always played a significant role in man's worship. They were regarded as the abode of spirits and of supernatural power. Special divine qualities were attributed to them, more particularly if they were meteorites or as outstanding by their monumental size as were those used at Stonehenge.

But even more significant was the use of sacred circles in man's veneration of the gods. They existed in the land of Canaan. The Bible tells of rites practiced in Gilgal, a name that now describes a geographical site but originally meant a "circle" of stones. There were many Gilgals. Best known of all is the site of identical name, on the east border of Jericho, at which Joshua made the Israelites encamp after their crossing of the Jordan. Significantly, it was there he set up twelve stones when celebrating the Passover (spring) festival at that very spot. Long after Joshua and the Israelites had passed through Gilgal, it continued to serve as a pagan sanctuary. Its cult was gravely denounced many centuries later by the Hebrew prophets.

All these considerations, parallels and further finds have led to generally accepted conclusions.

Stonehenge undoubtedly was built as a temple to the sun. This solar body was worshiped from its magic circle of stones by men who recognized in the heavenly disc the supreme giver of life and growth.

The construction of Stonehenge was commenced as long ago as the late Neolithic times—four millennia ago. The monument did not attain its final shape and dimensions at once. It was changed through the centuries. It is obvious now the builders followed a method of trial and error in certain parts, and that the original plans were altered during the actual construction.

In addition, Stonehenge also reveals unmistakable Minoan-Mycenaean traces and therefore it is not a purely local structure but incorporates features imported from that ancient civilization which flourished in the Mediterranean area during the second millennium. It was in the great Homeric days of the Achaean culture that Stonehenge reached its present-day monumental appearance.

Whatever its origin and the data of its construction, Stonehenge is a timeless, mysterious monument of man's veneration of the supernatural. Awed by the powers beyond, with superhuman strength and magnificent cooperation and coordination, he built this cathedral at the dawn of history—a feat of supreme enthusiasm and architectural genius. Its huge stones indeed look like symbolic gateways into a dimension still beyond man's grasp.

## THE DRUIDS

As Stonehenge, so the Druids have presented many mysteries and have been subject to misunderstanding. But their influence and their legacy cannot be disregarded. Their beliefs and practices have made their mark on the history of religion and magic, and the world of the occult owes them a tremendous debt.

Two millennia ago, the Druids were so powerful that wherever they made their home—in pre-Roman Gaul, Britain and Ireland—they could not be ignored. Out of their midst came the Celtic priesthood so adept in magic.

Druids believed in the immortality of the spirit and its indestructibility. They also were convinced that it migrated after death from one body into another. Such view gave life a deeper meaning and simultaneously took fear out of death.

A horrifying aspect of the early Druid cult was their original offering of human sacrifice. It was so repugnant a custom that the Romans prohibited it and made it their main reason to ban the faith. Probably, then, Druids, while discontinuing the actual sacrifice, symbolically offered effigies in its stead. These they enclosed in huge baskets which they burned in honor of their gods.

One theory strongly suggests that when British children burn effigies of the wicked Guy Fawkes on November 5, they are not actually celebrating the anniversary of an aborted political plot to blow up both king and Parliament, but are unknowingly reinacting the human sacrifice, one of the most gruesome of Druid rituals.

The training of Druids was very intense and extended over a period of many years. Yet their traditions were never entrusted to writing. They were handed down orally. This was done for the obvious reason, so Caesar maintained, that no unqualified person should ever be able to come into possession of their secrets and work their magic. This makes it difficult to assess the Druids' place in the history of man.

More than a thousand years after their having become outlawed, the Druids experienced a revival. In 1717 the Most Ancient Order of Druids was established. Its members claimed to take up and carry on the noble practices of the Druids. They regarded and called themselves their legitimate heirs. Among their most publicized ceremony nowadays is the annual celebration of the summer solstice at Stonehenge.

## The Druids' Name

Many opinions have been voiced as to the true meaning of the Druids' name which originally was not a term for "a master of knowledge" and "a wise man" as is now generally assumed.

The name has been linked with several significant features of Druidic tradition. True or false, the derivations have much to tell of the Druids' fundamental beliefs and customs.

Their worship was generally held in ancient oak groves, and the oak tree occupied a central place in their cult. It was regarded as sacred, believed to enshrine a living spirit and to work magic. Why this was so is easily understood if it is recalled that oak forests were common all over Europe at the time, and that man was aware of how his life depended on the tree.

Its fruit, the acorn, nourished his cattle. Its wood provided him with shelter, warmth and the means of transportation across water. Its parasite mistletoe's viscous berries in their white waxen color reminded him of his own semen which caused him to believe they contained the gods' life-giving sperm. And as the oak rooted deep in the soil, with its branches reaching out toward heaven, it was seen as a powerful link between earth and sky.

Thus, the Druids looked upon the tree with awe, conscious of the blessings it could bestow. In devout prayer they acknowledged its power and with sacrifices implored the tree to supply them with its abundant bounty.

The Druids' very name echoed the oak and was derived from the Sanskrit for "wood"—*drus*. The identical linguistic root was also responsible for the Gaelic "oak" (*darach*) and even the English "tree."

Another phenomenon of the Druids' cult was its association with the wren and the role this bird played in their preoccupation with the occult.

They hunted to catch and to keep the wren for their solemn ritual of divination. By interpreting its twittering, the Druids claimed, they were able to foretell the future. They partook of its flesh, eating the wren sacramentally, as the Christian does the host. They believed that by doing so they absorbed the bird's mysterious gift of divine power into their own bodies. Convinced they became like the wren, they took on its name.

"Druid," this theory claims, goes back to the Welsh word for wren—*dryw*. This root, it is interesting to know, also gave birth to the English "true" and the German *treu*. Hence, a Druid acquired from the wren not only his name but, literally speaking, its deeper meaning as well as a "truth teller." It was a very appropriate choice of title for men who claimed the privilege of being able to contact the divinity to learn from it what the future held.

## Seeing and Molding the Future

No matter whether the Druids' name spoke of the divining bird or the sacred oak, they were renowned for their ability to foretell the future.

They did so not only from the singing of a bird but from the sneeze of a man and the babbling of a brook. Another of their methods was to enshroud themselves in the hide of a newly slain bull. This, they believed, would transfer all the animal's strength to them. Lying down then near a site that they regarded to be inhabited by a spirit, they imagined to commune with it, gaining the information they sought.

Most descriptive perhaps of their manner in foretelling the future was *baile*, a Gaelic term applied to them. Very similar to the biblical Hebrew *nabi* for "prophet," it actually described utterances of an uncontrolled frenzied nature.

Druids claimed not only to have the power to look into the future, but also actually believed they were able to influence it by their charms and spells. This they did on varied occasions. They accompanied armies in wars, for instance, so that with their spells they could create confusion among the foe, causing his defeat.

Their "appointment" anticipated that of modern army chaplains who originally must have served a similar purpose. What otherwise could account for their presence on the field of battle among the opposing forces? Any religion—at its best—taught peace and not war, and decried any killing as murder. But as on both sides men of God led soldiers in prayer for victory—to whose voice should God listen? It amounted to blasphemy: to a competitive spiritual tug-of-war with the deity at the center.

No wonder Druids were in great demand even by royalty who made them their most trusted counselors. Their secret knowledge was regarded as so precious that Scottish kings sent their sons to be trained on the Isle of Man, one of the strongholds of Druidism. And Druidic magic was employed in the rivalry between kings who hoped to gain supremacy by means of it.

The bards of Wales and Ireland may well be authentic successors of Druid singers. Their poetry intended not merely ecstatically to celebrate the feats of national heroes of the past but to foretell the future.

## The Druids' Origin

Who the Druids really were, whence they came and when is still an unsolved mystery. All that can be given is a short summary of some of the possibilities.

That they had been a priestly class created around the fourth century B.C. by Celtic settlers in Gaul was the hypothesis proffered by T. D. Kendrick. These "original" Druids had then mixed their own Celtic traditions with those they found among the native Gauls. When later on they spread out yet farther afield, this time to Britain, they added to their already enriched lore elements of the cult and culture they encountered in their new domicile.

After intensive research, Sir John Rhŷs came to another conclusion. In his *Celtic Britain* he traced Druidism back to an earlier age. The Druids had been a pre-Celtic aboriginal race whose home had been both Gaul and Britain.

Lewis Spencer in his *History and Origin of Druidism* voiced the view that the Druids dated as far back as 2000 B.C. They had their beginnings in the food-gathering age, when oak forests first began to cover great parts of the European continent.

Other authorities saw in the Druids non-Aryans who had come all the way from ancient Egypt.

Wherever their original home had been, Druids finally had become firmly established in both Britain and Gaul where the Romans clashed with them in their conquest of the north. The Romans were so appalled by their practices, which then included human sacrifice, that they were determined once and for all to put an end to a faith which, in their eyes, was unenlightened, primitive and inhuman.

However, they could not really eradicate beliefs that dwelt deep down in the soul and the mind of a people and molded their hopes and fears.

Druidism thus never completely died out. It merely went underground. As was only natural also, its clandestine existence caused many of its former notions, if not to disappear, at times to take on new features and change almost beyond recognition. Essentials were forgotten and incidentals assumed an unjustified, central role.

As Druidism also preceded by many centuries Christianity in the very countries where it flourished, it can be taken for granted that, when adopting the new faith, former Druid priests came to occupy similar positions in the new hierarchy and preserved in their new office (or cleverly adapted to it) their previously Druidic beliefs and customs.

### Druidic Legacies

There are numerous examples of the survival of Druidic thought and practice.

Many of the later witches may have been defrocked Druidic priestesses.

In those far-off days, Druid women had their own rights and, distinct from other cultures and religions of that time, had their acknowledged place in their society. Like the men, they not only participated in, but also led the religious cult and acted as priestesses. When eventually the Druids' faith was outlawed and suppressed by the Christian Church, the Druidesses might well have continued their duties as witches and thus made their lasting contribution in the field of the occult.

It cannot be by mere accident either that *Walpurgisnacht*, Lammas, Halloween and Candlemas—the four great Sabbats of the witches—coincide with the four great annual feasts of the Druids.

### The Tonsure

Druid priests shaved part of the hair of their head. It was a peculiar custom which led J. Rhŷs to suggest that the Catholic priest's tonsure was actually also a Druidic survival.

### The Star of David

Some authorities have claimed that even the so-called Star of David originally was a Druidic magic seal. This hexagram, they said, was first employed by those Celtic priests in their supernatural rites.

Only later ignorance and the erroneous rendering of its name came to link "the star" with King David. In reality, it should be called—as the earliest spelling is said to have been—the star of the Druid. In Hebrew lettering, this would imply a minute change in lengthening the upper bar of just one letter and rounding its corner. This would make out of the "V" (the Hebrew *vav*) of David the "R" (the Hebrew *resh*) of Druid, and it must be remembered that early Hebrew was written without vocalization, using consonants only.

## Kissing Under the Mistletoe

To kiss under the mistletoe is a welcome custom at Christmastime which few people realize is derived from the ancient Druids. Its original purpose was not just to steal a kiss and do so duly authorized by an established tradition. On the contrary, it is a relic of the Druidic belief in the fertility-promoting qualities of this divine "golden bough," which they might have looked upon as the oak's genitalia.

The mistletoe, a parasitic plant, grows in bunches entangled with branches of the holy oak which by its mere association made it sacred. Its seed had been carried there by birds. The magic potency of the branch, according to the Druids' belief, extended far beyond the realm of fecundity. Thought to cure almost any disease, the mistletoe frequently was referred to by the name "all-healing." Sprigs fixed above doorways of homes were said to keep away lightning and evils of many kinds.

No wonder the Druids treated the mistletoe with utmost awe and venerated it in solemn rites. Clad in white robes, they cut it off with a golden sickle and distributed its bunches among the members of their congregation.

There is a striking parallel, if not a causal chain, between this ceremonial of the severing of the branch and the partaking of the holy eucharist in the Christian Church. Just as only gold was regarded pure enough to touch the sacred plant, so the inside of the chalice serving the consecrated wine (said either to represent or actually to have changed into Christ's blood) had to be of pure gold.

## THE GYPSIES

Gypsies have always been misunderstood. Their name is even a misnomer. It is all that is left of "Egypt." When they migrated from India, their homeland, around the year A.D. 1000, they stayed for a while in Egypt—or so it is claimed. And people, indifferent to the true origin of gypsies, called them after their last port of call—Egyptians. Soon this name became corrupted to gypsies.

The gypsies arrived in England in the sixteenth century, in Shakespeare's time. It is well to remember that in *Antony and Cleopatra* he referred to the Egyptian queen (who really was Greek) as a "gypsy." He did so for two reasons: not only did she rule Egypt, but also because she had deceived Antony "like a right gypsy."

People have always looked down on gypsies. They saw in them rootless vagabonds roaming the countryside who could never be trusted. Their low reputation is reflected in the fact that in English "to gyp" became synonymous with "to cheat."

As if to save the face of the gypsies, other derivations of the ugly word have been suggested, though all of them are spurious. The verb was traced to "gee up," a local English dialect term for to treat roughly. Another rescuing attempt linked the cheating "gyp" with "gippo." This was the name of a seventeenth-century jacket worn as part of the uniform of servants who looked after Oxford undergraduates. Eventually, it was identified with the valets themselves who were renowned for their dishonesty and thefts.

Gypsies themselves shun the name gypsy for it expresses only contempt and dislike. They call themselves Roms or the Romany people after their native language. It is actually a Hindi dialect related to the ancient Sanskrit. But, just as in the case of Yiddish, it contains numerous words picked up from the tongues of the people through whose countries they passed on their wanderings. Romany is derived from the Hindi word *rom*, meaning "man."

Gypsies generally are dark-skinned and slightly swarthy nomads, with jet black hair and dark eyes. They love their freedom and never settle down. Moving about all the time, their wagons are their castles. But the very fact of their being so strange and withdrawn added to the mystery of their existence and to the suspicion with which they were viewed and treated.

Romanies are proud people and, where still unassimilated, exclude from their midst anyone who has married a person not of their race. Such banishment is regarded as the most severe penalty in their unwritten code of law.

A non-Rom they call a *gaujo*. This word, very much like our "barbarian," described an uneducated "rough peasant." (Is there any connection perhaps between this gaujo and the *gaucho*, the Argentinian cowboy?) Thus they paid back in like coin the feeling of condescension and comtempt shown to them.

## The Gypsy as Fortune-Teller

From the East they carried with them a gift of the psychic and a predisposition for the occult. They claimed special magic powers of "glamour" and "fascination." Their amulets and talismans were thought to be effective in warding off evil and attracting good luck.

To "tell fortunes" became their special trade, which they usually did from the lines in a person's hand or by means of cards.

The gypsies' renown in the realm of magic and witchcraft was unsurpassed. A Scottish Act of Parliament in 1579 spoke of "the idle people calling themselves Egyptians [!] . . . that fancy themselves to have knowledge of prophecy, charming, or other abused sciences." One medieval tradition oddly asserted that the Magi who had come to Bethlehem from the East had actually been gypsies who had told the fortunes of the holy family by palmistry!

It was their way of life that created in gypsies their special aptitudes. Moving about in wagons, they came to know all about horses. Horse-dealing became one of their occupations, especially at fairs. Above all, by their constant outdoor living, they acquired a closeness to nature now lost to other men. The earth was their "divine mother," their supreme deity. And it was their being in touch with the soil, roaming among trees and plants, that gave them an intimate knowledge of things beyond the ken of ordinary people. This applied particularly to their discernment of the medicinal qualities of herbs and berries which they used in healing the sick. Their acute sense of observation intensified their unique faculties in fortune-telling and magic.

It was not only their heritage from the East, however, but also the treatment they had experienced from the West that gave their faces an inscrutable look that, at the same time, appeared uncanny. Even back in their original home, more than a thousand years earlier, they had been downtrodden by their own countrymen and compelled to belong to the lowest cast of untouchables.

Mostly illiterate, they passed on all their traditions by word of mouth, a fact that made them even more mysterious. Lacking an alphabet, they invented secret signs of their own which deepened the suspicion that surrounded them. In their code of secret markings, they made use of any material or natural growth at their disposal. It could be a simple piece of rag of a definite color, leaves, a wisp of grass arranged in a certain shape or branches, again placed in a special way.

### Gypsy Music

Even more expressive than their sign language was the message of their music, their songs and their dances, which they handed down from generation to generation. However, there has been much controversy over the authenticity of modern "gypsy" music.

The gypsies' violin has its own occult story. It was said to have been Satan's gift and specially created by him in a proper transaction in which he fulfilled the desire of a gypsy girl who had fallen deeply in love. Unfortunately, the man she wanted was not of her race, and he did not return her feelings.

Desperate, the love-sick girl turned to the devil for help. He promised to arrange the match, if she would pay for his services with the souls of her own family.

Nothing was too dear for her to gain the object of her love. And the bargain was made. Duly the devil used the souls of her nearest kin to create the first violin ever. The father he turned into the sound box, the four brothers into four strings and the mother into the bow.

Finally, the devil presented the finished product to the girl. With the souls of her people, as it were, she produced the most divine (!) soul-stirring music on her devilish instrument and thereby was able to ensnare the alien youth who had ignored her.

No sooner had the two become united than the devil reappeared to carry them off into hell. He left behind the violin, which had served its purpose. It fell into the hands of a gypsy boy who made it his own. And ever since gypsies have been masters in bewitching the world with the music of their violins.

## The Gypsy's Names

Every gypsy has three names. The first is heard only once. The mother says it so softly at the moment of her child's birth that no one else can hear it. And she will never entrust this name to anyone. It is the gypsy's "real" name. So that the devil may never learn it and thereby gain power over the person, the name is kept secret.

The second name is that by which gypsies call each other. They will never reveal it to, or use it in the presence of, strangers.

The last and third name is one of many aliases. Gypsies make use of it only for "public relations" and "the authorities."

## From Birth to Death

Like most primitive races, gypsies regard pregnancy as a period of great danger and ritual impurity, and they attach to it a strict taboo. A mother giving birth must never do so "at home"—in the wagon or tent. If she did so, the site would be defiled and would have to be burned with all it contained. For a month and a day after having given birth to a child, she must not touch, let alone cook, any food, except that which she will eat herself.

The mystery of "bread and salt" has its special significance at the marriage ritual. A loaf is broken on this occasion and a portion of it, along with a pinch of salt, is given to both bride and groom. The couple thereupon will solemnly exchange their portions, eating them like a sacramental rite. The celebrant (usually a renowned member of the group) reminds them then that if ever they became tired of bread and salt, they would tire of each other.

Death like birth must never take place inside the home. For any gypsy to die is regarded not as merely a personal loss but as a bereavement suffered by the entire group. Consequently, grief is expressed openly in common, and given much conspicuous publicity.

Most gypsies will never return to the grave in which they have buried one of their people. Another tradition makes them dispose of all personal effects of the deceased. Heirlooms, often a bone of contention among Western people, are unknown to the Roms. At times, gypsies even break up or burn the wagon of the dead. They do so to make it impossible for anyone else to occupy the caravan. This might be resented by the departed gypsy's spirit, who would come back to haunt the living.

## "God's Own Children" and Devil Worshipers

God in the Romany language is *del* or *devel*. Of Sanskrit root, it means "a shining one." Yet who could fail to notice the similarity with "devil" and hence identify gypsies with devil worshipers? To make matters worse, gypsies reached Europe in the sixteenth and seventeenth centuries at the height of the witch trials! Both witches and gypsies shared the common fate of being suspected, decried and persecuted. Was it any wonder they joined forces?

It was natural that the mystery of the gypsies' life and their fate as wanderers caused people to ask what actually had made gypsies what they were. Of course, there were those anxious to defame them. All that the gypsies had now to suffer, these said, was in punishment of a terrible crime which their ancestors had once committed. People only differed in their identification of this "original sin."

Some said that gypsies were the direct descendants of Cain who had murdered his brother.

Others claimed that a gypsy had forged three of the nails with which Christ was crucified.

Yet others believed that all gypsies were despised because their Egyptian forebears had met the Virgin Mary on her flight to Egypt but had denied her and her family the hospitality and help they so much needed.

Gypsies were truly "God's own children" and the most perfect he ever made relates another legend in a much happier vein. Not surprisingly, this one originated among the Romany people themselves.

A story tells of how God, in his early efforts to make man, had not been successful at first. He had shaped him out of chalk satisfactorily and then put him into an oven. But preoccupied at the time with so many things of creation, God forgot all about him and came too late to remove the "finished" product which was burned. And so the black man came into existence.

God was anxious not to spoil man for a second time, and in his concern, he removed him from the oven too early. Being completely underbaked, he lacked color. And thus, white man appeared on this earth.

"Third time lucky," God carefully watched the oven and took out "man" at the very moment he was properly "browned." This was the perfect product. It was the gypsy who ever since, as the faultless divine creation, has wandered the earth which belongs to God.

## ROBIN HOOD IN FAIRYLAND

Robin Hood who traditionally befriended the wretched and downtrodden, robbing the rich to help the poor, is one of history's great legendary figures. He is the hero of countless English ballads. The earliest literary reference to his alleged existence dates back to William Langland's second edition of *The Vision of William Concerning Piers Plowman* in 1377.

It is possible that Robin, too, has been greatly misrepresented and, far from being a human being, belonged to fairyland. Much that is told about him would bear this out.

His home was Sherwood Forest—like that of other fairy people, a dark wood. He and his gang, too, were clad in green. Like all elves living outside the law, he was a deadly shot with the bow and arrow.

Robin was a name frequently bestowed on a fairy. Even the "Hood" might well go back not to an original surname but to the hooded garment or pixie cap the fairies were supposed to don. Therefore his unabbreviated name could have been "Robin with the hood."

An inveterate foe of the Establishment, like the subjugated aboriginal fairies, he made its members and those serving it the target of his constant attacks. A friend of the common people, they cherished him as they did the nature spirits of the original old religion.

Even Robin's death would fit in with the tradition associated with the fertility gods of paganism. It is told that he bled to death by the treachery of a nun. She had claimed that she would restore him to vigorous health by bleeding him. Perhaps, as in the case of the ancient fertility gods, his blood was meant magically to fructify the soil and to ensure the rebirth of nature.

## THE CHANGELING

So much in the life of man is still unexplained. By constant study and indefatigible research, he tries to reduce the power of sickness and conquer disease. Sometimes it happens that by intelligent correlating of observations he finds a cure or the answer to a problem along the most unlikely and unexpected avenue. Who, for instance, would have ever guessed that a child could be born deaf or with heart trouble, if, during a certain period of her pregnancy, the mother had suffered from measles?

We still largely grope in the dark and have only partial answers as to what causes some children to be backward, to be born as mongoloids or as spastics. The problem is aggravated by the fact that usually such abnormalities do not appear or manifest themselves right away, nor without special diagnostic tests.

Can one therefore blame parents in past generations who were bewildered if a child suddenly acted strangely, or stopped growing physically or mentally? Certainly they noticed it and were sure there was a reason for it. But they differed in the explanations they gave and the realm in which they looked for them. It was all the fairies' doings, they said and firmly believed this.

Surely, the child now in their possession was not theirs. The one to which the mother had given birth, had been stolen by the fairies. They had done so either to bring it up as one of their own or worse still to sacrifice it to the devil. But in exchange and to deceive the mother, they had left behind in its stead a fairy child. And that is how the myth of the ''changeling'' was born.

The suspicion and accusation were apparently supported by the fact that children thus afflicted were undersized and distinguished by peculiar features such as a high-domed forehead. That they often died young only confirmed the conviction. A pixie child would look like a freak. It would never grow tall nor live long.

## HALLOWEEN

Many a feature of modern religion and secular celebration is a take-over of occult customs, and often only very thinly disguised at that. This applies to all the great festivals and celebrations, and not least among them is Halloween. Though as a public holiday it is hardly known nowadays outside the United States, modern "witches" continue to observe it universally and they do so as one of their major conventions.

It all began more than two thousand years ago, among the Druids, as a holy communion with spirits. The Druids' New Year was November 1. It marked the beginning of winter and therefore was a date which deeply concerned people with the dying and rebirth of nature. The harsh cold and the weakening strength of the sun had to be counteracted. Man had to make sure that life would not end by everyone freezing to death. To keep the people alive, he made use of all the powers he could summon.

At this juncture of summer and winter, the entire world seemed agitated. The spirits of the dead, witches and ghosts of every description, were at large on that night. They roamed the earth, tried to make contact with the mortals and, possibly, to do them harm.

Huge fires were lit on the eve of that day. First, they were meant to warm and reinvigorate the sun. Second, they were intended to act as a powerful deterrent to all the malevolent forces, warlocks, witches and devils around, threatening man but known to be scared of fire.

The Druids, in their preoccupation with the occult, took special note of the occasion. They solemnly observed the day and its eve as Samhain. Though the term was interpreted later as merely identifying the calendar date with the "summer's end," it really recalls the "lord of death" and November 1 was his feast. On that day, so the Druids believed, he summoned the spirits of the departed to judge them and determine the type of existence they were to lead thenceforth.

For people to go to bed during that night would be the wrong thing to do. There was strength in numbers and thus, gathering in groups, men and women tried to reassure each other in what they knew to be the invisible presence of the ghosts.

And so, to frighten the spooks away, they lit fires. Worried that by doing so they might only rouse or aggravate the spirits' ill will, they also sacrificed a black sheep to the dead and poured libations to the spirits of those who had died during the previous year.

Their major concern on that night, however, was the sun. They had to make sure that the divine luminary would return in full strength in the spring. For this purpose they not only worshiped it but offered it the most precious gift of all: man himself. And that is why they burned

the human sacrifice in huge wicker baskets. When the Romans outlawed the custom, they replaced the live being with an effigy and
eventually substituted a horse.

Eventually, witchcraft took over the Celtic tradition and made
Samhain one of its four great Sabbats.

## The Christian Adaptation of Halloween

People could not help but be deeply impressed and almost overwrought by the atmosphere of a night in which huge fires were blazing
and it was believed that all the spirits and ghosts were abroad. With
awe and devotion and not a little anxiety, they took part in occult rites
to safeguard their future.

Christianity became greatly perturbed by the attraction exerted by
those pagan practices. In spite of all its efforts and threats, it was
unable to suppress what it condemned as a heinous heathen custom.
And "if you cannot beat them, join them" is not only a modern
political slogan and practice. Religion has learned its wisdom no less.

That is why Christianity adopted and adapted the very festival it had
strongly condemned. In 834 it made Samhain its own, christening it
"All Saints' Day." The faithful were told that on this day they should
honor the saints, particularly those of the Church who had never been
identified and hence never been allotted an individual day in the
Christian calendar. It was only logical to assume that through the ages
there must have been thousands of men and women who lived the most
exemplary holy lives but did so completely unrecognized and therefore were known to God alone. And it was to them that All Saints' Day
was to be specially dedicated.

An alternate name for "saint" was "hallow." The day thus became
known as well as All Hallows. Subsequently, the celebration of its eve
was called All Hallows' Eve, which was eventually shortened into
Halloween.

## THE CORN SPIRIT AND LAMMAS

Lammas falls on August 1. Its name is hardly known to the average
person today. Yet once, as the beginning of the harvesting season,
Lammas dominated life, so much so that its observance and celebra-

tion continue in almost every land, though in forms so different that no one would guess the connection.

Only witches preserved the original name and did so as that of one of their four annual Sabbat conventions based on the ancient Celtic agricultural calendar. The day survives in new guises in Britain's August Bank Holiday and America's Thanksgiving.

It all started thousands of years ago when man, aware of his dependence on the soil, recognized that corn did not grow of its own accord. There was so much more to it than the seed, the sunshine, the rain and his own plowing of the field. Just as he himself had a soul, so, he was sure, the grain had an indwelling spirit. And at the time of harvest when he cut down the corn, the spirit had to move on to take refuge in the ever smaller portion that remained standing on the field. In the end, the spirit was confined to a last, minute "retreat." Indeed, it was literally "cornered."

No one would dare cut down that corner by himself and thereby make completely homeless the spirit on whose goodwill his daily bread and therefore his very existence depended. Only collective action would wipe out any personal feelings of responsibility and of guilt as well as fears of punishment and reprisal. It is a psychological phenomenon well known in modern persecutions.

Therefore, reapers jointly, or in turn, threw their sickle at the spot where the spirit had taken its last stand. Some primitive races actually felt that to pacify the corn spirit they had bereft of its rightful home, they had to make proper restitution. To do so they brought sacrifices to it as recompense. Among the Aztecs, so used to offering human beings to their gods, this took the form of the ritual murder of a young girl. Only she would be the right price, they thought, to make up for the loss of home suffered by the corn spirit.

Other races adopted less cruel methods. Though cutting down the "corner," they would not destroy this last refuge of the spirit by "processing" the corn. The moment they had reaped the last corn-stalks, they would bind them together into a sheaf, often plaiting it into a female figure. Thus personified, the "corn doll" or "great mother," as it was called, solemnly and joyously was carried away. At the ensuing harvest thanksgiving feast it was given a place of honor. The reapers might then take it home to their barn or to a sacred shrine where they paid homage to it as a divine being.

They kept the corn spirit, thus caught in the last sheaf, in safe custody throughout the winter. But when in the following year the time of sowing came, they took it back to their field for it to reenter the soil, to bless and fructify it.

There was another way in early times to evade possible retribution from the corn spirit for having cut down its last refuge. None of the people would ever try to undertake the ominous operation. They themselves left the corners standing, so that others, the hungry and needy, might do the work for them and at their own peril.

This is the long forgotten basis of the significant social legislation found in the Hebrew Bible which actually commanded "at the harvesting of your land" not totally to reap the corner (Lev. 19:9; 23:22). It should be left for the poor and the stranger. Originally, the law was not as well intended as it now appears. To start with, it had cleverly shifted a dangerous and thankless job to those who had little to lose and all to gain.

## A Corn Feast Becomes a Lambs' Mass

Nothing could give greater joy to a man than the safe ingathering of a plentiful harvest. It meant that in the year to come he would not go hungry. And gratefully he acknowledged the divine gift of food. Apart from verbal expressions he did so by giving to the deity something he greatly treasured in the form of offerings and sacrifices.

It was this recognition of supernatural help that gave Lammas its name. However, its true meaning has mystified people and led to various derivations.

Once again those steeped in the lore of the ancient Druids recognized in Lammas one of their festivals. This was celebrated to pay homage to Lugh, the Celtic sun god whom they also worshiped as the bountiful giver of harvest.

Early in August nature began to show the first signs of fall. The sun had spent itself and seemed to die. And very much concerned with its fate, the Druids introduced the festival to honor the memory of the sun god. Appropriately, they called the day dedicated to him Lughnasadh, a word that referred to the "commemoration of Lugh." But when later generations could no longer make any sense of the rather cumbrous name, they shortened it into the more easily pronounced Lammas.

Even if the memory of an early Celtic god originally had its place in the Lammas, he did not stay there permanently. Man in his "progress'' evicted the deity to replace him with his own ''bread'' (and butter).

Having ground the first corn they had gathered, people baked it into loaves which they took to their shrines to dedicate to their gods.

Christians adopted the pagan custom. In the Old English tongue a ''loaf'' was *lam*—from the Saxon *hlaf*. Consequently, the day of thanksgiving on which the faithful brought their loaves to the service came to be known as the ''loaf's mass.'' Later this was shortened and ''loaf's mass'' became Lammas.

Eventually people forgot the early tongue. Many communities no longer lived solely on the soil but raised sheep as well, just as their ancestors once had done. And when Lammas came along, its name no longer reminded them of the original ''loaf'' baked from the first corn but, by its very sound, of their ''lambs.'' These they now took to the service!

# CHAPTER TEN

# Astrology and Astronomy

It is not difficult to realize how thousands of years ago man looking up to the sky came to worship its luminaries and to imagine that they actually determined his destiny.

So high up in the heavens, they seemed to him the all-seeing guardians of his fate. Unapproachable, they were invulnerable to any attack and thus almighty. Therefore he saw in them powerful gods on whose every will and whim he depended. All he could do was to try to obtain their goodwill by worshiping them and doing his utmost to understand what they were saying to him.

Once such an attitude took hold, human imagination began to read into the various natural features displayed in the skies a definite message from above. If properly deciphered, it would make all the difference between good and bad fortune, between life and death.

## LUNAR REFLECTIONS

The most typical example was the many phases in which the moon appeared. Was it not almost inevitable to assume that its growth would magically ensure an identical waxing of synchronized action on earth, for instance? That is the origin of the superstition still practiced by some people when at the moment they see the new moon they jingle coins in their pocket. It was a sure means of multiplying their own fortune: as from its thin crescent the moon grew ever fuller, so one's own pocket of money would surely fill up likewise.

Conversely, it was inadvisable, if not potentially outright fatal, to commence any task of consequence, such as a construction, an expedition or a battle, during the period when the lunar body was waning.

Early Assyrian astrologers took note of any strange or peculiar features of the moon. The authorities were well advised to apply their observations to the conduct of state affairs, particularly so regarding war and peace.

Carefully watched were the brightness and color of the moon, the shape of its "horns" and the chance appearance of any halo or ring. The ring, for instance, was interpreted as the omen of a forthcoming siege, while any break in it foretold a happy escape.

No one should underestimate the powers of observation of early man, for it was far keener than our own minds which in their sophistication have become blunted to the wonders of earth and sky.

Man eventually came to recognize that a definite link existed between the phases of the moon and the tides. Women erroneously came to believe that their own flow of menstrual blood as well was determined by the waxing and waning of the moon. They were led to this assumption by the almost identical time that elapsed between each of their periods and the rebirth of the moon.

Somewhat unkindly we continue to describe any person whose mind is unstable as a lunatic. This is based on the belief that his abnormal behavior is due to some disturbing influence of the lunar body. Doctors have actually observed that people who suffer from nervous ailments might show a worsening of their condition at the time of the full moon.

## SEASONAL CHANGES

There was another, even more important observation man made early in his watching of the stars. Undoubtedly, the coming of the various seasons coincided with the recurrence of specific positions of sun, moon and stars. He could read in the skies what happened on earth, since spring, summer, fall and winter occurred at the same time as the celestial bodies took up those "stations."

And since seasons were related to and indicated the times of sowing and reaping, they also determined the cycle of life. In Egypt, for instance, the rising of the dog star Sirius coincided with the anxiously awaited inundation of the Nile Valley. This was essential to their life, since if it did not happen, the land would lie barren and the people go hungry.

It was almost inevitable, therefore, for men to recognize in this parallelism and juxtaposition not a mere coincidence but rather a causal chain of events. The stars in their courses, man assumed, were responsible for his very life. That is why he worshiped them as living gods, in order to influence their movement for his own good and to make sure that they would take up their right position at the proper time to ensure the return of spring or whatever else was expected and needed.

Surely, man reasoned, the sovereignty of the sky was not concerned only with the natural phenomena of the earth. It must have equal influence on each individual. And in his eternal quest to know and to learn of his future, man was anxious to ascertain what the stars had to tell about himself.

After all, why should man be exempted from the iron rule apparently governing the upper regions? Terrestrial phenomena ought to be as predictably calculable as those of celestial heights—more so, for was it not logical that the latter caused the former? If only man were able to discern and rightly interpret the meaning of the heavenly signs, he would be able to know their earthly consequence and equivalent. Indeed, what happened above was bound to be reflected below.

Astrologers gradually realized that the movements of the celestial bodies followed fixed paths and were governed by a definite law. There was an orderly system of regular stellar recurrence. It was the earliest concept perhaps of a universe, in which one law ruled the entire world. Altogether it seemed—in the words of the 19th Psalm —that "the heavens declare the glory of God." And, certainly, their orderly arrangement and pattern gave man confidence, trust and faith.

Then suddenly something extraordinary happened that did not fit the accepted rules. People who had been lulled into a feeling of security by the apparent sameness and repetitiveness of stellar movements were filled with awe, terror and foreboding. A comet flashed across the sky. Stars seemed to fall from heaven. And, perhaps most frightening of all, there occurred what we now call an eclipse of the sun or the moon, when either of them appeared to be swallowed up. It was only natural then that man saw in those occurences a dramatic announcement of some stupendous event, maybe an impending disaster?

Astrology, therefore, originated not as a superstition and a fancy on the part of the uneducated and unenlightened. On the contrary, it owes its existence to the instructed and most learned. By exact observation and intricate calculations, they had become convinced of a causal chain between the events above and those below, and it was their unceasing endeavor to discover the import and implications of this significant link.

At first society was strictly divided between those who wielded power and their subjects, the common man. Only the former really mattered. Hence, in the beginning, astrologers were merely concerned to seek out the fate of kings, princes and other important leaders. But with the emancipation of slaves and the growth of democratic ideas, it was realized that the stars did not differentiate between people and classes but mattered for each and everyone.

Astrological predictions now extended to each individual. But apart from trying to perceive their future, they claimed as well to recognize character.

It was not surprising that those representing religion were greatly perplexed by the implicit fatalism of astrology. If the stars actually determined fate, then all which religion taught of man's responsibility did not apply. Nevertheless, Augustine, the fourth-century Christian theologian and most famous of the Latin Fathers of the Church, still accepted in his *De Civitate Dei* the existence of planetary influences on the world as a whole. He maintained, however—rather paradoxically—that this did not impair man's freedom of action and will.


## THE HOROSCOPE

Once man's faith in the stars was accepted and their determination of his fate and character recognized, astrologers were ready to produce the horoscope.

The term is a combination of Greek and Latin roots. It spoke of man "observing" (*skopos*) the "hour" (*hora*). This referred to the specific moment of time concerning the birth of a person, the occurrence of an event or an occasion of national importance on whose behalf the heavens were consulted.

The resulting horoscope presented a geocentric map of planetary positions in relation to the Zodiac and subsequent calculations about the future or character of the subject under review.

This presented its own problems which have not been satisfactorily solved for those who believe in this area of the occult. As any astronomer knows, our calendar has changed, and the maps of the skies and stars still in use are largely erroneous.

More significant still is the question, if the constellation of stars determined a person's fate, which grouping of stars should be used? The general assumption and choice of the actual moment of birth seem inadequate. After all, a child's life began nine months prior to its delivery. Why should the stars only "count" when the mature embryo leaves the mother's womb? Should it not really be the split second when the sperm found its target in the ovum and fructified it? But who ever would be able to time this moment of conception exactly?

## STARS IN THE HEBREW BIBLE AND BEYOND

The Hebrew Bible has little to say on astrology. Certainly it does not express any definite and explicit view.

However, the prophet Isaiah scoffingly spoke of the Babylonians' "astrologers, star gazers" and compilers of the monthly calendars of lucky and unlucky days (47:13). Their magical arts would prove powerless to avert their country's destruction. Jeremiah reminded his people (10:2) not to be "dismayed at the signs of heaven" as other nations, especially as the Babylonians were, among whom this passage was probably written.

It was to be expected that astrology would somehow figure in the book of Daniel, whose story took place in Chaldea. It tells how Nebuchadnezzar called on his astrologers to interpret his dreams and how Belshazzar asked them to explain the mysterious writing on the wall.

One passage of the Hebrew Bible has been quoted often to prove that even the early Israelites believed in the stars. When in the battle by the waters of Megiddo, Deborah had defeated ''the kings of Canaan,'' she broke forth in a triumphal song. She referred in it to the fact that the fighting had been so fierce and bloody that even ''the stars in their courses fought against Sisera,'' who had led the Canaanite army. Yet, as commentators were quick to note, this phrase did not reflect an astrological view but was a powerful metaphor to express the vast extent of the fight, which had taken on cosmic proportions.

Opinions on the rights and wrongs of astrology greatly differ in Jewish postbiblical literature. Some books of the Apocrypha and several rabbis of the Talmud completely denied the possibility that stars had any influence on or control over man. Others qualified the idea. Though generally believing that stars determined human fate, they oddly excluded the Jewish people from their sphere of influence.

A great number of Jewish authorities, on the other hand, accepted astrology as an undeniable fact without qualification. They taught that the destiny of individual men and nations depended on the movements and positions of the celestial bodies. They attributed King Solomon's wisdom to his capacity to interpret the constellations correctly. In one case, quoted in the Midrash, the library of collected Jewish sermons, astrological belief is carried to its very extreme. There was not even a blade of grass, it was said, which had not its own star in the sky, responsible for its growth.

Nevertheless, it was equally believed that man was so limitel in his understanding that he was unable to read the signs correctly and therefore to predict the future.

Josephus, the famous first-century soldier-historian of *History of The Jewish War*, recorded that astrological belief was widespread among the Jews of his time. However, he claimed that it was their misinterpretation or ignoring of significant celestial signs that was partially to blame for the wrongly timed outbreak of their rebellion against the Roman invader with its consequent fatal end, the destruction of the Temple, Jerusalem and the entire Jewish state in A.D. 70. The people, and especially those in authority ''did not attend, nor give credit, to the signs that were so evident, and did so plainly foretell their future desolation. But, like men infatuated, without either eyes to see or mind to consider, did not regard the denunciations that God made to them. Thus there was a star resembling a sword, which stood over the city, and a comet, that continued an entire year'' (*War* VI, 3).

## FROM MAZEL TOV TO SHLIMAZEL

Jewish mysticism and particularly so the Kabbalah incorporated astrology in their systems and made no secret of their belief in the stars. But generally, like all other "enlightened" men, Jews came to deny its validity. And yet in one significant feature the ancient astrological belief survives and unknowingly is literally reiterated on each happy occasion of Jewish life.

Jews congratulate other Jews whenever there is reason to do so by wishing them *mazel tov*. Mazel tov generally is assumed to mean "good luck." However, the wish goes much deeper or, one should say, much higher. It reflects firm belief in the influence of the stars.

*Mazal* (which is the correct spelling) originally was the Hebrew technical term for "a constellation of stars." Hence, to wish a person mazel tov actually expresses the hope that, whatever the occasion, it should coincide with a favorable (*tov* for "good") constellation of the stars.

That, too, is the true background of all *shlimazel*, a Yiddish term describing misfortune. Actually, it is a hybrid, a fusing of two words: the German *schlimm* (for "evil" or "bad") and once again the Hebrew "constellation" (*mazal*).

Shlimazel in its meaning of bad luck actually indicates that it is not the fault of the people experiencing it but the result of the unfavorable constellation of stars.


## THE STAR OF BETHLEHEM

Few, indeed, are the passages that deal with stars in the New Testament. Mostly they are religious symbolisms, such as the reference to "the bright, the morning star" in the Book of Revelations (22:16). The description of Satan falling from heaven as lightning (Luke 10:18) most likely uses the picture of a comet or shooting star.

No star has dominated Christian thought and lore more strongly and permanently through the ages than the star of Bethlehem. Matthew tells (2:1-12) of how it actually guided the Magi coming from the East to Bethlehem, to the very crib in which the Christ child rested in the stable. Whether myth or an astronomical phenomenon, the mere fact that the men are described as Magi, those wonder-working, Persian astrologers, reflects the Gospel writers' belief in the guidance by a star.

Some see the entire tale as a legend. It was used to stress the supernatural nature of the event. However, it also was meant to emphasize the cosmic significance of Jesus' birth and how it was destined to influence not just the Palestinian Jewish community but the entire pagan world, including the heathen magi! A common feature of many legends is the sudden appearance of a star at the birth or death of a great figure.

That Jesus' birth should thus be announced was all the more understandable because those believing in his Messiahship well remembered a prophecy of the Hebrew Bible. In the Book of Numbers of the Pentateuch (24:17), Balaam had foretold that "there shall come forth a star out of Jacob." Christians believed this spoke of the future Jesus, the Christ. According to Jewish interpretation, however, the passage referred not to him but to King David or Bar Kochba.

Other suggestions have been made to explain the story of the star. It really was not a star at all that the Magi had observed in the sky, some said. It had been an exceptionally bright meteor or fireball. This would not tally with the Gospels' account that the "star of Bethlehem" stayed in the skies for a time so much longer than a shooting star or fireball ever would do.

A further theory advanced suggested that "the star" referred to an extraordinary comet. It is not such a farfetched idea, as the appearance of comets throughout the ages have been a source of awe to many people. Calculations actually proved that comets appeared in the sky in both the years 4 B.C. and earlier, in 11 B.C., when it was the famous Halley's Comet. Later times could have easily confused their dates with that of the birth of Christ. Nevertheless, the theory is untenable. Comets have always been regarded as an evil omen, a harbinger of misfortune, of war and of pestilence and have never been seen as an indication of a forthcoming event that was good and would bring blessing.

There were, of course, those pious people who were convinced that the star of Bethlehem could have never been a mere natural phenomenon. Worthy of the savior who then entered the world, they said, it was a supernatural miracle.

In yet another school of thought, still assuming the veracity of the

Gospel story, great pains were taken to explain that what Holy Scripture called a star was really an entire conspicuous planetary conjunction, a like of which had never been seen before.

Among those anxious to prove the case was Johannes Kepler, the great German astronomer. Between December 1603 and February 1606 he observed a certain conjunction of stars and was struck by the sudden appearance of a brilliant new star which then gradually faded and vanished. He was convinced that what he had seen was the exact repetition of the phenomenon known as the star of Bethlehem. And calculations he made subsequently seemed to prove his point.

Modern astronomers have taken up Kepler's lead. They tried to ascertain with their immensely increased knowledge whether any out of the ordinary astronomical phenomenon did occur (such as the sudden coming into view of a bright nova) at the time of Jesus' birth which might have given rise to the Gospel account.

New difficulties were added which rendered the astronomers' deliberations most problematic and their quest to identify the star of Bethlehem almost impossible.

We now know that our modern calendar is very inexact. It certainly does not give the correct amount of years that have passed since the assumed birth of Christ. Taking into consideration data now commonly accepted as true and based on historical records, such as the extent of Herod's rule and the periods of tax collection by the Romans, it seems definite that Jesus must have been born several years "Before Christ," certainly not later than 4 B.C. but most likely in 8 B.C.


## ASTROLOGY AND ASTRONOMY— WHERE THEY MEET AND PART

Astrology and astronomy come from the East, most likely from Chaldea once situated at the site of modern Iraq. Its rulers and people were so preoccupied with the stars and what they said that the "Chaldean" became synonymous with stargazer, soothsayer and astrologer. As such the name appears in the Bible.

As words, however, both astrology and astronomy are Greek. They say almost the same thing. *Astron* referred to any "star."

*Logos* was the Greek word which, through St. John, became

all-important in Christian theology as the description of God the son in the holy trinity.

*Nomos* (the root of *nomy*) described to Greeks the majestic "law." In the realm of faith this was to take on a fatal role, when the Greek translators of the Hebrew Bible, for lack of any better and more appropriate term, used it to render inaccurately the difficult Hebrew word for "*Torah*."

Astrology thus was merely "the telling of the stars," while astronomy spoke of studying their law—"the arrangements of the stars," their distribution. Accordingly, an astrologer was a "star discourser" and an astronomer a "star arranger," not in the skies but on stellar maps.

Only very gradually did astrology become a separate study and as late as the seventeenth century finally assumed without a single change of the "word" (*logos*) its present-day meaning. Its observation was now exclusively applied to divination.

Astronomy, on the other hand, entered the realm of pure science. The two words, once used interchangeably, now were strictly separate. It was a division jealously observed between the men who tried to learn what the stars told and those who made it their task to tell what they foretold.

## STARS IN OUR SPEECH

It was not only the Jews who preserved and applied unknowingly ancient astrological beliefs. They have left their conspicuous mark even more so in the English tongue.

That is why we thank our "lucky stars" for good things and put the blame for misfortune on being "ill-starred" or having been "born under an unlucky star." There cannot be any doubt as to the original implication of expressing the view that a person's "star is in the ascendant." Any disaster equally—and very obviously so to those learned in Latin—attributes its cause to the antagonism (*dis*—"against") of the "stars" (*astra*).

Dwelling further on the "dismal" side of life, this description is tied up with astrology and its view that each day whether good or ill is subject to a star. Stellar influence predestines an effort to be successful or a failure. Dismal, from the Latin *dies mali* speaks of "the evil days." We do not make them so, but they exist so in advance and are the result of the stars. Bringing misfortune, they should be shunned for any new venture or enterprise, whether marital, martial or commercial.

Our calendars still indicate the "red letter days" of the year. Ancient nations equally marked the "evil days" as foreboding no good and therefore being "dismal." The Roman calendar distinguished two "dismal" days every month. In some parts of Europe these kept their unfortunate association well into medieval days.

To "consider" a situation seems so objective and detached. Yet if we were really to mean or know what is implied each time we "consider" a matter, we ought to consult an astrologer! Also hailing from Latin, the word "consider" literally says that we relate the subject "with" (*con*) the "star" (*sidus*), making its position the decisive factor of our final course of action. Consideration thus is the contemplation not so much of our mind but of stellar vicissitudes.

Becoming even more specific, our language attached concepts to individual planets. "Jovial" people are related to Jupiter. War and strife are regarded as "martial," because they were seen as the direct effect of the planet Mars.

Less common nowadays is the use of "saturnine" for people of a gloomy, sluggish and taciturn nature. These were once astrologically linked to the planet Saturn. Mercury gave us those individuals who, like quicksilver in their "mercurial" personality, are quick-witted and volatile. Venus, which personified the goddess of love, has fared rather badly on the loom of language and has come down from her lofty heights. This planet chiefly survives in the evil effects of (loving) promiscuity, as "venereal" disease.

Language, indeed, has built a colorful variety of lasting monuments to man's astral associations and his belief in "star power."

## THE SUN

The sun was recognized by primitive man as the mighty ruler and source of life, in fact, of the entire universe, and it was worshiped as the supreme deity from very early days. But merely to pay homage and bring offerings to it was regarded as insufficient. Man watched the heavenly body and its daily movement across the sky with utmost awe. So many of its features puzzled him, and some occurrences connected with the sun created not just worry in man's mind but filled him with terror.

The sun's notable decrease, of power in winter frightened him. Would the sun die altogether and thereby cause him to freeze to death? When a solar eclipse occurred, he feared that the end of the world had come. Therefore, man used every magical means at his disposal to seek to aid the solar body at its moments of apparent grave crisis. He felt certain that unless he did so his own life was endangered, since on the fate of the sun surely depended his own future. And he pursued this endeavor in various forms. These were the beginning of many still-observed customs which, with their original reason now completely forgotten, appear so far removed from man's early anxieties and desperate battle for survival.

## BONFIRES

Wintertime was the most frightening period. The sun sank ever lower and became so weak that it seemed just a matter of time before it burned out altogether. It needed help to nourish its dying fire and to renew its strength. It was obvious that only other fires lit on earth could magically achieve this aim and cause the sun to rise again, reinvigorated and reborn. And it was these considerations that caused man to institute—all over the world—the first fire festivals. They were not joyous celebrations but thoughtful ceremonies to provide the sun with essential fuel. And that explains the origin of the bonfire.

The term "bonfire" was later applied and is derived from the bones burned. All its present-day cheerful associations vanish when it is realized that originally it referred to the pyres heaped and nourished with humans burned to death—whether as sacrifice, heretic or criminal is not important to the story. And it was their bones that were the last to be consumed by the flames. The choice of bones, to begin with, had an additional magical reason. But when King Henry VIII in his battle against the Roman Church burned its sacred relics which included the bones of its saints, bonfires lived up to their name.

The grim and gruesome birth of the bonfire has now been mostly forgotten. Out of its embers rose the cheerfully dancing flames of happy gatherings.

Hard to believe but nevertheless true is the fact that the bonfires lit all over England on Guy Fawkes Day with so much enthusiasm and childish glee have little to do with the celebration of the abortive gunpowder plot in 1605 and the preservation of Parliament. The blazing fires of the night of November 5 had anticipated that historical date by many centuries and had been lit long before the existence of any English monarchy and Parliamentary system. These fires stem from the ancient sun ritual practiced by the Celts in celebration of Samhain which marked the end of summer. Lit every night for the first week of the new month which inaugurated the winter, the fires were meant to ward off evil spirits, to burn all the anxieties of the past and, above all, once again to serve the sun by their magic.

## THE FIRES OF CHRISTMAS

Is it any wonder that with all the magic of fire the Christian faith was unable to quench it? By using lights on the Christmas tree, Christians adopted the light of the pagan world to brighten up the darkness of winter. The new interpretation it gave, however, was merely thin camouflage that could not hide the original meaning and purpose of those now beautiful customs and the vital role they played at the winter solstice.

Lighting up the Christmas pudding with brandy-fed flames seems so decorative and gives extra flavor to the pudding and the celebration. However, this fire too is pre-Christian and recalls the fervent pagan prayers and magic ritual aimed at the dying body of the sun to help it in its fight for survival.

The yule log of Christmas—both in name and as a custom—was taken over from the Scandinavian pre-Christian feast of Juul, which was observed at exactly the same time as Christmas.

The original meaning of yule is still doubtful. It might well speak of a "wheel," and therefore reflect the annual revolution of the sun, hopefully implying that after having gone down for a while it surely had to come back. Another view saw in yule an Anglo-Saxon and

Gothic root which referred to the ale drunk on that festive occasion, adding, as it were, extra spirit to the log.

The significance of the burning of the yule log is not in doubt, however. It was done to ensure the return of the sun at winter's end.

## EARLIEST OBSERVATORIES AND THEIR PRIESTS

Astrology was one of the earliest universal faiths. The belief in astral religion was so strong that rulers six thousand years ago spent fortunes to have their fortune told from the stars in their courses.

All over the world, astrology became a venerated and essential pursuit. No cost was spared to construct observatories. In some notable cases these bear witness to very advanced mathematical and astronomical knowledge in the remote past.

In Chichén Itzá, Mexico, for instance, the early Mayas had constructed an observatory with such erudite care that its openings were accurately aligned with certain constellations at a given time. One such "window" was focused precisely on the setting sun on March 21, the vernal equinox.

Stargazers belonged to the government service and were officially appointed. Theirs certainly was no easy task. They worked then without the help of the telescope. Their full-time profession demanded advanced mathematical knowledge and unending patience.

The expert astrologer was fully aware of his responsibility in guiding those in authority. But he was equally conscious of the power he wielded. In his hands lay the destiny of men and nations. His "ruling" determined the planting of seeds, the embarking on important missions and the making of peace and war.

The astrologer's profession was one of the first specialized vocations in the world. It created its own closed circle of initiates and, at times, in some parts of the world, was hereditary.

There are astrological tablets and texts among some of the oldest excavated documents. Translated from the ancient Akkadian into Egyptian, Hebrew, Greek, Arabic and Latin, they eventually reached the Western and Far Eastern world. Apart from the Bible, no other "scriptures" have had a stronger hold on people. From King Sargon of Akkad to Hitler, would-be conquerors of the world believed in the stars. Even C. G. Jung, the world-renowned psychologist of modern times, used to study his patients' horoscopes. He did so not to predict their future but imagined that it would help him to understand their character and possibly the underlying cause of their neurosis.

## ASTROLOGY IN MYTH AND HISTORY

Myth and history tell many stories of how the scanning of the skies paid high dividends to all concerned. Taking due note of all they saw above and making their calculations, the astrologer-priests of ancient times seemed to prove the validity of astral religion which they guarded and guided so faithfully.

King Sargon who ruled in the third millennium B.C., was one of the earliest world conquerors. His rich kingdom, situated in the fertile two-river valley, Mesopotamia, seemed a valuable prize to neighboring tribes and nomads. They were anxious to share the wealth and happy existence of a country so favored by nature.

Well aware of the threat to his land and rule, Sargon was determined, once and for all, to destroy those adversaries and to put an end to their constant menace.

To do so, he planned—as other "great" leaders did after him—to extend his rule over the entire known world. He would make all people like "one flock under one shepherd." He intended to unify the language of all those countries. Their people should speak with one tongue and the entire earth thus become one large dominion.

And his well-laid plans succeeded. With the battles won, he established the hoped-for peace and introduced a universal tongue over the vast area he ruled. Alas, it was not permanent.

But the significant feature in this stupendous undertaking was the fact that Sargon had timed the complicated operation not according to advice given by his generals or military experts, but had consulted instead the royal astrologers. They had watched out for the most propitious constellations of the stars to embark on the venture. And the timetable they had suggested had led him to victory.

A totally different example comes from China and the reign of Emperor Tehuen-Hio. The official astrologer of his court was also the "minister of agriculture." It was his duty to inform the people of the most favorable moment to commence planting the seeds. And his calculations were based on the situation of the stellar bodies.

In the Himalayan mountain kingdoms rulers were crowned and the dates of marriages fixed on the advice of those who scanned the skies. Their word was law and no one would have dared to ignore their prognostications.

Greek legend tells that when Olympia was about to give birth to her son, she was carefully watched by Neoptolemus, her father, the king of Epirus. He was steeped in the arts of the occult and particularly so in astrology. Having cast the horoscope of his grandson to be, he knew that, should he be born at a given hour, he would be destined to become the master of the world. And thus, he caused his daughter artificially to delay the birth till the propitious moment had come. And the child born later became Alexander the Great!

## THE ZODIAC

Man has always had a vivid imagination. At times his mind saw figures and objects that really did not exist. Modern psychology used this capacity for its own purpose and devised a diagnostic technique popularly known as the Rorschach or ink-blot test.

Ancient man, looking up into the night sky, was awed by the splendor of its countless stars. Also aware of their movement, he felt they were interrelated. And populating the celestial heights with earthly creatures and creations, he recognized there the fancied resemblance of living beings or well-known objects outlined by the stars. Divine power, he believed, had put them there. The reason for it and the way it had been done became the subject of numerous myths.

The various figures discovered in the sky and identified by a definite name were called by the general term constellations. This simply recorded, by the fusing of two Latin words, how "together" —con—"the stars"—stella—had formed these special twelve groups. The choice of this specific number no doubt was motivated by the sanctity of the figure 12 in the Babylonian tradition of numerology.

It sometimes happens that what appears to our eyes as real is only an illusion. That is how for thousands of years—until Copernicus—the view prevailed that our earth was the very center of the universe around which everything else rotated: literally and metaphorically as well. Around the earth thus also moved the sun, the moon and the planets.

Further observation seemed to show that it took the sun one day to travel about the earth and one year around the sky where, with the moon and the five planets, it made its path among fixed stars which formed its background.

The Babylonian priest-astrologers discovered yet another phenomenon. Those seven celestial wanderers (sun, moon and five planets) each month met a different group of those fixed stars—the constellations. And comparing notes over the years, they further realized that, on their annual itinerary around the sky, the seven heavenly bodies appeared within the identical set of stars at exactly the same season of the year. The sun seemed to rise every month in a different constellation. (And into each twelfth section they sought to interpret a feature from their treasury of legends.)

With this knowledge, they were able to fix on their stellar maps well in advance the annual march of those seven divine bodies through the twelve different stations which, by that time, had their well-known names.

The entire procession around the sky was assumed to move in a circular track. All that was now left to do was to give this imaginary belt, to which all the movements were confined, a proper name. This was not really difficult. The majority of its twelve segments, the constellations, were named after animals. Hence the belt spoke of them and therefore has been known ever since as the "animal circle." Using the ancient Greek tongue, it was translated and perpetuated as *Zodiac*. This combines the Greek "animal" *(zoon)* with *kyklos*, the Greek "circle."

The individual signs of the Zodiac, like the majority of our astrological concepts, go back to Chaldea.

## Aries—The Ram

That the ram—in its Latin form *Aries*—is the first in the order of constellations is not accidental. Rams were among the first animals man worshiped even in prehistoric times. The great number of ram gods in existence in many parts of the world in early times testifies to the importance of the sheep in ancient cultures. The replica of a mummified ram was featured on artifacts in the first Egyptian dynasty. The Bible tells how Isaac's life was saved by a ram which got caught by its horns in the thicket and took the place of the young boy as a sacrifice.

If the ram has thus occupied an eminent place in the life, thought and worship of man, it is not surprising that it was given a commensurate position in the skies. Earliest astronomers gave it priority to all other constellations by choosing the ram as the name of the group of stars through which the sun passed at the vernal equinox: the beginning of spring, when the renewed power of life asserted itself and the days began to grow longer.

When the Greeks adopted the celestial and zodiacal ram, they immediately linked its lofty existence with one of their own myths. This presented a ready-made and feasible explanation as to why the ram was so honored.

The ram in the skies was indeed not an ordinary ram but the most famous of all: the winged ram renowned for its precious, golden fleece. In the Greek myth, the ram, at the bidding of Hermes, had saved Phrixus and his sister Helle from the altar when, in consequence of a vicious intrigue, they were about to be offered to Zeus as a sacrifice.

The ram had carried them away, to take them through the air to Colchis. But on that flight, while crossing the waters separating Asia and Europe, Helle had slipped off the ram's back into the straights where she drowned and ever since they have been called the Hellespont after her.

The ram, however, succeeded in taking Phrixus safely to his destination. After landing in Colchis, Phrixus had sacrificed the ram to Zeus. Its golden fleece he presented to his new father-in-law, who fastened it to an oak tree and had it guarded day and night by a dragon that never slept till, in spite of the precaution taken, the Argonauts were able to retrieve it.

Zeus was so deeply moved by the sacrifice of the ram that he bestowed on it the highest distinction and elevated it to the heavens. There it has stayed ever since as the gateway of the sun in spring and constitutes a group of stars that is easily recognized and continues to this day to honor that primal ram.

Apart from giving its name to the first sign of the Zodiac, the ram has been perpetuated in the language of warfare: both in the Roman nomenclature as Aries and in English as the battering ram. In its primitive form this was a long heavy beam spiked at its end with an iron head. Obviously it received the name in recognition of the irresistible force of a charging ram that could knock down solid walls.

### Taurus—The Bull

It was not a fancied likeness of the constellation to the bull, of which there is hardly any, but the supreme importance of the animal in life and myth which caused early man to call the most brilliant and exquisite group of stars by its name. In Latin this is *Taurus*.

Man must have felt that no other creature was worthy to be so honored. From prehistoric days the bull symbolized the treasured powers of reproduction, and its likeness appears among the earliest cave paintings. Its presence was meant magically to ensure fertility among cattle and men. The Egyptians, for the identical reason, paid homage to the sacred bull, which they called Apis.

The bull was worshiped all through the East. Traces of its deification can be found even in the Bible. When the Israelites felt lost during Moses' prolonged absence, they began once again to pray to an idol which was in the form of the golden calf. (The ancient worship and sacrifice of the bull actually survives today in Spanish and Latin American lands in the bullfight. This did not, as is mistakenly often believed, start as a bloodthirsty sport, but has its roots in a potent and awesome fertility rite.)

When the Greeks took over this tradition, they linked it as well with one of their legends. They told that when Zeus had fallen in love with beautiful Europa, daughter of the Phoenician king, he abducted her by assuming the shape and color of a snow-white, golden-horned bull. All the way from the shore of her country he had swum to Crete, carrying Europa on his back. And it was to preserve for all time this romantic ride and swim that both a continent and a constellation received their names. The princess survives in the name of Europe, and Zeus in his bovine disguise is Taurus.

## Gemini—The Twins

The values of loyalty and deep affection are highlighted in the skies by the constellation known as "the twins," or in their Latin rendering as *Gemini*. Greek legend identifies them with Castor and Pollux, two brothers who were so attached to each other that they not only lived but wanted to die together.

When Castor was slain in battle, Pollux was so overcome by grief that he entreated Zeus either to revive his brother or to make him share his fate. Life held no meaning for him without his beloved twin.

Zeus would have been only too happy to fulfill the request so expressive of brotherly love. However, even with the best will in the world and in heaven, he could not do so. While Castor was a mortal and hence subject to death, Pollux, as Zeus' own son, was immortal.

Nevertheless, Zeus was determined to do anything in his power to help Pollux, even if it was a compromise. His action is described in two versions.

One tradition tells how in answer to Pollux' prayer, Zeus had permitted him to divide his time. He was to spend his days alternately: one with his brother in Hades and the next with the gods in Olympus.

The more popular version believed that Zeus, to honor the wish and acknowledge the twins' mutual devotion, had placed both their images into the sky. There they have stayed together as shining lights to the world, as heavenly twins, just as they had lived with each other on earth.

That is how Gemini, the constellation of twins, came into being. It tells men in every age not only the story of Castor and Pollux, those two noble youths, but how nothing excels true, unselfish brotherly love. Indeed, the two shining stars must have caught people's attention from earliest days and caused them to wonder what had created their outstanding brightness and strange link.

Though so highly elevated, it was not the end of the honors bestowed on the twins. Poseidon, the god of the seas, is said to have rewarded them by putting them in control of the waves and the winds. And, aware of their power, sailors duly made them their patrons. They especially invoked their help at perilous moments of unexplained phenomena or of danger to their lives—when they were shipwrecked or saw a mysterious flame around the masthead of their ship, later referred to as St. Elmo's fire. Sailors used the light and position of the twin stars as navigation aids before the invention of the compass.

There is a suggestion that the mild oath and exclamation of surprise "by jiminy," stems from the sailors use of the phrase "by Gemini" when appealing to the twin stars on all kinds of occasions. It is more likely, however, that the invocation was not at all addressed to those two figures of pagan myth but to "Jesus Domine"—Jesus, the Master. But fearful that the call might be resented as being blasphemous, the words were changed beyond recognition and thus camouflaged.

The twins of so long ago gained new fame in modern times with the conquest of the skies and of outer space. When the Americans launched the first spacecraft ever to carry two men into orbit toward the stars, they called it, imaginatively, Gemini!

### Cancer—The Crab

The names by which the various constellations were called link them not only with ancient myths but show the migration of ideas from one country to another and from one period to the next. They equally bear witness to man's early powers of imagination and observation. This applies particularly to the "cancer" and the story of how its name, nowadays chiefly associated with malignancy, reached its celestial heights.

Cancer is the Latin rendering of the Greek word for "crab"—*grapsias*. The Greeks, in turn, had adopted this crustacean description of the constellation from the Chaldean stargazers. It is interesting to note that in German one word is used for the animal, the disease and the constellation. They all are known as *Krebs*.

The choice of the crab for this group of stars goes back to earliest maps of the sky. Thousands of years ago it formed the background for the sun when this luminary reached the summer solstice. This was the moment when the sun, having attained its most northerly position, reversed its direction to begin its journey southward. And it was its apparent going "backward" that suggested the movement of "the crab." In the case of the "cancer," therefore, it was not an imagined likeness with the figure but a movement that gave birth to the constellation's name.

But the ancient Greeks, always anxious to link the heavenly lights with their myths, supplied an additional story. It was to explain why the crab had climbed up all the way to the skies.

One of Heracles' (Latin: Hercules) twelve labors was to kill a monstrous dragon, the many-headed Hydra. The task was formidable, as the moment one of the creature's nine heads had been severed, two new ones immediately took its place.

But as Heracles had proved himself master of the most impossible situations, the goddess Hera was much concerned for the dragon. Therefore she sent a huge crab to its aid which, while Heracles was fighting the monster, nipped his foot. The hero, undaunted and hardly taking note, crushed the crab to death.

In reward for the crab's valiant and suicidal deed, Hera raised it to eternal life and gave it an appropriate place among the stars of heaven.

It is an interesting observation how quite coincidentally cancer has thus been linked with death from antiquity onward and in completely different spheres.

The Egyptians represented this stellar sign with the figure of a scarab. According to their myth, this beatle possessed the power of perpetual renewal of life. Therefore it became their symbol of eternity and of resurrection. Anticipating the modern custom of bestowing a decoration on people of distinction, the ancient Egyptians presented a special scarab medal to those they wished to honor. The purpose of the badge went far beyond a mere decoration; it was meant also as a magical means to give the person "a long life." Likewise, to ensure their resurrection, Egyptian dead were entombed with a valuable scarab ornament, often enclosed in the mummy wrappings.

## Leo—The Lion

That people imagined they saw the outline of a lion in the night sky was no wonder. Its majestic figure has always produced in man feelings of awe and fear. Yet views still differ as to why a constellation was called by this animal's name.

An early opinion was that the burning heat of the sun, when passing through this celestial "sign," reminded people of the fiery ferocity of a raging lion. Therefore, they had called the constellation after the king of beasts.

But the Greeks, ever mindful of their gods, had their own story which linked the making of the constellation with Heracles (Latin: Hercules) and the first of twelve labors he had to perform while serving Eurystheus, King of Tiryns.

A fearsome lion was ravaging vast areas of the country near Nemea in Argolis. All attempts to kill it had been unsuccessful, as this mystical creature was invulnerable to stone, iron and bronze.

After meeting a peasant whose son had fallen victim to the murderous beast, Heracles was all the more determined to slay it. He pursued the killer and the moment he caught up with it, attacked it with his arrows, sword and club. But none of them could harm the lion which, unhurt, withdrew into its lair.

But Heracles did not give up the fight. When he detected that the animal's hideout possessed two openings, he immediately blocked one and entered by the other. And then, confronting the Nemean lion, he strangled it with his bare hands. He carried its body back to the mourning father and together, in gratitude, they brought an offering to Zeus.

To perpetuate Heracles' valiant deed, the god placed the lion high up among the stars, where it has dwelt ever since. Now known by its Latin name, *Leo*, it belongs to the Zodiac. With great imagination you might still recognize in a sickle of stars the head and the front part of the body of the lion.

## Virgo—The Virgin

In spite of the traditional view that woman counted for nothing until modern days, the fact is that she was worshiped and highly esteemed in antiquity. It was thought that, paradoxically, both her virginity and her fruitfulness ensured the survival of the world. However odd and contradictory it might seem, both were therefore honored and fostered among women. In ancient Rome a status symbol was attached, though, of course, of different kinds, both to the vestal virgins and to women engaged in holy prostitution.

The respect paid to woman was not restricted to any single region but was practically worldwide. When man began to identify the various groups of stars, he naturally reserved one of the twelve houses of the Zodiac for a woman. She was not merely an ordinary female but the most illustrious, possibly divine, figure of her sex.

Babylonians chose Ishtar—the mother of all life and the goddess of love (who oddly enough survived in the Hebrew Bible by the name of Esther, the Jewish queen of Persia and savior of her people). It was almost a foregone conclusion that the Egyptians would similarly elevate and honor Isis. The most familiar figure of their pantheon, she was the archtype of a devoted mother and a loyal wife whose faithfulness to her husband extended beyond his death.

In like manner, the Inca races of Peru identified the constellation with "the earth's mother." Moving east, even the Chinese recognized in the house a female figure. Though they called her rather strangely "the frigid woman."

A religious problem faced the Moslem people. Like Jews, they spurned making any pictorial representation of the human figure, since to do so was tantamount to idol worship in their eyes. This would apply even more so if the "image" was placed in the sky. And that is why the Arabs saw the constellation as an ear of corn which also symbolized fertility. Each of the women placed in the sky by the various cultures had carried in her arms a sheaf of corn. All the Arabs really did was merely to eliminate the woman and to retain the corn.

The reason why ears of corn have always been linked with the maiden of whichever name is because the sun passed through the constellation at the very season when the harvest was ripening. In fact, in classical times, the house was known by the name of Ceres. Ceres was the protector of corn and the goddess of grain to whom we pay homage by calling our breakfast food after her—cereal.

Eventually, however, strict Moslem religious scruples waned and the ear of corn gave way to what the Arabs then came to call "the innocent maiden."

They followed the Greek tradition which by then had been adopted throughout the vast Mediterranean region and beyond, seeing in the constellation a virgin, *virgo* in Latin.

But she was not just any virgin. She referred to a specific well-known figure. Because of her renown, there was no need at the time to identify her further by name. Everyone knew who was meant. (Later on, the same practice was repeated by the Roman Catholic Church. Catholics spoke of the "Virgin" without having to mention Mary's name.)

The stellar virgin's name was Astraea. She had experienced the Golden Age of former days, when the world was young and gods dwelled among men. Though a goddess, symbolizing innocence and justice, her abode was the earth. But the purity of life soon vanished and sin began to raise its ugly head. There seemed no further place for a being of her kind, so unsullied and so virtuous. To keep her out of harm's way and the corruption of a permissive and law-defying generation, the gods rescued her. Raising her out of the moral mire, they placed her into the skies. which were so immaculate and pure. There she took up residence in the house that has been called after her ever since—the Virgin.

There is yet another and very gruesome explanation the Greeks gave for the virgin occupying the special part in the Zodiac. It was linked with the Greek peasants' first experience of drunkenness.

Icarius, a citizen of Athens, had been instructed by Dionysus in the art of growing grapes and making wine, and had proved a most apt pupil. Soon he shared his product with many of his countrymen who drank plenty of it. Having never known what it felt like to be intoxicated, they imagined that their Athenian ''friend'' had poisoned them and consequently killed him. To cover up their murder, they buried him under a pine tree.

When Icarius did not come home, his daughter Erigone became worried and went out to look for him. Led by her father's howling dog, she found his corpse in its shallow grave. After discovering the heinous deed, she was so overwrought with grief that she took her own life by hanging herself from the very tree under which the peasants had dug the grave to hide their crime.

As if to add a happy ending to this dismal tale, Greek myth told that her body did not stay underground on earth. It was duly taken to heaven to become there a constellation of stars—Virgo.

### Libra—The Scales

*Libra*—the Latin for ''balance''—became the description of the seventh sign of the Zodiac. Going back only to the sixth pre-Christian century, it differs from all other constellations in three aspects. It is the youngest of all symbols. It is the only one that does not represent a living figure but an inanimate object. And there is no Greek myth to support or explain its place in the skies.

Scales almost always have served as a symbol of justice. Weighing man's deeds and his soul, they determined his innocence or guilt and thereby his final destiny.

The choice of the scales for a constellation may be based on a natural phenomenon. At the time the sun passes through this part of the celestial arc, day and night are of more or less equal length and therefore properly "balanced."

A variety of other objects had preceded the scales as the symbol and name given to this house. They included among Chaldeans the picture of an altar, among Egyptians a yoke, most probably the beam of the instrument used to measure the inundations of the Nile, and among the Greeks a scorpion's claws.

## Scorpio—The Scorpion

Fossils show that as long as four hundred million years ago the scorpion lived on earth. This makes it all the more intriguing that this ancient terrestrial being preserved in stone is immortalized in the skies as well.

A combination of several factors gave the scorpion a unique place and meaning in the picture gallery of stars. Of all creatures in the sky, the scorpion, and most of all its striking tail, is easiest recognized. Very little imagination and inventive power are demanded of the viewer. This explains why, from earliest days, diverse cultures independently trying to identify the constellations could not but help catching sight of the "scorpion," after which they duly called the eighth sign of the Zodiac.

It was a Greek myth once again that gave it special meaning for the entire Western world.

The scorpion's elevation into the sky was due, so says the myth, to Artemis, goddess of fertility and of all wildlife. She wished to acknowledge in perpetuity the scorpion's deed of having killed Orion, the mighty hunter, by its sting. It had done so at the bidding of the goddess who had wanted to punish Orion for his boast that he was superior to even the fiercest animal in stamina, strength and speed.

The constellation thus is also one of the earliest monuments that honors a murderous act, no matter how justified.

## Sagittarius—The Archer

*Sagittarius* is the Latin for "the archer." The majority of ancient cultures recognized in this constellation the features of an archer, or of his bow and arrow. The Babylonians, those pioneers of astrology, had done so in very early days.

Quoting the Bible, later generations felt that the constellation represented, and in fact, contained, the very bow God is said to have placed into the skies after having saved Noah and his kin from the deluge. It was meant as an everlasting token of God's covenant with man "and every living creature" that never again would he send such a catastrophic inundation. Sagittarius was a divine life assurance against death by flood.

Greek myth identified the archer with Chiron. His place among the stars, it explained was the result of his unselfishness.

Chiron was the most famous of centaurs, that mythological race of monsters, half horse and half man. His skills were manifold and outstanding. He excelled in the arts of healing, teaching, prophesying and, not least, hunting. But he had also no equal in performing acts of kindness, and was thus an exception among the centaurs.

Quite by accident and sheer misfortune, a poisoned arrow from the bow of Heracles pierced one of Chiron's legs. Heracles, greatly agitated and deeply grieved by the misfired shot, immediately removed the missile. But the wound never healed.

Chiron was in constant pain. As he was born immortal, not even death could help him. Then, at last, release was offered, yet for a price not less torturous.

It concerned Prometheus, who stole fire from Olympus and brought it down to man. Fettered to a rock by Zeus in punishment for his "crime," Prometheus suffered terribly. At last Zeus relented and was prepared to give the Titan back his freedom. However, he could not do so until some other immortal being was willing to take his place in Tartarus, that deep, dismal and sunless abyss far below Hades. Chiron believed this would end his own suffering from the wound and gladly volunteered to be the sacrifice. To reward him for his noble deed Zeus elevated Chiron to the stars.

### Capricorn—The Goat

The presence of the goat in the sky, in the Latin guise of *Capricorn*—"the horned goat"—is at first puzzling. Why should it be chosen—next to the ram, the bull, the lion and the crab—to constitute part of the Zodiac as it already was among Chaldean stargazers?

The explanation lies in its "position," not in the animal world but up in the sky. Its house is situated in that part of the Zodiac that, to ancient Oriental peoples, was the place occupied by the sun at the winter solstice. Having traveled farthest south from the equator, the solar body then began its climb up. And was not the goat renowned as a climber? It served so well to symbolize the very constellation through which the sun passed at the moment it had reached its lowest point on its downward course and, turning around, had to start its laborious ascent.

When the Greeks got hold of the climbing goat of so much older and alien tradition, they lost no time in making it their own, tethering it to a story of their past.

The "apparent" goat, they suggested in their myth, was not really an animal but Pan, the god of the countryside and patron of shepherds and goatherds.

One day while enjoying himself in the company of other gods on the banks of a river, Typhon the hundred-headed monster attacked them. To save their lives the entire group of divine revelers jumped into the water and, to make sure their escape, took on other shapes. Pan disguised himself as a dual being: his head, chest and arms were that of a man, while the rest of his body was that of a goat. And as such Zeus had placed him into the sky.

### Aquarius—The Water Carrier

The name of Aquarius—the eleventh house of the Zodiac—is easily identified even by those not very conversant with classical languages. Everyone knows, from the aquarium, if nothing else, that Aquarius, an almost identical word, is linked with *aqua*, the Latin for "water."

Earliest civilizations recognized in the water, whether in the form of rain or the inundation of a river, the very basis of life. Its absence or scarcity could spell death. Cosmologies of old thus told how God or the gods created the waters first of all, or at least simultaneously with the earth. It has been suggested that the story of Genesis in the Bible likewise really first had said that "in the beginning God created water and earth" (and not as the authorized version has it, "heaven and earth"). "The heaven" (*shamayim* in Hebrew) took the place of "the waters" (*mayim* in Hebrew) merely by a scribe's error caused by words so similar in sound and spelling.

Water belonged so much to man's existence that, when inventing his first alphabet, he made it one of its elements. The letter M of our present-day alphabet actually stems from the original picture portraying water in the stylized form of a wave. It is still discernible in the Hebrew character *mem* (the ancestor of the M).

People soon realized that water poured down from heaven or equally miraculous came up from the river at specific times of the year. They also recognized that these fixed seasons always coincided with the passing of the sun through the identical part of the Zodiac. And using the experience and imagery of daily life on earth, they felt that there existed a celestial water carrier. Stationed at that very spot of the imagined band of stars, he was responsible for the supply of the power which fructified their fields and thereby saved man and his cattle from drought and consequent famine.

That is how almost all cultures fancied to see in that zodiacal house a man with a pitcher or a vase, pouring water downward toward the earth. The only difference consisted in the choice of presentation, whether it was carried, stored or emptied. The Chinese adopted for the constellation the "filled vase." Chaldeans saw it as a "watering can." To the Greeks and Romans it became a "water pourer" or "water carrier," eventually called Aquarius.

As with almost every other part of the Zodiac, the Greeks were determined to personify and identify the figure. They were not satisfied to see in it a faceless water carrier. Thus they discovered in Aquarius the famous youth Ganymede, whose ravishing beauty had taken the fancy of Zeus. The chief of gods had become so enamored with the lad that he assumed the form of an eagle and carried him off, away from his father with whom he left in his stead exquisite horses, a rather odd kind of compensation.

Zeus jealously kept Ganymede for himself and installed him as his personal cupbearer. This was a very ancient and coveted office at royal courts, still recalled in the biblical story of Joseph.

In his new profession Ganymede was responsible for the ample supply of intoxicating liquid. But it was equally his duty to look after and ensure the annual flooding of the Nile.

His friendship with Zeus and well-carried-out obligations gained Ganymede the highest award. He was given permanent occupancy of the celestial house known as Aquarius.

### Pisces—The Fish

Water certainly dominates the last quarter of the Zodiac. It does so in such abundance that the ancients described that part of the sky as the heavenly sea. By its very name, Aquarius proclaimed its exclusive concern with water, to make things grow on earth. The cycle of the Zodiac ends with the creature most closely associated with the water, without which it could not live—the fish.

Gliding silently through the water, with its glistening skin reflecting light, fish must have mystified and filled early man with awe. He came to worship them as gods. They served him as a staple food. Recognizing their gift of reproduction with its wealth of progeny, man made fish one of his early aphrodisiacs.

It was only right and just that the fish that occupied such high status in the mind and hopes of man, by his very existence and perpetuation of life, should be given appropriate recognition by reserving for it a place of honor in the sky. Thus fish joined the illustrious company of other celebrated figures to become the twelfth and last house of the Zodiac.

In the early pictures of the sign, two fish are shown swimming in different directions, with their tails joined by a ribbon. Other ancient representations retain the two fish, but place one above the other, facing the opposite way.

Immediately two questions present themselves. Why, first of all, were the fish given the last of the twelve houses of the Zodiac? This position was not meant as an afterthought. On the contrary, it stressed the fish's significance. Just at the time when the sun reached this constellation, the fish in the Nile were growing so large and fat that it became the fishing season. Look at the sky, it could be said, and if you see that the sun has joined the "fish," you will know that they are ready to be caught in terrestrial waters.

The second question concerned the choice of two fish. Why their duplication? This was not accidental either, and two significant reasons have been suggested. It was meant to stress the eternal male-female relationship in the world of reproduction. But it also has been traced to an original close connection with the Babylonian calendar. This was based on the moon and not, like ours, on the sun. As lunar months are shorter than those of the solar year, a problem arose.

Festivals, linked with definite seasons, inevitably would move to the wrong part of the year, so that, for instance, a holy day dedicated to spring might fall in winter. To avoid such occurrence, Babylonians wisely introduced their own type of leap year in which they periodically added not just one day but an entire month to the length of the ordinary year. And they chose as the time for this additional month the very period when the sun entered the house of the fish. To record the fact and to remind the people that the moment had come to duplicate a month, they put two fish into the constellation, thereby doubling it as well.

Looking for a mythological reason for the fish in the sky, the Greeks found it in the incident that transported the goat heavenward to become Capricorn. It just so happened that when the frolicking gods were attacked by Typhon, the fearsome monster, Aphrodite was taking a stroll with her son Eros along the shore of the Euphrates River. And likewise threatened, they, too, sought refuge by jumping into the river and taking on a disguise. They became the two fish. To commemorate and perpetuate their life-saving metamorphosis, the goddess Athena placed Aphrodite and Eros—as they then were—as fish, into the sky where we still recognize them.

Though fish do not talk themselves, they certainly have much to say of man's early methods of calendar making, his fishing expeditions and his deep concern with fertility. Fish thus were truly worthy and fitting to conclude the celestial cycle of the Zodiac. They do so to this very day as the sign Pisces.

CHAPTER ELEVEN

# Mysticism

### THE KABBALAH

There has always been a religion for the masses, for the ordinary,
average person. He was satisfied with general rules and regulations.
So long as he could safely follow a pattern that gave sense to his life
and answered his spiritual needs, he found fulfillment and happiness
in his faith.

But there were others to whom this type of faith was insufficient
and, therefore, unsatisfactory. It lacked depth and true meaning.
Nevertheless, they were also aware that to gain the profound knowledge they really craved was beyond the grasp of man's limited intelligence. Only mystical vision and ecstatic experience could approach,
and in some exceptional cases, actually attain and preserve this state.

They were conscious of the inability of the majority of people to
follow and understand them, and the fact that their pursuit and preoccupation carried tremendous mental and spiritual dangers.

Such esoteric groups with their carefully guarded secrets existed in
various ancient cultures. The term "esoteric" itself stems from
Pythagoras and is very descriptive. This great Greek philosopher and
teacher delivered his lectures standing behind a curtain. Only those
students ready to absorb his profound message were permitted to share
his presence physically, to see his face and therefore to stay "within"
(the Greek *esotero* for "inner") the "veil"—the region of the
initiates. The others, anxious to learn from him but unable fully to
comprehend what he said, had to remain outside. Appropriately
Pythagoras called them his exoteric pupils. Aristotle adopted these
terms which, ever since, have been used for the two approaches to
acquiring learning and wisdom.

All esoteric knowledge was supposedly beyond the grasp of the uninitiated. Its daring speculations would at best be totally misunder-stood by them and, at worst, would cause confusion in their minds. From the very beginning, therefore, the exceptional men who steeped themselves in this type of search and mystical contemplation did not reveal it to outsiders. Their refusal to do so was not prompted by false intellectual and spiritual pride nor by the wish to create an exclusive, power-wielding circle of initiates.

This especially applied to the Jewish sages. In fact, the task and only justification for existence of all devout Jews was to try to comprehend the divine order of things and to seek to commune with and understand the supernatural. Few were able to attain the goal for which already the ancient rabbis had striven with all their heart, mind and soul.

Thus "to enter Paradise" was the very descriptive metaphor used for such superhuman effort to comprehend the incomprehensible, and do so by total concentration, intense vision and ecstatic experience. A report from the first half of the second century tells of four rabbis who embarked on this quest. And the fate each one met was most re-vealing.

One of the men could not withstand the pressure and died. The second went out of his mind, never to regain his sanity. The third, in illustration of the modern axiom that "a little knowledge is a dangerous thing," became a totally changed person. Immaturely trespassing beyond his mental capacity, this once pious and conform-ing rabbi assumed the role of a rebel and renegade or, as he would be called nowadays, of an aggressive atheist. Rabbi Akiba alone, the fourth of this unique quartet, had left "Paradise" unscathed—"in peace." His experience had greatly enriched him spiritually and given his life and his teaching an added quality.

Naturally, those who had acquired the rare and precious insight did not want to see it wasted. To keep it for themselves would have defeated the very purpose of their dangerous pioneering mission. To share the revelation they had received with those able to absorb it, became a sacred duty to them. Hence, the mystic scholars, with great care and caution, selected those they regarded worthy and ready for the message revealed to them, to become a link in the chain transmit-ting the heritage of esoteric tradition.

To "receive" in Hebrew is *kabal*. The volume of mystical knowledge handed down from one generation to another became known as *Kabbalah*, a term that could be rendered as "receiving" and "tradition." But in its specific meaning it referred exclusively to the carefully transmitted profound mystical insight. The Bible, so the Kabbalah believed, apart from the literal meaning of its text, had deep occult meaning, contained even in each of its words and letters. To interpret Scripture in mystical depth was the hallowed task of the Kabbalist.

To begin with, the speculations of the Kabbalah, because of their very nature and danger of falling into wrong hands, had been taught orally. But in fear of their getting lost, eventually they were recorded. They became the contents of some significant works. These included *The Book of Creation*, *The Alphabet of Rabbi Akiba* and *The Book of Splendor*—the Zohar which has been called the "Bible of Mysticism." Other manuscripts of similar kind were discovered among the Dead Sea Scrolls.

The knowledge of the Kabbalah and of its most treasured details, however, remained the exclusive property of a few individuals who claimed the special gift of mystical intuition. They further developed the occult message they had received and became experts in supernatural art and practice. Greatly revered, they were at times looked upon as "wonder workers." But as was only to be expected under the circumstances, the secret lore presented a fruitful field for abuse as well. Unscrupulous men exploited it for their own enrichment and power.

The Kabbalah was assiduously studied by many mystics and searchers after supernatural wisdom, no matter of which faith. It helped them in their exploration and possible application of the profound secrets of existence. The Kabbalah has proved a truly rewarding source for devoted study and has left also its deep imprint on the art and teaching of the occult.

## CABAL

It is very odd indeed that the Jewish Kabbalah should have come into the English language as "cabal." Cabal has become part of politics, and was linked with people least interested in matters of the spirit and the mind, nor at all concerned with ethical conduct. Those secretly plotting to undermine authority are now said to form or join a *cabal*.

One explanation sees in the cabal a historical acronym and associates it with events that occurred during the reign of King Charles II. Five members of the ministry connived in political schemes which they pursued without Parliamentary knowledge or approval. Among the plots was a secret treaty of alliance with France in 1672 which stampeded the country into war with Holland.

The intriguing group became known, it was said, as *cabal* by a combination of the initials of their five names: *C*lifford, *A*shley, *B*uckingham, *A*rlington and *L*auderdale. Their underhanded and clandestine perfidy justified in making cabal a word so despised that it led Thomas Macauley, the renowned British author of *The History of England*, rightly to say that "these ministers . . . soon made the appellation so infamous that it has never since their time been used except as a term of reproach."

However, though the story of the five men is correct, the acronymic interpretation of their cabal is apocryphal. Actually, the word reached England from France long before the five ministers had joined together in their scheming. The French had derived the "cabal" straight from the Hebrew Kabbalah and had done so because of its secret nature and effective use of occult practice. They applied the new word first to groups in their country that were known to be engaged in intrigues and conspiracies. Nevertheless, it was through the British junta of the 1670s that the cabal was popularized and became a word included in all dictionaries as the strangest scion of the Kabbalah.

To make things stranger still, a hypothesis has it that the modern "Cabinet" evolved out of this cabal "committee for foreign affairs" of 1672.


## THE ZOHAR—THE BIBLE OF MYSTICISM

The Zohar is not only the Bible of Mysticism but a mysterious book in itself. It has been described both as a divine revelation second to none and as a crude forgery. Scholars denounced it as "a book of lies" and people exalted it as the key to the most hidden secrets. Some saw in it only feverish fancies and childish ideas, while others treasured it as a volume of unsurpassed wisdom. It was claimed to have been written both to open men's hearts and their purses.

Of all Jewish literature, the Zohar is least known. Yet its teachings have exerted an enormous influence on the Kabbalah and on the occult generally.

Zohar means "brightness." However, it is one of the great paradoxes that a book so called should be lost in darkness. The obvious implication of its name was that the study of the work would enlighten the reader on the fundamental secrets of life, the mystery of creation, man and the universe. The title was derived from a passage in the book of Daniel (12:3). This spoke in poetic hyperbole of those who were wise and who would "shine as the brightness [*zohar*] of the firmament."

The Zohar is not a single book but embodies writings of great diversity and scope. Its main part presents a unique commentary on the Five Books of Moses, aimed to reveal the hidden sense of individual passages which must never be just taken literally. But included in the Zohar is a vast amount of additional philosophical and mystical speculation. This appears almost haphazardly, certainly without any systematic order or arrangement. Indeed, the Zohar is a very labyrinth of occult speculations.

Its language is not Hebrew but a peculiar type of Aramaic. First published in Spain in the thirteenth century, it was claimed to be the work of Rabbi Simon ben Yochai, a second-century Jewish luminary renowned as a great mystic. It was said that Rabbi Simon had composed it during the thirteen years he had lived in a cave in northern Palestine, hiding from the Roman occupation forces who had condemned him to death. The Zohar recorded the result of his solitary meditations and communion with the divine, as well as discourses he had held clandestinely at that time with other mystics.

No one before him had gained such wealth of mystical insight and esoteric knowledge. Therefore, the Zohar was a companion of greatest value to all concerned with the occult. It was the complete guide to a life of spiritual fulfillment.

The mystery of its authorship has never been settled. Most likely, the Zohar does contain some early passages by Rabbi Simon himself.

However, it was completed by Moses de Leon (d. 1305), its Spanish publisher, who incorporated many other mystical works then at his disposal. This would explain the great variety of style, the many anachronisms, contradictions and repetitions. Harry Sperling and Maurice Simon in 1931-1934 published in five volumes an English edition of its major parts.

The Zohar deals with almost every aspect and theme of the occult. It speaks of man's quest to comprehend the unknown and unknowable—the mystery of mysteries. Only at rare and short-lived moments of supreme intuition could he catch a glimpse of it—"just as sunbeams play on the surface of water."

In detailed and numerous metaphors the Zohar discusses the "ten spheres" (the *sefirot*), those ten stages leading from "the root of roots" to its penetration of the entire universe. It asserts that nothing in life is separate or isolated. "Everything is linked with everything else down to the lowest rung on the chain." Life thus was a continuous stream in which every individual counted. Even his most minute action could change the destiny of the world.

Indicative of the vast extent of the Zohar's esoteric speculations are the very titles chosen for some of its subsections. These include "The Book of Concealment" and "The Secret of Secrets." They range from "The Child" to "The Discourse of the Old Man." Subject matters discussed extend to the mysteries of prayer and the existence of evil, angelology, chiromancy, theories on the soul, its preexistence and transmigration and "the world to come."

The mark of Zohar left in both Jewish and Christian thought and mysticism cannot be exaggerated. The Zohar motivated and inspired the modern movement of Chasidism with its emphases on love and the unbroken relationship between the world of the divine and that of man. The Besht, founder of Chasidism, could well have said (as he has been alleged to have done) that "when I open the book, I behold the whole universe."

Chasidism, in turn, deeply effected the theology of our time and is reflected in works like Martin Buber's *I and Thou*. The Zohar—this Bible of Mysticism—continues to assert its influence on man. The very obscurity of the work and its many still unsolved enigmas give ample room for further investigation and speculation by both the scholar and the seeker in the world of the occult.

## THE TEN SEFIROT

Well-known and acknowledged is the influence that the Hebrew Bible and its tradition have exerted on Western civilization. But there are very few, outside those steeped in the world of the occult, who realize the equal importance played by Jewish mysticism, of which even Jews in their great majority are ignorant.

Fundamental in the world of mysticism is the belief in the "ten sefirot." Sefirot is the plural of the Hebrew "number," "cipher" (*sefirah*), though some authorities have derived the term from other sources such as the Greek *sphaîra* for "sphere." It reflects the idea, explicitly propounded by the Greek Pythagoras, that we do not only *count* with numbers but that each figure has a meaning in itself and is of great mystic and cosmic significance.

First of all, the ten sefirot enumerate the ten primordeal figures, each of which conveyed not just a cipher but a dynamic concept of universal dimension.

Still echoing this early tradition is the idea of unity of the "one world" in which everything depends on the other. Descriptive of this interpretation of life was the popular and well-known modern observation that one man's sneeze in the subcontinent of India could change the entire course of world history.

Dualism is expressed by the figure 2. Throughout life, man is made to recognize the juxtaposition or strife between white and black, good and evil, left and right, above and below.

Pythagoras had called 3 "the perfect number." It expressed completion and fertility. That the words three and tree sound so much alike is not accidental. They have the identical root which is buried in the ever-active power of reproduction. The idea of trinity has played its significant part in the world of mystic contemplation. It was a fundamental belief in the Egyptian pantheon which combined into "one" Isis, Osiris and Horus. Hinduism taught the *trimurti* with its three members of Brahma the creator, Vishnu, the preserver and Shiva, the destroyer. And there is the Christian dogma of trinity. Man's total being, too, has been represented as constituted of body, mind and soul.

The remaining seven ciphers, in like manner, were seen to possess vital and dynamic attributes, meanings and influences.

Jewish mystic belief went much further. Those ten numbers did not exist independently. Exactly as in counting, one figure followed the other and was its result (for example, 1 plus 1 made 2, and twice 2 made 4), so there was a causal chain between the first and the tenth. The ten sefirot thus represented the uninterrupted flow of divine revelation and manifestation. It led from the most complete and incomprehensible "one"—referred to as the *ayn sof*: the "unending," the "infinite"—by successive stages or grades to the most "basic" level of existence.

Out of the supreme One emanated, like out of an overflowing fountain, the entire world, which in itself presents in ten interrelated "spheres" the various manifestations and qualities of God. However, the further they are removed from the source, the less divine substance they contain.

Overabundant are the metaphors in which the literature dealing with the sefirot tries to explain this philosophy of emanation.

The ten sefirot were depicted in the form of a tree. Did this not show how one part grew out of the other—from root to crown—each embracing and being fed by the divine sap? And they all formed one essential unity.

Another simile used is that of the human body. Its various parts symbolized each of the ten divine qualities. Their positions indicated their particular virtue and meaning.

As in the Aristotelian picture of the universe, the ten sefirot were compared with ten concentric spheres or "shells," one encircling the other. The further removed from the vital and dynamic center, the less it would retain of its radiating force.

In this chain, each sefirah symbolized one of the divine qualities or attributes. They could be compared with the many colors of a prism which joined together to form the universe of the shining, all-permeating, divine light.

The way the sefirot have been identified and the sequences in which they were presented differed in the various traditions. The most popular and generally accepted order is as follows:

1. The Supreme Crown
2. Wisdom
3. Intelligence
4. Love
5. Power or Judgment
6. Compassion or Beauty

7. Lasting Endurance
8. Glory or Majesty
9. The Basis or Foundation of the World
10. The Kingdom or Diadem

If duly imbued and dedicated, man has potentially the gift of a mystical, spiritual ascent. This will lead him from the lowest level of the tenth sefirah, through all the others, each possessing its individual character—finally to reach and experience union with the great First, the One—the Infinite and Divine Spirit.

# CHAPTER TWELVE

# Divination

## LOOKING INTO THE FUTURE

Man has always been anxious to know his future. Even today, this longing is so strong that newspapers—even those catering to assumedly intelligent people—include a regular feature on "what the stars foretell."

Whether it was the ancient biblical prophets or gypsy fortunetellers, pagan soothsayers or modern clairvoyants, there has been no epoch nor part of the world without this desire to look beyond the curtain that hid from man's gaze the things that were to come. And a variety of reasons accounts for this universal and perpetual quest.

Curiosity is an innate human quality, and not least so when applied to the mysterious. And what could be more mysterious than the future—the great unknown.

There was a more important factor, however, that urged man on in this pursuit. Almost paradoxically, he believed that once he knew what the future held for him, he might still be able to change it. A great number of so-called prophecies contained in the Bible never came true. This was not because the "seer" failed in his vision, or was a fake. It happened because the people, having been warned of what was to come, took heed, changed their way of life and thereby their destiny.

A psychological factor greatly contributed further to man's longing to know what was in store for him. It is symptomatic that this should be so, especially at times of crisis when existence seemed precarious. The need reveals a sense of deep insecurity. If he felt sure of himself, man would be less concerned with what might happen.

The entire complex of prophecy and foreknowledge created a problem that has greatly troubled philosophers and theologians since antiquity. If the future could be foreseen, did this not imply that it already existed? Was it not perhaps (as a modern metaphor put it) like a man standing on an upward moving escalator who has turned around and thus faces backward? He can only see the way he has traveled up so far. However, behind his back there already are the steps that lead farther to the very top. And at certain moments, perhaps for only a split second, he might glance over his shoulder and catch sight of what is to come.

But if that is really so, what of man's free will? The most common and obvious answer given was that the "seer" did not influence the decision. Neither was the future predetermined nor foreordained. Only the psychic gift of the "prophet" had enabled him to recognize the eventual course of events and to "guess" how man's free will would make him act.

Constant search for portents and omens occupied man's mind. No dimension of life or death was excluded. Nothing that ever happened was merely accidental or due to natural circumstances. Everything tried to convey a message.

An entire dictionary could be filled with scientific descriptions of the various types of divination, a word which itself implies that the knowledge of the future was a "divine" gift.

## FUTURE EXPERTS

Those claiming to have the gift to see the future have been known by many names. Each has its own story to tell and paradoxically reveals much of its past which is not only enlightening but, at times, surprising. Not least, the etymology of the names shows the trust those prophets (or those listening to them) had in their powers of prediction. None of the terms left any doubt as to the veracity of the pronouncements made.

### The Misunderstood "Prophet"

One of the most misunderstood and then misapplied names is that of the "prophet." Everyone now takes it for granted that the prophet knew and foretold the future. But this assumption is wrong.

His calling and the Greek etymology of the word have nothing to do with prediction. A prophet merely says that he is a "speaker" (the Greek *phetes*) who voices a message "for" (*pro*) or "on behalf" of another. (The prefix pro certainly in this contest is not temporal!). He is a spokesman and the mouthpiece of God. Therefore the correct rendering of the prophet in English should not be a foreteller but a forthteller.

In actual fact, the Hebrew word traditionally translated by "prophet"—*nabi*—means "announcer." How odd that such a simple and straightforward concept as that of the prophet completely changed its original meaning and, in the sense now used, its entire function.

## The Forgotten Truth

The soothsayer has traveled the opposite way from that taken by the prophet. His title began as a forceful assertion but then deteriorated into a mistrusted occupation, taken not very seriously. The soothsayer literally told "the truth" which is the root meaning of *sooth*. (This original sense of the word was maintained in the now rarely used *forsooth*, "in truth.")

A soothsayer therefore was a man or a woman who "said" what was "true." Eventually this was applied specifically to matters concerning the future alone. Maybe because people do not like hearing the truth or, more likely still, because crooks took advantage of people's gullibility and shammed the profession of the soothsayer, his once honorific title assumed its present-day tarnished connotation.

## The Original Madness

One type of seer, renowned in classical Greece as much as in primitive societies, received his knowledge of things to come in a state of frenzied ecstasy. This enabled him to make contact with mysterious sources of information "beyond," to interpret oracles and discover what was hidden from the ordinary, normal mortal. He was "out of his mind" then or, as the literal meaning of ecstasy says, "standing beside himself." His violent, uncontrolled emotions caused people to look at him with tremendous awe. To them he was "possessed" by a supernatural power.

Madness then was not regarded as sickness but seen as a privileged state of those endowed with the precious talent. And the Greek term for this abnormal condition was *mania*. A person experiencing it was called a *mantis*, which is the Greek for "prophet." It was from him that we still call the many types of divination as practiced through the ages, by Greek terms which all end with *mancy*. It stems from that ancient sacred "madness" which has also given us the "maniac."

## Auguries

When a new scheme is "inaugurated," when a meeting is held "under the auspices" of a certain society, or when we feel that the time is especially "auspicious" to introduce a new policy, most people do not realize that on each of these three occasions the very words we use reflect occult belief. They are based on the conviction that unless we choose the right moment, our venture will fail. In each case, as well, the choice was originally determined not by logical or psychological considerations but by a supernatural message obtained from birds: one of the most ancient forms of divination. Looking into the future by aid of birds was the source from which "inauguration," "auspices" and all that is "auspicious" have come.

Early man must have wondered what caused birds to soar high up into the air far beyond his reach. He was equally mystified by the unpredictability of their flight, its direction, its various speeds, turns and twists. What made birds suddenly, and for no apparent reason, take off or come down to earth? The peculiar formation in which they flew and veered when in a group or the manner in which all on their own they hovered high up in the sky, as it were surveying a vast area of the earth, were other features that added to man's awe of them and to his puzzlement.

More intriguing still were the sounds birds made. What did they try to say with their cries, croaks, songs, calls and twittering?

Man was convinced that behind it all was the wish to convey some message. And because birds moved at all times between heaven and earth, they belonged to both those two dimensions and people came to regard them as divine messengers. They rose into the skies, man believed, to receive instructions from the gods.

For the sake of his own life and his future, man had to find the key to understanding what it was that the birds were telling so expressively, but in a language and in movements beyond the comprehension of ordinary human beings.

That is why in antiquity special functionaries were appointed whose responsibility it was to watch carefully the flight of the birds and then rightly to interpret the omens. They came to be known as "augurs" and their name clearly defined their professional duties: the divining by the flight of the birds. Augur is a contraction of the original Latin word for "bird" (*auger*, which preceded *avis*) and either the verb *gerere* for "to manage" and "to perform" or the verb *garrio* for "to talk" and "to chatter."

There were so many "signs" the augur had to observe. They ranged from the direction of the flight and the quarter of the sky in which the bird appeared to the type of bird it was and the grain, worm or meat on which it fed.

The augur fulfilled a most responsible function in the national life of the Romans. No government would embark on an important venture without having first consulted the appointed official. His considered opinion and "view" of the birds would determine the course of action. And this ancient "augur" is still part of our modern in *augura*-tion. Likewise, "auspices" speak of the "bird" (*avis*) being "watched" (*specio*). This also explains why we always wait for the "auspicious" moment to ensure success. What was really meant by the term was the approval given by the gods and duly conveyed by their messenger birds.

Systems of augury naturally varied in different cultures and epochs. The Druids paid special attention to the wren. The Celts selected their new settlements by watching where the crow touched down. And Aztec legend claims that the site of the Aztecs' capital city Tenochti-tlán (the present-day Mexico City) was chosen in the identical way. It was the very spot where an eagle with a snake in its beak was seen to alight on a cactus. The modern Mexican state recalls the incident in its coat of arms which is embossed on its coins and incorporated in its flag.

## THE TEMPLE

The influence of man's feathered friends has gone much further and deeper. Those who have worshiped or gathered in a temple, whether pagan, Jewish or Masonic, have without knowing it really paid homage to birds and respect to the Roman augurs.

Though the word temple reached us from the Romans and their Latin tongue, they had taken it over from the Greeks. The Greek *temenos* defined a "sacred enclosure" which was literally "cut off" (*temnein*) from the surrounding, unconsecrated area. The Romans applied *templum* not to any region on the ground but to air space.

*Templum* was the technical term that described the area in the sky marked out by the outstretched arms of the Roman bird-watcher soothsayers and declared sacred. The birds' flight within that confine was thought to foretell the future. And therefore it was on that "temple" that the augurs focused their attention.

Eventually, this "outline" of the upper region was applied to its earthly equivalent: the area on the ground specifically chosen and restricted for divine worship and speculation. It was fenced off for that purpose as holy territory.

Only much later the term temple was transferred to an actual building erected in this "out of bounds" compound. And that is how the temple came down from celestial heights to earth. At first it was applied exclusively to pagan shrines. But then the Jews took it over and called their sanctuary in Jerusalem dedicated to the One God "temple" as well.

Modern Masonic lodges, and Liberal and Reform synagogues continue to use this term of the augurs of Rome for their meeting places in which to worship and do the workings in honor of the invisible God and the Architect of the Universe.

Countless were the ingenious methods man applied to try to learn of his future. They represent an important chapter in the history of the occult. The many ways of divining all came to be known as "auguries." The original meaning, which was restricted to birds, expanded to embrace almost everything in the sky, on earth or below the ground that could serve in foretelling the future. The multitude of divinations is so immense that only a selection can serve as examples.

## DEAD MEN TELL TALES

Death always has haunted man. To cope with its dread, he devised all types of precautionary measures. Many of them we continue to practice under the guise of so-called mourning customs.

The power of the dead, however, was thought to go far beyond the ability to send their spirits back from the grave to harm those who neglected to look after them properly.

It was believed that the dead were especially gifted to foresee future events. No longer constrained by the limits of mortal existence, the horizon of their vision included the things to come.

That is why from earliest days man has tried to make contact with the dead to get the information he so deeply desired.

The art was practiced in ancient Mesopotamia, and the Assyrian magicians who engaged in it were known by the title of "raiser of the departed spirit." The famous Babylonian *Epic of Gilgamesh* (which influenced, if not suggested, the biblical story of Noah and the Flood) tells how the hero, aided by god, summoned Ea-bani, his dead companion. Odysseus, in Greek legend, goes to Hades to have his future told by Tiresias, the blind Theban seer who by then had joined the spirits of the underworld.

Greeks esteemed this pursuit so highly that according to their tradition a goddess, Hecate, looked after it and Euripides, the great Greek fourth-century B.C. dramatist, referred to her as "the queen of the phantom world."

Necromancy became almost a permanent feature, practiced in every generation of man. The term itself means in Greek "prophecy" (*manteia*) by the "dead" (*nekros*). With its roots in antiquity, it survives in the ritual of the séance in which the medium claims to commune with the spirits on "the other side."

Well known is an example of necromancy in the Bible. Unfortunately, like others of its stories and records, it has come down to us rather slanted and inaccurate. And certainly not accidentally so.

The incident is that which tells of King Saul on the eve of the battle of Gilboa, the decisive confrontation of the Israelite forces with the powerful Philistine foe. Saul was greatly perturbed and worried about the final outcome. Disguised as an ordinary man, he called on a woman who, he had been told, was able to contact the dead. He hoped that by her occult gift she would gain for him from the dead Samuel the information he sought.

The Hebrew text refers to her simply as "a master of *ov*." *Ov*, from the Hittite, originally described the "pit" out of which the spirits of the dead were thought to rise. Eventually, *ov* became the description of those very spirits. Thus the passage spoke of the woman as "a master of the spirits" or, as we would say in modern parlance—a medium.

The Authorized (King James) Version of 1611, however, mistranslated the phrase and called the woman "a witch." And as such, as "the witch of Endor," she has survived in people's minds ever since, though the Hebrew Bible never said so.

Certainly, the translators did not choose the term deliberately to falsify Scripture. But at the same time a person gifted with psychic power was regarded as being in league with the devil and therefore considered and condemned as a witch. And that is why without compunction the translators submitted to the prevalent opinion and rendered the text accordingly. They changed its meaning and did so without even indicating that what was presumed to convey the literal wording was in fact a paraphrase that fitted in so well with the attitude and prejudice of the age.

The Revised Version somehow mitigated the calumniation. Yet even its rendering of the passage remains inexact. It changed the nonexistent "witch" of 1611 into "a woman that has a familiar spirit."

No doubt the woman of Endor was a medium who practiced necromancy. The Bible further relates how she actually succeeded in contacting Samuel's spirit. He accurately foretold the imminent total defeat of the Israelite forces and the death in battle of Saul and his sons.

Mistranslations can play havoc. And it was not only the nonexistent witchy part of the original Hebrew text that has left its permanent imprint. Necromancy seemed to be fated. When the Greek term eventually was expressed in Italian, it appeared there as *nigramancia* which became known as "the black art."

Many of the features of attempts to contact the dead appear obnoxious and terrifying to the healthy mind. They included the desecration of graves and exhumation of bodies, preferably of people recently buried. Murders were actually committed to use the corpse, in all its freshness, to reach the realm of the dead in order to gain from there a knowledge of the future.

Necromancy was one of the reasons for the revolting sexual perversion to have intercourse with the body of a deceased woman. Such copulation, it was thought or claimed, would revitalize her through the life-giving potency of the semen. Thus reinvigorated, the corpse—no longer so dead—would answer the call and supply the information asked for.

Through the ages a vast and exacting ritual was developed to summon the dead, and it was applied by the sorcerers who became experts in necromancy. They made use of magic circles, special bells, an altar and tripod, magnetized iron, the sign of the pentagram and mystical incantations, to mention just a few.

## URIM AND THUMMIM

Of all divinations the most concise was that which demanded a definite, unequivocal "yes" or "no." It was a method practiced in ancient Hebrew times, and it was included in the duties of the high priest. Its origin goes back much further, most likely to the Babylonian religion and its "tablets of destiny."

How the oracle was actually worked is still a matter of conjecture. The Bible tells little about it. The "apparatus" used and referred to as the "Urim and Thummim" was attached to the high priest's breastplate which, part of his official garb, was more fully and aptly known then as "the breastplate of decision."

Questions put to the oracle had not only to be specific, but also had to be worded in such a way that the answer given would be one of two alternatives. When David consulted the oracle of the Thummim, wanting to know whether or not the men of Keilah would deliver him and his followers into the hands of Saul, the answer was definite: "And the Lord said [by means of the breastplate]: 'They will deliver you!' " (1 Sam. 23:10-12).

Most probably the Urim and Thummim were some kind of lots, made of stone or wood. That they might have been "sacred dice"— symbolizing "truth" and "justice"—has been suggested by actual examples of that type which were excavated in Egypt, where they were found around the neck of a mummified priest.

Another hypothesis explains the Urim and Thummim as flat stones, colored white on one side and black on the other. The way they fell indicated by the color the divine affirmative or negation. Implying their magic potency, some authorities even claimed that it was the appearance of the stones (their sudden luster or their becoming completely dull) that conveyed God's approbation or disapproval.

Equally uncertain and mysterious is the etymology of their name, as shown by the variety of explanations given for Urim and Thummim. These range from Hebrew words standing for "curse" (*arar*) and "integrity" (*tum*) to others for "lights" and "perfections." In the Thanksgiving Psalms discovered among the Dead Sea Scrolls appears a very similar term, though spelled as one single word—*urtum*, which was applied to express "divine enlightenment."

The name has also been linked with the magic use of the oracle, and it has been noted that it could not be merely accidental that the Urim and Thummim commenced with the first and the last letter of the Hebrew alphabet.

That the oracle was worn next to the priest's heart was meant to indicate and to emphasize its truly sacred mission. The Urim and Thummim could only be consulted in questions that concerned the fate of the community. To do so in matters of a personal nature was strictly taboo.

With the passing of time and the further spiritualization of religion, the Urim and Thummim lost their original function. Though still worn as part of the priestly regalia, they were no longer consulted. Like a diadem, they now served as a conspicuous symbol of the high priest's authority and of his right and gift to interpret God's will, but now doing so by inspiration alone, without the aid of an instrument.

## THE FUTURE IN YOUR HAND

So much of what a man does or possesses has been used to gauge his character and to gain information of his past and future. His gait and facial expression, the way he talks, the quality and pitch of his voice, its softness or loudness—they all have been carefully noted and assessed. But none of his features, manners and physiognomy have played a more "telling" role than his hands. How often do people jump to conclusions about a person by merely shaking hands and observing whether he does so with a hearty, firm grip or limply and casually?

Man's hand seems to embrace an entire world. Without it civilization could not exist. The Greek philosopher Anaxagoras, who lived in the fifth century B.C. and possibly taught Socrates, was convinced that man owed his supremacy to his hand. And this became his matchless tool because of its "outstanding" thumb.

We could not even talk without our "hand"—and this is not meant in the sense of gesticulation but quite literally.

People "hold hands" in love. If generous they are said to have an "open hand," but they conspire together "hand in glove." Effortlessly they might achieve their goal "hands down" or be forced to live and work with a "handicap." Some must be satisfied to accept things already used, that is "secondhand." Those greatly disappointed, "wash their hands" of a responsibility they previously cherished. They might "hand it over" to someone else. Others, however, showing great interest in a cause, "take a hand in it" and likewise acknowledge the merit of a person by admitting that they have to "hand it to him." When things "get out of hand," one must take "a firm hand" or lose one's grasp.

Going beyond the realm of conversation and its countless idioms, man could not have spelled all his words either—again meant very literally—without the aid of the "hand." The letter J owes its very existence to the hand which it portrayed when characters were still pictures. *Yod*, the Hebrew name of this letter (the tenth in line in its alphabet) recalls the original presentation of the now stylized picture of the "hand." Used as a number, *yod* signifies 10, that is, the fingers of two hands.

Equally near "at hand" is all that is strong or weak, good or evil. The word "dexterous" is rooted in the Latin for "right," *dexter*, because the majority of people do things best with the hand on that side. Consequently, it was their strong side.

A thinking person has many questions that concern the hand. He wonders why at moments of great anxiety people's hands get so clammy. This physical reaction to an emotional situation most likely goes back to the dawn of history. Humans then, like their simian relations, still lived in trees. To fall out of a tree endangered their lives, as beneath in the jungle or dense forest they could easily become the prey of the wild beasts roaming around, always ready for a feed.

Therefore, should a man slip he needed some extra safety device to help him stay up and survive. To enable him to grip a branch and to hold on to it firmly, nature provided him with glands that secreted moisture as an ingenious immediate reaction. And thus his instantly clammy hands would save his life. Now regarded unpleasant, uncomfortable if not embarrassing, the clammy hand is a vestige of our early tree-dwelling ancestors and man's eternal quest to hold on to life at all costs.

### Palmistry

Man detected other distinctive features about his two hands, among them the numerous lines that crisscrossed his palms and the odd formations of miniature "mounds" and "dales." Comparing notes he came to realize also that no two hands were ever alike.

Convinced that everything in life had a purpose and meaning, he felt that this mystifying discovery must have some message for him. To explore it became a highly specialized task and occupation.

That is how palmistry came into existence. Using the Greek word for "hand"—*kheir*—it is also but more rarely referred to as chiromancy. (The Greek *kheir* survives as well in chiropodist, one who looks after both the "hand" and the "foot" (*poûs*), and the chiropractor who manipulates patients with his "hands.")

Palmistry is the oldest of the divining arts that chose a part of the human body for fortune-telling purposes. Later on there followed physiognomy, judging man's character by his facial features, and phrenology, which concerned itself with the configuration, the "bumps," palpable on his skull.

Palmistry goes back at least five thousand years to China and India. The Bible contains numerous references to the hand and has been quoted as a divine support of the art and as God's "charter" of palmistry. In Job's words God "seals up the hand of every man, that all men may know his works" (Job 37:7). Medieval chiromantics asserted that this verse clearly indicated that the imprints in man's hands had been especially provided by God for the purpose of palmistry.

264 • STRANGE CUSTOMS

Greeks believed in and studied its art. A story tells of how Aristotle had discovered among archaeological remnants in Egypt an ancient manuscript written in Arabic letters of gold on the science of "hand reading." Deeply impressed by it he had forwarded it to his patron, Alexander the Great, and urged him to study it because it was "worthy of the attention of an elevated and inquiring mind."

In their portrayal of God and his influence on this world, medieval artists used to picture an impenetrable cloud in the sky, from which a hand—God's hand—was reaching down. With this they tried to convey how the unknowable divinity was concealed from man by his human limitations. However, God did reveal himself by the hand—a divine instrument. It not only signified God's workings recognizable by the senses, but presented a gift of unending potential which has not yet fully been grasped.

The palmist was the expert who claimed the gift either intuitively to grasp or by acute observation to detect and then rightly to interpret the coded message held in a person's palm. Every line, mound and marking had a meaning. To assess the meaning correctly careful note had to be taken of these features' depth, size and dimension, the figure they formed and the position in which they were placed. If rightly done, it would give profound insight into the person's character, his past or his future and even the state of his health.

Maps were drawn of the outstanding marks for which to look, and each was given its individual connotation. Among them were the "line of life" and "line of heart," names that are self-explanatory. The mounds of Venus and of Mercury clearly indicated by their names that they concerned characteristics of sex and mercurial quickness and changeableness.

The two hands of a man, it was further reasoned, would not give the identical message. God and nature were too economical to repeat in one hand what the other had already shown. Evidence of this claim was again found in the Bible by quoting the statement made in the Proverbs (3:16) that "length of days is in her right hand, in her left hand riches and honor." This was not just a metaphorical statement, it was the divine acknowledgment of the distinctive function of each hand for divinatory purposes.

Subsequently, there was a tradition that while the left hand "contained" everything that belonged to a person in innate qualities, tendencies and endowments, his right hand registered what he had done with them, that is, his actual achievements. With this information in mind, Osbert Sitwell chose as the title of the first volume of his autobiography, *Left Hand! Right Hand!*

There was another significant observation those studying a person's hands were able to make. People can be divided into two groups according to the manner in which they clench their hands into a fist. Many, when doing so, will put their thumb inside their fingers, as it were, they hide it within. Others—equally instinctively—will always superimpose the thumb and let it rest on top of the clenched fist.

The clasping of the fingers, too, can be done in one of two ways, and a person will never change the method he has adopted. Either he puts the right thumb over the left or vice versa.

It was a foregone conclusion that the type to which an individual belonged was thought to convey a special message and reveal some definite characteristics. Even psychologists claim so, though they are not unanimous as to the actual meaning of this conspicuous variation in the manner of clenching fists and interlacing fingers.

At times it was felt that palmistry in combination with astrology would be even more effective as a means of divination. By joining forces they would be able to penetrate further and deeper the mysteries of the future and man's mind. But then palmistry experienced a setback which was not of its making. Charlatans discovered that man's curiosity to know his character and his future could easily be exploited. And "fortune-tellers" became a favorite attraction at country fairs. Thus cheapened, palmistry lost much of its standing and many people came to look down upon it.

Nevertheless, chiromancy has not died out. It has gained an entirely new look and meaning by its application in modern medical science which has learned in its diagnoses to take note of the hand. To the doctor a man's hand, his fingerprints and even his nails can indicate significant features, proneness to or the presence of certain diseases and his general state of health.

The personality of a hand thus has contributed its share to divination. It reflects the occult view that just as man is the microcosm of the universe, so is his hand the microcosm of man. And in many ways he cannot disguise it. People can deceive others about their age by making up their face or undergoing cosmetic surgery. But their hands will still give them and their age away.

Confronting the uncertain future man continues to use his hands.

Whether he does so actively or in speculation depends on the view he takes on the validity of palmistry. This, along with alchemy and astrology, constitutes man's unholy trinity.

## THE OUIJA BOARD

From earliest beginnings man has used "natural" means to catch a glance beyond the curtain that hid from him the future and to get into contact with the supernatural. But in modern times he also devised artificial aids to help him in his endeavors. One of the more popular ones in spiritualist circles is the Ouija board.

Manufactured in various forms and designs, the board is generally made of polished wood or a plastic substitute. Arranged in diverse pattern on the board were the letters of the alphabet, the numbers zero to nine and significant one-word "answers," like "yes," "no" or "maybe."

The board in itself only "works" in conjunction with the marker or pointer which is known as a planchette. This is the most important instrumental part in the entire procedure. Actually, it existed before the board and, as its name indicates, originated in France.

Planchette is the diminutive of *planche*, the French for "plank" and therefore refers to a small piece of timber. The French came to apply it to a specific gadget they invented to facilitate "spirit communication." It was a little board of wood mounted on casters and holding a pencil. By lightly resting the fingertips on it, the medium would put it into motion without actually or noticeably directing it. The planchette then would trace out on paper with its pencil written "messages" or "spirit pictures."

The addition of the board merely further mechanized and accelerated the process. The message received was now no longer written out or drawn, but "pointed out" by the marker which did so by moving from one symbol to the other on the board.

Like a modern Telex machine it spelled out information reaching us "here" from "there," only the "there" was assumed to be the "beyond."

"Communications" of course, could only be received by an operator—at the "mechanical" end of the line—who was psychic. Highly sensitive to the invisible impulses produced by the power beyond, his action very much resembled "automatic writing." However he did so not with a pencil on paper but, much more streamlined, by means of the planchette which moved from one character to another on the board. He was thus able to "spell out" quite literally and immediately the "replies" given to the questions put.

Obviously, explanations of this phenomenon differ according to the individual's point of view. Spiritualists recognize in the procedure a genuine communication from the other world. Another interpretation sees in it not a message from the supernatural but the articulation of subconscious thoughts and wishes. A third group "explains" the operation with the Ouija board as the fraudulent manipulation both of the planchette and of gullible humans.

The name of the Ouija board, which was patented in the United States, is actually a hybrid. It is a very odd double affirmation of the positive in two languages. In one word it says twice "yes" and does so first in the French *oui* and then in the German *ja*. Some cynics have taken this as an indication that the answers given by the board are exactly what the inquirer wants to hear.

However modern the Ouija board is, its origin goes back to a technique of divination practiced in many parts of the world—from Japan to Greece—thousands of years ago.

In the sixth century B.C., Greek augurs traced a circle on the ground, dividing it into twenty-four sections, each of which was marked with a letter of the alphabet and covered with a grain of corn. A cock then was let loose. Due note was taken of the pattern, the sequence of characters, in which he selected and ate the individual grains. Just as in the case of the Ouija board, it was thought to spell out the answers to the questions put. The name given to this type of divination was "alectryomancy," called after the Greek rooster, *alektryon*.

## CRYSTAL GAZING

Crystal gazing also goes back to the far-distant past and has been practiced in many parts of the world. It is just one more variety of the many applications of "penetrating the veil." This assumed that a clairvoyant gift possessed by man could be activated by his fixing his gaze at a shining surface for a prolonged period. Thus "entranced," the viewer could see what was hidden from ordinary mortal sight.

Early Babylonians knew that staring at a glistening surface could reveal secrets. Hidden objects could thereby be discovered, stolen articles retrieved and other desired information gained.

A great variety of so-called *specula* (Latin for "mirrors") serving the identical purpose preceded the modern crystal ball. Any kind of polished, shining, light-reflecting article might be employed. This included the nail of one's thumb, a man's shiny bald pate, an animal's liver, the flashing surface of a pool, a blot of ink, the sharpened iron edge of an arrow tip or a bowl filled with oil or treacle.

The "demon of cup or thumb" (as the Jewish tradition called him) was thought to reveal the information sought to the spellbound visionary. The "magician" himself was often a young boy placed within a magic circle.

Those claiming the gift of crystal gazing do not actually "see" the future or the answer to the question inside the object on which they fix their eyes so intently. The focusing of their mind on it and its light refractions are merely a method of concentration which "switches on" their clairvoyance. It enables them to discover in their mind, and not in the actual glass, the knowledge they seek.

This explains why centuries ago the term "scrying" was chosen to describe crystal gazing or some related pursuit in the realm of fortune-telling. Like "descry," the scrying referred to the act of "catching sight of" and "discerning." The word "crystal" is derived from the Greek *krystallos*. The Greeks gave this name to the nature-made mineral because this looked to them like "clear eyes." Crystal was a very apposite choice for its later application in the occult, to "clear up" mysteries and to penetrate a hitherto opaque situation.

Crystal gazing evolved through the years as a complicated affair in which every aspect had to be considered carefully. Each feature associated with the practice was intended to create the right type of atmosphere and to bring about the proper conditions in order to assure success in the occult pursuit.

As it was believed that the information gained came from a spirit, this had to be invoked in a manner that would prompt it to divulge the secret. The crystal gazer himself had to be a person known for his integral and pure character and dedication to the occult. Prior to commencing his task he had to cleanse himself. And to do so both physically and spiritually he underwent ritual ablutions, abstained from food and spent considerable time in meditation and invocation of invisible cooperators.

The very site chosen for the consultation had to be a secluded spot where there was least likelihood of interference from any disturbing noise. Equally important was the timing. The operation had to take place at the most propitious moment and therefore meticulous observation of the planets was essential. Their constellation had to be just right, and the procedure had to be initiated at the time of the waxing moon.

Finally there was the crystal itself (or whatever took its place). If possible, it should be inscribed with sacred magical symbols and had to be positioned firmly, preferably on a stand.

There were several reasons for the eventual choice of the crystal glass. First of all, there was the psychological consideration. Crystal was a very precious substance which added to the "value" of the entire affair. The boundless spherical shape of the crystal ball gave it extra mystical and cosmic significance. The endless lines brought man into contact with the infinite. For the identical reason, at times the egg, too, was used for divination and some of the crystals were egg or pear-shaped.

Mostly, though, fortune-tellers came to substitute the real crystal with common glass, and not on account of any monetary cost. So-called witches, especially men and women already under suspicion of having contact with the occult world, would rarely own a crystal. For one to be found in their home would be irrefutable proof of their nefarious work with all the dire consequences this implied to loss of their property and their lives.

Instead they made use of other, everyday objects which would draw no attention. Among them were fishing floats made of glass. They fixed their gaze on these.

Crystal gazing was not reserved for fairs or for odd people and the unenlightened. It was a highly regarded art. Queen Elizabeth I had on her staff her personal occultist, the famous Dr. John Dee. It was according to his astrological advice that she fixed the date of her coronation. Dee frequently made use of his crystal ball to which he referred as his "shew-stone." Still in existence is his detailed description of it as a flat, circular, black stone with a highly polished surface. When not in use, he stowed it away in a leather case.

A scryer staring at a crystal might visualize the appearance of a substance which initially was foggy and blurred. Soon, however, he would recognize in it an actual picture or symbolic pattern. Each case demanded careful, individual interpretation which rendered crystal gazing highly specialized and in no small measure subject to the scryer's way of thinking and looking at the world.

Interest in crystal gazing declined as people realized that the effect of crystal gazing was not due to the work of a demon as the ancients had thought or the gift of a benevolent spirit as medieval society had assumed. It was a psychic communication received in a state of trance attained by the prolonged gazing at a shining object.

Modern science offers several explanations for the revelations experienced by crystal gazing. They may be the result of mind reading or of telepathic communication. A state of visionary hallucination or self-induced hypnosis might likewise account for them. No matter which it is, they all are the ultimate product of the prolonged gazing at a selected object, just as a Buddhist monk achieves his aim of spiritual enlightenment by focusing his eyes on his navel.

### Breaking of a Mirror

There might even be a link between crystal gazing and the superstition that it is unlucky to break a mirror. Just as the crystal was thought to reveal the future, so was it imagined of the mirror. The fact that it broke was taken as an ill omen. The gods did not want the beholder to foresee the bad that was in store for him.

## CARTOMANCY

To play cards in any of its many forms may be an innocuous pastime. Yet if the cards are used for gambling, they can make or break a person, gain or lose him a fortune. But playing cards have from the very days of their invention many centuries ago fulfilled a much more ominous role, in the literal sense of the word "omen." The universal language of symbolism used in a pack of cards, this "book without words," if rightly interpreted, it was claimed, could tell volumes about man's fate and future. However, only those highly skilled and endowed with psychic power were able to discern the message.

"It's in the cards" is a remark made occasionally. Used generally to express a belief in fate, fundamentally the phrase reflects one of the most favorite forms of divination—cartomancy.

Why did cards come to play such a significant role in such diverse spheres as gambling and fortune-telling? The answer is really simple. Both contain the element of chance, appeal to man's love of risk and cater to his fascination with the mysterious.

Views differ as to which of the two came first: amusement or divination. Man has always been anxious to pierce the veil of illusion and to penetrate the mystery of the future, so playing cards must have been used for fortune-telling from almost the very beginning. In Europe, cards used for fortune-telling, nevertheless were called "playing cards"; this was not done ignorantly but deliberately. It was a camouflage to keep away the uninitiated, the unenlightened and, most of all, those dangerous to anyone engaged in the pursuit of the occult.

## THE PSYCHIC ELEMENT IN TAROT CARDS

Of all decks of cards used for divination, none excels the tarot cards in significance and complexity.

The discovery of the message contained in the cards could be compared with the deciphering of a cuneiform inscription. Each of its individual picture graphs may have several meanings. Which of these applies may differ on each occasion and depends on the context in which the figure appears. Only those steeped in ancient Babylonian-Assyrian culture and lore, and gifted with special skill, could ever attempt to read even a simple cuneiform text.

Thus the adept in tarotology must be fully cognizant of what each card might represent and then how its meaning is changed by the very sequence in which it is picked and in the way it is laid out on the table. This task calls for a tremendous amount of study and is easily subject to error and misinterpretation.

But cartomancy goes far beyond a decoding of symbols, since it concerns the psychic world.

Man has often been led to wonder whether there is such a thing as chance. No one can deny that those knowing how to "grasp" it can change it into providence. May it not also be that an occurrence we call chance actually is the result of a causal chain of factors still unknown to us? We are so used to taking things at their face value. Many of us are as ignorant of and insensitive to the subliminal world as the tone-deaf and color-blind persons are to a great part of reality which they miss.

Churchill once gave the telling example of a man leaving his home and then turning to the right. In so doing he met on his way the very woman who was to change his entire life. The man then gratefully thought how lucky he had been. He could have just as well turned to the left and thereby would have missed the fortunate "chance encounter."

Churchill pointed out the fallacy of the argument. It only had relevance with "all other things being equal." But how did the man know? Could it not have happened that if actually he had turned the other way—to the left—the young woman would have come from that side?

There are no chance coincidences according to occult belief. Those who "pick" specific cards by what is termed "mere chance," do not do so "accidentally" after all. There may well be some still unknown factor that determines the selection of this particular card as distinct from all others. The apparent random choice is not random at all.

For example, people trying to get hold of an object in the dark without really knowing its position may nevertheless direct their hand straight toward it. They do so by some mysterious, instinctive sense of direction. Likewise, people may "accidentally" open a book they had never consulted before at the very spot that contained the information they needed.

Events are never independent. There is always a connection among past, present and future. Interaction is a universal and cosmic law. Pascal's reflection that had Cleopatra's nose been shorter "the whole aspect of the world would have been changed," was not an entirely fanciful observation.

Invariably we react to one another and are susceptible to our surroundings. In different company we become a different person. Almost like a chameleon we take on the color of our environment. Just as the letters of the alphabet when arranged in different se-

quence spell out diverse and at times contradictory words, so do cards
vary in the message they convey. This depends on the particular card
that is picked, on the how and when and on the pattern into which it
eventually falls.

Not everyone would be able to decipher what each card tries to say,
not individually but in the sequence in which it is "chosen."

To complicate matters further, methods of divination vary according to the several schools of the occult that are being followed. The
most common way is to ask the "consulter" to shuffle the pack and
then to pick a card, and to repeat this procedure several times. The
tarotologist then arranges the selected cards in a definite pattern
according to the tradition he has adopted, making things even more
complex. It may take the shape of the Hebrew tree of life, of a pyramid
or of King Solomon's seal. The practitioner then reads out of them or
into them the answers to the questions put by his "client."

Other problems arise. Did some mysterious power emanate from
the inquirer that determined the choice of cards? Are those claiming
the gift of "reading" them influenced by some spiritual contact which
goes far beyond telepathic communication?

Furthermore, the actual pictures and even the way in which they
follow each other in their "chance" sequence may have little significance as such. Their paramount purpose could well be to serve as a
stimulus, to rouse a latent psychic gift and open up in the tarotologist a
sixth sense of viewing a world that is hidden to the ordinary mortal.

By concentrating on the various pictures on the cards and their
combination, his power of recognition may be activated. As in crystal
gazing, the pictures may create a hypersensitive state in his mind,
receptive to ideas that would normally escape others. It is exactly as
with sounds and colors that are inaudible and invisible to the ordinary
human senses because their decibels and wavelengths are beyond his
reach. Looking at the tarot symbols may unlock memories long
forgotten (perhaps even of previous lives) and fire a chain of thought
buried in the subconscious.

Reading the past, the future and fortune from tarot cards thus is not
the mere decoding of a message by mechanically following certain
rules and traditions. The revelation received depends on a psychic
rapport going far beyond man's ordinary senses.

Considering the countless and diverse factors that relate to the
practice of divination and the possibilities contained in a pack of tarot

cards, a famous retort seems applicable. A viewer at an exhibition of modern art could not make out what a picture represented. The artist, when asked what it meant, replied, "It means whatever you find in it."

## The Tarot Pack

There are altogether seventy-eight tarot cards. These are divided into two distinct groups. One pack of fifty-six (eventually reduced to fifty-two) is known as the "minor arcana." The Latin term *arcana* refers to the "secret" and "mystery." Immediately, therefore, the very name stresses its supernatural purpose, though it is surprising that it is from this deck that our modern playing cards evolved.

The fifty-six cards, in turn, are divided into four suits. This number has been interpreted mystically in several ways. It was said to represent the four elements, the four corners of creation and the four worlds of the Kabbalah. The suits were originally known as cups, coins, swords and wands and are the predecessors of the modern hearts, diamonds, spades and clubs.

Each suit consists of fourteen cards. These are made up of the ten digits (the "pips")—the usual ace to ten—and "the royal house." This has, in addition to the king, queen and knave, a "horse." This equestrian figure has been "discarded" or merged with the knave. The usually unnumbered "fool" also was part of the original pack, to be changed later into the "joker."

Much more important in cartomancy is the second pack, appropriately called the "major arcana." It is the real tarot. The number of its twenty-two trump cards itself has caused much speculation that it was not mere accident this coincided with the number of letters of the Hebrew alphabet with its profound importance in mystical circles and the Kabbalah.

The cards carry a colorful variety of allegorical figures and symbols. All are typical of the customs, fashions and emblems known in medieval times. They include the Juggler (1), the Emperor (4), the Pope (5) and the Devil (15), as well as the Star (17), the Moon (18) and the Sun (19).

Gypsies recognized in the series a pictorial record of their wanderings and their fate. Churchmen interpreted the sequence as a dramatic illustration of man's moral and spiritual progress with its culmination in "the Judgment" (20). The tarots served as an ingenious aid to memory (a "mnemonic" device) was yet another explanation and possible rationalization. It might have been chosen to make acceptable and respectable the so suspected "book of the devil." Finally, it was said that the cards were meant to recall fundamental sacred truths which had been represented in their manner already to the members of early Gnostic sects.

### An Analysis of Tarot Cards—an Enigma Within an Enigma

Some of the cards seem to have obvious meanings. The Wheel of Fortune, for instance, is so universal that anyone will easily get its message of either hope or forewarning. Things never stand still and inevitably will change for better or worse.

Other tarot cards, though their symbols are easily identified, are not as self-explanatory as at first appears. The Sun foretold not only the clearing up of a problem, nor did the Hermit (an itinerant aged man with a lantern) point merely to waywardness. The Fool may not refer at all to "stupidity" but to a child's purity and innocence. The Tower, many centuries prior to Freud, was seen as a phallic sign and all it conveyed.

A card usually has not a single, simple and unambiguous meaning. It is open to every type of interpretation, which is why during the last five hundred years countless explanations have been given for each individual picture and symbol. Perhaps nothing exceeds the mystery of and the problems presented by Number 12—the "Hanged Man."

The young man hanging by one leg from a horizontal beam at first seems to present so straightforward, though morbid, a message: imminent disaster and death. But looking at him more carefully, striking and contradictory aspects are revealed. The man does not really hang down from the gallows. Only one of his feet is bound to its crossbeam or perhaps merely touches it. The other foot is bent at right angles and thereby creates the sign of a cross. His face, which obviously should show anguish and suffering, looks placid and serene.

No wonder that some tarotologists were convinced that the so-called Hanged Man was not hanged at all. The "suspension" was a printer's error. What had happened was that carelessly he had reproduced the picture upside down. In reality the man was standing with one foot on the ground while watching out where to put the other one. Hence the card was meant to convey not horror and death but the virtue of prudence.

And thus a picture of doom had suddenly changed into one symbolizing sagacity. But then it was realized that, when this card was first produced, it was not printed at all but painted. Therefore the theory of the reversal of a printing block fell to the ground.

Another school of thought claimed the "topsy-turvy" aspect of the man was still a misconception. It was due to the faulty Latin knowledge of an early card maker. The man on the card was meant to represent prudence. For this reason special instructions had been given to the artist to portray him in a cautious position. The card maker was to depict the man *pede suspenso*—"with (one) suspended foot"—holding it up. But the printer had misinterpreted the direction as saying that he should draw the man "suspended by his foot."

There are other numerous views of what the card really was supposed to tell. Eliphaz Levi saw in the Hanged Man the true Prometheus—the eternal sufferer. With his feet in heaven, he only slightly touched the ground. Another opinion found in the picture the message of the link that should exist between the infinite spirit and the finite earth. It was meant to impress the complete reversal of life, was yet another view. Man should learn the true value of life and substitute spiritual force for his material love. A further interpretation explained the Hanged Man as representing not the ultimate fate of a condemned man but a stage of initiation into sacred, esoteric rites.

By paying attention to other incidental details in the picture, this becomes even more complicated. What was the meaning of the gold coins that seemed to drop out of the man's pocket? Was it to show his contempt for riches and that we should replace love of money by the "golden rule?" Or did it recall the thirty pieces of silver for which Judas Iscariot had sold his master, subsequently hanging himself in repentance of his crime? Some say that what appears to be a halo around the man's head is not that at all but just a crude depiction of his hair.

The mysteries multiply the more attention is given to the card. The one lesson it does teach is the infinitude of meanings it can suggest even to an unbiased observer, interested only in "facts." But if used in cartomancy by an imaginative clairvoyant interpreter who is saturated in the tradition of fortune-telling and has psychic rapport with the questioner for whom he is trying to look into the future, the ideas this one picture can conjure up defy description.

Added to it is yet another complication. The value of the card on its own is not its final message. The card appears in tandem and therefore its interpretation is modified by the "pictures" that precede and follow it. Furthermore its particular position in the pattern chosen must be considered. Attention must be given to whether any of the cards in front or behind, above or below, instead of being placed right side up, accidentally were put down in the reverse.

## The Mysterious Origin of the Tarot

As enigmatic as is the meaning of tarot cards, so is the story of their origin. One claim asserts that they were the surviving leaves from the ancient Egyptian *Book of Thoth* which had been brought from the Nile Valley to Europe by gypsies, those experts in magic and mystics. But there is no substantiation of this theory. Tarot cards certainly existed prior to the arrival of the Bohemians, by which name gypsies were frequently called.

Others traced the tarots to the Hebrew Kabbalah or thirteenth century Arabs. Leonardo da Vinci, that great genius in so many spheres, has also been credited with their invention. People loathing "cards" and all they stood for in gambling and fortune-telling honestly believed and so stated that they were the creation of the devil. Going to the other extreme, enthusiastic card diviners discovered in the tarots the ancient "tablets" which the Hebrews consulted in their quest for divine guidance. Others again linked them with astrological and numerological pursuits.

It is most likely, however (and can be supported by much evidence), that the cards were first designed in the East. They were certainly known in China before A.D. 1000. They then carried pictures from the domino game and from chess, and were produced in oblong and circular shapes of wood, ivory, plant fiber or even metal. Card packs existed early in India and in Persia, each with their individual features. And it was from the Far East that eventually cards reached the Middle East. From there they were taken, like so many other Oriental practices and traditions, by the crusaders to the West, where, Europeanized, they soon caught on.

It has been suggested that the crusaders had concealed their arcane employment and had done so to avoid persecution by antioccult authorities, so they especially stressed the cards' entertainment value. The cards were described as a splendid device for amusement and gambling. According to one strange tradition, the "original" purpose of their introduction into Europe was due to the wish to help concubines pass their time during their "off hours."

Tarot cards, as they now exist, stem from fourteenth-century Italy. (An Italian Renaissance game was actually known as *Tarrochini*.) From there they found their way all over the continent to be used both for amusement and divination.

### The Etymology of the Tarot

Like the origin of the tarot cards, so their very name is shrouded in mystery. Opinions still vary greatly as to what or who gave them their peculiar designation.

Those linking this type of fortune-telling with the gypsies discover in the tarot the Hungarian gypsy word *tar*, itself derived from the ancient Hindustani *taru*. Very much to the point, this merely said what it really was—"a pack of cards."

A grid of lines that once marked the back of the tarot cards was the origin of its name according to another hypothesis. Either continuous or dotted lines, they crossed each other diagonally, thereby forming a shape described in French as *tarotée*. And it was this simple pattern "on the other side" which had been responsible for the name of the tarot.

Other authorities discovered in it a Hittite root. *Tarrh* in ancient Mesopotamia was the name of the mysterious "force" that controlled life. The tarot, therefore, was said to speak of the "powerful" one.

Those who condemned the cards as evil and devilish had their own derivations to offer. Tarot recalled the god Tar, a member of the Egyptian pantheon whose dominion was the netherworld which made him fiendish and unfriendly. Hence his name would be the perfect choice for cards that proved equally inimical to man.

Unconvincing, though sharing the same attitude and location, is the suggestion of those who saw the Greek *Tartaros* as the source of the tarot. This infernal region abounded with devilish spirits and truly was likely to lend its name to the cards.

Sylvia Mann in her *Collecting Playing Cards* links the cards to a geographical site. She points to the fact that the tarots were first popularized in the north Italian valley of the Tarot River, a tributary of the Po. And it is a common occurrence in word-making that an object, profession or person is called after the very city or region of their first appearance.

## Modern Playing Cards in the Making

Though present-day playing cards evolved from the early fortune-telling pack, they differ in various aspects and reveal interesting changes and adaptations.

Playing cards now are double-headed. This feature was introduced in the nineteenth century for the sake of convenience. It enabled players on either side easily to recognize the identity of the card. In the earlier pack, each carried a full-length portrait and card users had to learn to see things upside down.

Originally, the king, queen and knave, because of the elaborate robes they wore, were known as "coat" cards. It was so easy to err in this case by their association with the royal court. Soon they were mispronounced and erroneously called "court" cards, which they have remained ever since.

The modern "trump" goes back much further. It is a telling monument of early triumph in warfare. The trump recalls the *triumphal* processions by which Roman generals celebrated their victories.

The pictures on the cards were never updated; thus they continue to reflect the fashion, the way of life and symbolism of the time in which the cards came into existence.

Originally, the four suits were meant to represent the four social classes which made up medieval society. The present-day clubs, hearts, spades and diamonds are a later evolution and partially a misunderstood interpretation of the early designs. To indicate the four strata of society for which they stood, these showed chalices for the clergy, swords for the nobility, coins for the merchants and staffs or wands for the peasantry.

In spite of their apparent appropriateness, the "spades" have nothing to do with the agricultural tool used to dig up the ground. From the Spanish *espada*, it really referred to the "sword" and as such symbolized the warrior class. Oddly, the English retained the old Spanish word and possibly did so because the shape of this sword looked very much like a spade.

The early chalice or communion cup was not retained. It was replaced by the heart. It is not certain what actually caused this substitution. Some believe that it was to express the supreme position of ecclesiastical power. Were not the bishops and clergy the very "heart" of the community? Their station in life would bring home the message so much better than a communion cup.

"Clubs" were not, as the word might suggest, wooden implements used as weapons. They were trefoil symbols meant to remind the player of the three-leafed clover and thus represented the peasant, significantly doing so in a luck-spelling way of the trinity.

"Diamonds" seem so plainly to be associated with the moneymaking merchant class. But they, too, are not what they appear to be. They recall the checkered floor of diamond-shaped stones with which the exchanges were paved where important business transactions took place.

Few players realize that in every pack one of the aces is especially ornamented. There was a valid and costly reason for this, and to players at the time the "decoration" was first introduced not a welcome one.

Governments, always anxious to raise funds, do so conspicuously in taxes and seem to be never at a loss to find new avenues for their revenues. Eighteenth-century Britain put a levy on playing cards, and the duty stamp (adding insult to injury) was incorporated artistically inside the ace of spades which thus metaphorically dug into players' pockets. That the tax has been paid for a pack of cards is nowadays indicated by a sticker on the wrapper outside. Nevertheless, our packs retain the original "tax receipt," and it continues to take part in every game and in cartomancy in general.

The earliest European cards preserved (of which there are altogether seventeen) stem from a pack painted in Paris in 1392 for therapeutic purposes. They had been made for King Charles the Mad of France in the first stages of his mental sickness. It was hoped that they would help to relax and distract his mind. Despite the unfortunate circumstances, the mere fact that cards played some part in the royal household gave them standing and led to their vast popularity.

However, their association with both gambling and divination caused their use to be prohibited by official edicts. The ban was welcomed by many. Aristocrats had lost huge sums of money gambling with them and were threatened with bankruptcy. Unfaithful spouses and corrupt officials in high quarters believing in the efficacy of the new art of cartomancy feared that the "pack" might bring to light what they tried to keep dark: their adulteries and dishonesties.

But the prohibitive measures were counterproductive. The very desire and effort to suppress cards publicized them all the more and gave them a special attraction. Card reading and playing became the fashion, and people have never lost their fascination for them.

## HYDROMANCY

Water has always been regarded as an element of truly cosmic dimensions. It is no wonder that many cosmogonies believed that the world was created out of water. And, as noted earlier, if the first words of Genesis really contained a copyist's mistake of the Hebrew text, this, too, might have originally read that "in the beginning God created [not 'heaven' but] 'water' and earth." The rarity of water in certain regions of the world added to its preciousness and its value. This explains also why one early type of sacrifice offered the gods not slaughtered animals but a libation of water.

Water has mystified man in so many ways. It could bestow life and bring death. It might flood vast areas or, by its absence, cause drought and death. It could taste sweet or salty (and salt added its own essentially occult property). In the form of rain, water descended from heaven, the divine realm. The tides, with their irresistible bodies of water surging forward and then receding, showed up an element of innate mystical power no man could stem or retain. The depth of water at some places was as unfathomable as all that was associated with it.

Because of its cleansing properties, too, water was endowed with magic. It was believed to purify man from his sins and other defilements. This is the origin of baptism and the reason why the devil and all evil forces were thought to be allergic to water. The consideration of the devil-repelling quality of water was responsible for the introduction of one of the most infamous practices in the medieval judicial system—the ordeal by water (or "swimming").

No wonder that water, too, became a significant means of divination, known as hydromancy, a word derived from the Greek *hudor* for "water." Those adept in the art observed and interpreted "ominously" and mantically every detail of the water: its movement, the direction of its flow, its calm or restlessness and what happened to a ring which, attached to a string, was dropped into it.

Was it really surprising that those who claimed the ability to gauge psychically concealed messages would find an almost limitless source of information in this "noblest of elements" with all its power to cleanse, to give life and prosperity, as much as to create chaos, destruction and death?

## THE ROD

Sticks and branches have always served man in a multiplicity of forms. They belonged to his primitive weapons. With his club he beat his human and his animal foes. By way of fences or living hedges, branches gave him extra protection. As message sticks, they were his original bush telegraph.

It was the way in which they grew and then mysteriously suddenly sprouted that made man look upon them with tremendous awe. They were not just dead wood, he reasoned, but even if cut off retained some miraculous, supernatural power. More so, their resemblance to a phallus bestowed on them in his imagination extra life-giving qualities. That is how from the beginning, those very rods, sticks and branches found a place in man's occult pursuit.

### The Power of the Rod

Rods in the right hands could work wonders, so man was convinced from the dawn of history.

Egyptian lore told how Pharaoh Nectanebo of the Thirtieth Dynasty, by manipulating an ebony rod, moved models of his entire fleet to attack and defeat the enemy naval force. This was not a war game or an innocuous pastime, but the practice of sympathetic magic.

Well known is the frequent use made of a magic wand in the stories of the Bible. In their confrontation with Pharaoh, Moses and Aaron tried to convince him of the divine power which would protect and deliver their people by "wielding" the stick. Significantly, in some cases Egyptian magicians were able to emulate their performance. Commentators have suggested that Moses' rod actually was his shepherd's crook. Therefore, it was his psychic gift that had invested it with its supernatural quality.

## A Rod as a Unique Charter

A different type of branch served Aaron to quell a rebellion among a faction of his own people directed against his hierarchical monopoly and which could have easily cost him his supreme ecclesiastical position. They resented and openly questioned Aaron's right to appropriate to himself and his family the priestly rights, privileges and vested interests they carried. Aaron then, so the Bible relates, "demonstrated" the legitimacy of his divine appointment by the miraculous budding of a rod, ever since referred to as "Aaron's rod" (Num. 17:1-13). And, like a modern charter, he is said to have kept it in safe custody in the sanctuary itself.

## The Healing Rod

By their magic quality, rods were thought to be able to cure disease as well. Often they were linked in this special mission with the snake which, when stiff, was so much like a rod. A representation of such a "healing rod" with serpents coiling around it was discovered in an ancient Sumerian artifact, going back to the third millennium B.C.

The United States and British Army Medical Corps have retained this very rod as their emblem. It is known as the caduceus. In ancient myth the caduceus served as a herald's staff. The messenger was, however, not an ordinary one but the god Hermes. He carried the staff to guide disembodied spirits to the other world and to restore to life those who were dead.

Originally, the wand was an olive branch, symbolic of immortality. Its power then was reinforced by the twin serpents. The regular shedding of their skin was seen as representing and magically ensuring rebirth and constant renewal. And that is why, thousands of years later, doctors continue to treasure the rod, and the Masonic craft to use it in its initiation rites to bring home to the candidate the message of everlasting life.

## Water Divining

In yet another form, in equally ancient days, the rod became a life preserver. It did so in the role of a divining tool to trace hidden sources of water.

A telling example is known from the Bible. When the Israelites, lacking water in the heat of the desert, were utterly exhausted, they were once again about to rebel. It was then that Moses their leader, who no doubt possessed great psychic power, is said to have made a rock gush forth a spring which supplied them with water "abundantly" (Num. 20:7-13).

With his "magic" rod Moses struck a rock twice. To the discerning mind, the scriptural text describes—though rather distortedly—a typical case of water divining. In this particular incident, the effect of the discovered water was so powerful that it caused Moses' hands holding the rod to react so violently that, to the people watching him, it seemed as if he actually had struck the rock.

That is the reason why the Bible record puts things in the reverse and tells that the water gushed forth because Moses had dealt a blow to the rock. In reality, it was a case of dowsing.

The practice of water divining in antiquity has been testified further by Herodotus who quotes examples from Scythian and Persian sources.

First explanations of the phenomenon assumed the existence of a miraculous magic power of detection in the rod itself. Like a modern Geiger counter, it was thought to indicate the subterranean presence of water. Others saw in it the working of contagious magic: the moisture in the green twig was "pulled" toward the underground water—like being attracted by like—and that made the twig dip.

That various types of wood, among them hazel, oak and elder, were used for the mostly cleft divining rod suggests that the actual power of finding the water (mineral, plant, coal or other substances sought) was not in the rod itself but in the person who carried it. He was an individual highly sensitive to some still unidentified type of radiation that emanated from the water or other object underground. This caused his involuntary muscular action which, in turn, made the rod in his hand jerk or vibrate. The entire process is well illustrated by Galvani's experiment in which the muscles of a frog's legs were made to twitch by the "invisible" currents of electricity.

The rod is not just a relic of ancient beliefs and a symbol in arcane and medical craft. It continues to serve as a practical tool in the hand of diviners to tap water or other hidden buried treasure.

## The *Book of Changes*

Rods certainly have ruled the world in many spheres. Their role extends from space to time. Apart from discovering what was underground, they have been used to reveal what was still to come.

By aid of a stick man has tried to "dig up" not just the past but the future as well. Like most methods of divination, this type also has been called by a Greek name which renders it all the more mysterious. The psychic application of rods in this context is known as rhabdomancy, from the Greek *rhabdos* for "stick."

As a well-known method practiced and popular in the East to this very day, it goes back to the far distant past and earliest Chinese civilization. Sticks (or in their place spills or coins) are tossed to the ground. And out of the pattern they form there, the anxiously sought information is gained. One way this might be done is very much like fortune-telling from the random shape formed by tea leaves in a cup. In the clairvoyant's mind it conjures up a meaningful picture. This is almost an anticipation of the modern psychological ink-blot test.

It seems all so simple, so primitive and misleading. And yet it is not really the sticks (or whatever is used in their stead) which, by themselves or even by the way in which they fall, supply the source of revelation.

It has been suggested that the individual "casting" them may possibly have subconscious control over the manner in which they fall by the amount of force he uses and the way he tosses them. It can be compared to someone throwing a dart. He will direct it in such a way that it hits the desired target. Only in this case it is not the result of dexterity or ruse but by the strange operation of some psychic gift and its involuntary manipulation.

It was equally thought that the erratic pattern that the dropped spills form on the ground is not accidental and meaningless, a mere chance fall. The configuration indicated the answer to the question put. The real problem was how to spell it out, to know its correct interpretation. To the psychic person the pattern that appeared on the ground, however, was not the actual message. It merely acted as a spark plug, firing their gift of divination.

And that is most possibly the way in which the "looking into the future" worked. It all happened in the mind of the person who did the forecasting and had little to do with the spills. Nevertheless (and this is unfortunate), people soon imagined that they could apply the interpretation of the various patterns in some generalized manner and hence divorced it from the "medium" who had hitherto been the intermediary to catch the message. All they needed was, so they believed, some kind of guidebook which gave them the key to the meaning of the various forms.

It was therefore assumed that the shape displayed had an independent significance and did not need a special individual and clairvoyant for its explanation. It was the latter opinion that gave birth to "dictionaries" in which you could "look up" what "fate" or "the supernatural" was trying to convey by the way it had arranged the sticks for you. Among the works used for that purpose, the most ancient and famous, and a favorite again in our time, is the *Book of Changes*, the *I-ching*.

Perhaps one of the oldest surviving Chinese classics, the work is said to date back to at least 1000 B.C. and is attributed to Wen Wang, the founder of the Chou Dynasty. Numerous commentaries have been written on it, one of them allegedly even by Confucius. Greatly venerated, they are but little understood. The very antiquity of the work and the obscurity of its style gave ample room for diversity of opinions. This made the type of rhabdomancy on which the *Book of Changes* was based even more difficult to perform and in its turn dependent on the individual interpreter.

The author of the book is said to have based its entire content on speculations made by Emperor Fu Hsi. He reigned at the beginning of the third millennium B.C. and, significantly, had invented a tool to split wood and thereby to produce the sticks needed easily. Studying the markings on the back of a tortoise, he had discovered eight diagrams which supplied him with a complete philosophy of life.

The *Book of Changes* in its simplest and oldest form consisted of sixty-four oracles based on those eight tortoise diagrams. According to the author two primary and fundamental forces exist in the world: "Light" and "Darkness"—*Yang* and *Yin*. But differing from the Zoroastrian view, they did not represent an ethical dualism of good and evil. Their distinction related to the solar and lunar aspects of life, the male and the female principles.

The graphs in the book (which it adopted from Fu Hsi's system as well) use the simplest possible method. An unbroken line represents *Yang*—the sunny side. *Yin*, the dark, lunar quality, is indicated by a line split up the middle. Each diagram or oracle is a combination of six lines: a hexagram of oblong shape.

Altogether there are, therefore, sixty-four different possibilities of joining into a hexagram figure both these divided and the continuous lines. To start with, their sum total was seen as a complete cosmological system, the sixty-four basic universal principles and fundamental conditions of life.

With the passing of time, however, the original symbolism with its depth of speculation got lost. People became more concerned with their own personal future than with ethical and philosophical contemplations. They employed the graphs now for purposes of divination alone. And thus the *Book of Changes* became a favorite "key" in the realm of fortune-telling, used solely to interpret the kind of life allegedly forecast by the pattern the spills or coins cast to the ground seemed to predict.

The "magic rod" of ancient days survived not only in the hands of the water diviner and fortune-teller, in the *Book of Changes* and as the medical emblem in the staff of Aesculapius. Its occult power was responsible also for the creation of the royal scepter, the officer's baton, the mace and in part the conjurer's wand. Even if now looked upon as mere symbols, originally they were believed to invest those holding and keeping them with supernatural, occult power: to reign, to command and to perform their magic art.

It shows how truly all our life, whether we know or admit to it or not, is deeply influenced, if not determined, by the occult. Whether it is so for better or worse depends on many factors: the circumstances of the situation and the individual. Whichever way, the first essential for anyone who is concerned and not merely intellectually curious is to find out how it all started and to what purpose.

# Index

Aaron, and pointing, 4–6; his rod, 282, 283

Abbreviation, Nr., 17; nickel, 57; Old Nick, 111; dybbuk, 120

Abel, 95, 166

Abracadabra, 5–8

Abraham, 103

Abraxas, 6–7

Acronym, Besht, 118; cabal, 245

Adam, 91, 97

Advertisement, for caul, 46

Africans, and man-animals, 76; and voodoo, 160–3; and magic hand, 172; and Stonehenge, 192

Age, of Bar Mitzvah, 24; coming of, 21–2, 27

Agriculture, and field corner, 209–10; and astrology, 226–7

Ahaziah, King, 107–8

Air-raid sirens, and banshee, 87

Akiba, Rabbi, 189–90, 244

Akitu, Babylonian New Year, 65

Alcmene, 150

Alectryomancy, 267

Alexander the Great, horned, 115; his birth, 227; and palmistry, 264

Alfonso XIII, King of Spain, and evil eye, 129

All Saints' Day, 208

Alphabet, and water, 32, 240; hand in, 262

*Alphabet of Rabbi Akiba,* 245

Altar, and candles, 18; measurements of, 19–20; thirteen steps to, 27; and blood, 82; its horns, 115; in Black Mass, 159; as constellation, 237

Amorites, 52

Amulet, of abracadabra, 5–8; and hunchback, 59; against Lilith, 94, 95; against evil eye, 130–3; definition of, 163–5; its forms, 165–7; in Judaism, 168; in Islam, 168; etymology of, 169; signet ring as, 181

Anaxagoras, 262

Anecdote, on Royal Garter, 53–4; on

flying witch, 146; on atheist, 184

Angels, and death, 14; and Azazel, 64; and fairies, 71; fallen, 103–4

Animals, in Ark, 21; peacock, 35–7; as scapegoat, 62; Kapporah *Hühnchen,* 65; man changing into, 76–7; and werewolf, 77–81; and reincarnation, 78; slaughter of, 82; serpent, 103; goat, 112, 173, 238; their horns, 114; Gadarine swine, 118; cats, 149–54; toad, 154–6; as mascot, 173; ram, 228–9; bull, 230; lion, 233

An-ski, S., 120

Aphrodite, 242

Apis, 230

Apocrypha, and Satan, 103; on astrology, 217

Apostles, twelve, 23

Aquarius, constellation of, 239–40

Arabic, for amulet, 168–70; for talisman, 169–70

Arabs, and numerals, 17; their oath, 21; and Virgo, 235

Aramaic, and, abracadabra, 6; Azazel, 63; Zohar, 247

Arcadia, 77

Arcane, the, 274

Architecture, and magic circle, 3; and pentacle, 176; of Stonehenge, 191

Argus, 36

Aries, constellation of, 228–30

Aristotle, on West, 40; and esoteric knowledge, 243; and palmistry, 264

Ark, and animals, 21; and figure "40," 30

Army, its insignia, 12; and three volleys, 18; and cat-o'-nine-tails, 22; and royal salute, 27; mascot, 173; and swastika, 181; medical corps emblem, 283

Artemis, 45

Arthur, King, 157

Asherah, 12, 171

Aspen, its tremble, 86

| DATE | | | |
|---|---|---|---|
| MAY 15 '78 | NO 09 '88 | DEC 1 5 1994 | |
| MAR 2 2 1979 | | | |
| OCT 2 7 1983 | OC 03 '89 | | |
| AP 29 '86 | AP 30 '90 | | |
| NO 24 '86 | NO 16 '90 | | |
| AP 10 '87 | SE 27 '91 | | |
| JA 05 '87 | AP 08 '93 | | |
| FE 09 '88 | | | |
| MR 07 '88 | APR 2 2 1993 | | |
| MY 17 '88 | | | |
| | | | |